29.95
70E

D1171071

Capitalism, class conflict and the new middle class

International Library of Sociology

Founded by Karl Mannheim

Editor: John Rex, University of Aston in Birmingham

Arbor Scientiae
Arbor Vitae

A catalogue of the books available in the **International Library of Sociology** and other series of Social Science books published by Routledge & Kegan Paul will be found at the end of this volume.

Capitalism, class conflict and the new middle class

Bob Carter
Department of Adult Education,
University of Leicester

Routledge & Kegan Paul

London, Boston, Melbourne and Henley

First published in 1985
by Routledge & Kegan Paul plc

14 Leicester Square, London WC2H 7PH, England

9 Park Street, Boston, Mass. 02108, USA

464 St Kilda Road, Melbourne,
Victoria 3004, Australia and

Broadway House, Newtown Road,
Henley-on-Thames, Oxon RG9 1EN, England

Set in 10/11pt Times
by Columns of Reading
and printed in Great Britain
by St Edmundsbury Press Ltd
Bury St Edmunds, Suffolk

Library of Congress Cataloging in Publication Data

Carter, Bob, 1949–

Capitalism, class conflict, and the new middle class.
(The International Library of Sociology)
Based on the author's thesis (doctoral) – University
of Bristol, 1980.
Bibliography: p.
Includes index.
1. White collar workers.   2. Middle managers.
3. Supervisors, Industrial.   4. Social classes.   5. Class
consciousness.   6. Marxian school of sociology.   I. Title.
HD8039.M39C37   1985   305.5'56   84-9956

British Library CIP data also available

ISBN 0-7100-9624-0

Contents

Acknowledgments

This book has its origins in a doctoral thesis submitted to the University of Bristol, 1980. Although much changed, it is fitting that those who helped in many different ways with that thesis be publically thanked. These include, in particular, Paul Anderson, Ian Gibson and the many ASTMS members and officials whom it would be impolitic to name. For supervision of the thesis and continued help and encouragement, I am deeply indebted to Theo Nichols. I would also like to thank Huw Beynon who read the thesis and made a number of suggestions which have been incorporated into this work. Thanks are also due to Pam York and Jyoti Chotai for typing successive versions. The greatest debt is owed to Pat Kirkham who has lived with the work from its conception, read and re-read various drafts, corrected errors and encouraged me at every stage.

Introduction

where?

There are numerous theories advanced by sociologists to explain why socialism is not a practical possibility, but few have found such a sympathetic response in everyday thought as that which holds that the growth in white-collar employment provides increasing security to the capitalist system. The argument has two variants. This growth either creates an increasing middle class, hostile to socialism, or, if white-collar employees are to be regarded as workers, their growth erodes the traditional, class-conscious working class. The examination of social theories concerned with white-collar employment and the consciousness of white-collar workers is therefore of some ideological significance.

Despite this, the works by socialists addressed to these problems are few. This has meant that the initiatives in social theory have come largely from conservative theorists. During the 1950s, for example, it was a widely held opinion that a fundamental change had occurred in working-class consciousness: *1950s* workers had become middle-class and their role as agents of radical social change had declined.[1] The impact of the theory was also reflected in, and reinforced by, changes that took place in the political culture of Britain. The failure of the Labour Party in the 1951, 1955 and 1959 elections led the leadership of the Party to examine the causes of its defeats. Part of the explanation accepted by the leadership was that the Party was too narrowly based on the working class, a class objectively and subjectively on the wane. In order to re-assume power, the leadership believed it necessary to widen the base of the Party's support to include the growing professional, scientific and technical groups.

It was further believed that a precondition for this wider support was the abandonment of the outdated ideology of class. By the 1964 election the appeal of the Party was no longer

1

directed to the need for socialism and the extension of nationalisation as its means, but rather on the need 'to make Britain up-to-date, vigorous and capable of playing her full part in the world'.[2] The vision of a socialist society was replaced by a technocratic one, dominated by the rhetoric of 'science' and 'modernisation'.[3]

The victory of this approach within the Labour Party was, of course, far from uncontested. Likewise in social theory there were rearguard actions to arrest and reverse the shift away from class analysis. There were, in particular, attempts to demonstrate the continued existence of poverty and inequality and to insist on the viability of working-class communities and culture.[4] There were, however, few determined attempts to tackle an essential part of the argument, namely the class nature of white-collar workers. Where examination of white-collar labour did take place, the approaches were dominated by neo-Weberian perspectives that held out little hope for radical change.[5]

The urgency of the need for a thorough-going socialist examination of the changing occupational and class structure of capitalist societies appeared to recede somewhat during the 1960s. The growth of working-class militancy and the possibilities for social change that appeared to be opened up by the 1968 May Events in France restored faith in the traditional role of the proletariat. As for the growing number of employees who were not part of the traditionally defined manual working class, it only remained formally to acknowledge their growth before asserting their real position as actual or potential members of an increasingly militant proletariat.

The failure of Marxist social theory to take seriously changes in the structure of capitalist societies had grave consequences. It gave space for those theories proclaiming the imminence of a post-industrial society in which the working class is reduced to an impotent minority, an idea given additional weight by the potential applications of recent advances in micro-computer technology. More importantly, and in spite of ritualistic claims that white-collar workers were part of the working class, Marxist theory reinforced the idea that the proletariat was synonymous with the manual working class by the absence of systematic studies of white-collar work. Recent analyses by socialists such as Jeremy Seabrook and André Gorz,[6] for example, that in different ways despair at the prospects for social change based upon the working class, a class defined only in terms of manual workers, are not therefore isolated aberrations, but reflect a failure of Marxism effectively to redefine the working class in accordance with changes in the capitalist labour process.

2

The outer signs of these changes are apparent in the occupational structures of the most advanced capitalist societies. In the United Kingdom, for example, in 1911, fewer than one employee in six could be classified as what is now conventionally known as a white-collar worker, but by 1971 the proportion was approaching one in two. In absolute terms this growth represents an increase from 3.4 million to 10.4 million, a three-fold increase in a period in which the total labour force expanded by only 33 per cent. Although in absolute terms the number of manual workers in the labour force remained almost constant in the period, by 1971 they represented only 54.7 per cent of the occupied population compared with 74.6 per cent in 1911.[7] The changing occupational structure has been accompanied by a change in the sex composition of the labour force. Whereas the proportion of female workers in manual employment has remained relatively constant, women workers have constituted a growing proportion of the expanding white-collar occupations, rising from 29.8 per cent in 1911 to 46.2 per cent in 1971.[8]

These changes are not unique to the United Kingdom and are reflected in the employment figures for Western capitalist countries as a whole. Indeed, in the United States by 1970 non-manual workers constituted the largest occupational category, outnumbering manual workers by a ratio of more than five to four.[9] This situation has yet to be reached in Europe, but the trend in that direction is rapid.[10] Similarly, the increase in the proportion of women workers has been a common development in both European countries and the USA.

There is still an urgent need for socialist analysis of these processes. This book aims to make a contribution in this direction by examining a specific section of white-collar employees and specifying a basis for their identification as part of a new middle class. In doing so it simultaneously implies which layers within the category of 'white-collar' should be regarded as part of the working class. The central perspective of this book is not concerned with white-collar workers in general, however; indeed, the heterogeneity of workers included in this category places severe limitations on the usefulness of the term. Nor, more specifically, is the book concerned with clerical, technical or scientific workers as such. Rather it focuses upon the class position of managerial and supervisory workers. A further qualification should also be added. Although women constitute an increasing proportion of the white-collar labour force, a general trend which itself deserves specialised study, women white-collar workers are not considered within this book as a separate category. This is primarily because the occupational

3

groups of managerial and supervisory workers on which this work focuses do not include significant numbers of women. In fact, the proportions of women workers in these categories are amongst the lowest in any occupational groupings and as female labour has been recruited to routine clerical and administrative work so the promotion prospects of male employees from those grades to managerial and supervisory grades has increased. R.M. Blackburn noted this development in his study of bank employees, where there was an expectation of career development and regular promotions for male appointees which was completely absent for female ones.[11] Similar findings have been recorded in studies of clerical work, one of which concluded that 'in future, the few men remaining in clerical jobs will be "juniors" working their way up'.[12]

It is not possible, however, to determine the class position of managerial and supervisory workers without reviewing the position of white-collar workers in theories of social stratification. Chapter 1 details the inadequacy of orthodox Marxist approaches to the class structure as well as sociological alternatives to them by an examination of social theory in both Germany and Britain. Attention is paid to the historically important debate on the class structure of Germany that took place between the beginning of this century and the coming to power of the National Socialists in 1933. Although generally unacknowledged, this debate rehearsed all the major positions subsequently taken up on the position and nature of white-collar workers. In contrast, the main debate in Britain took place after the Second World War. It was largely uninformed by the earlier German debate, being mainly influenced by neo-Weberian theories of social stratification that have dominated British sociology since 1945.

The conclusion that the treatment of white-collar workers in the class structure is inadequate leads, in Chapter 2, to a re-examination of the works of Marx in order to establish a satisfactory basis for the theorisation of a new middle class. The theories of recent Marxist writers who have identified such a grouping are then examined to ascertain whether or not their theories correspond to the elements of such a theory within the works of Marx himself.

Having established a framework for an analysis of the new middle class, Chapter 3 turns towards identifying the historical growth of managers and supervisors by an examination of changes in the organisation of the capitalist enterprise and the labour process within it. The consequences of the changes for managerial labour are also reviewed, particularly the growth of managerial hierarchies and the attendant growth in concern for methods of control of managers themselves. Chapter 4 continues these themes by examining the parallel growth and importance of new middle-class workers in the state sector in the context of changing state structures and policies.

One of the results of the changing structure of organisation and control in both private and public sector organisations has been the growing unionisation of white-collar employees. This development has been used by Marxist theorists to claim the increasing realisation of Marx's prognosis that the class structure of capitalist societies would tend to polarise. On the other hand, the dominant social image, reflected within sociological theory, maintains that white-collar unions are different from manual ones, being more conservative because of the middle-class nature of their membership. Chapter 5 challenges the opposing theories surrounding white-collar unionism, maintaining that they have imported from stratification theory inappropriate models of social class. The chapter goes on to put forward an alternative framework for the analysis of new middle-class trade unionism, corresponding to the perspectives on social class outlined in earlier sections.

The general hypothesis relating to the relationship between social class and unionisation maintained by the book is that if the work relations and experiences of new middle-class labour are significantly different from that of the working class, then where middle-class labour is organised in professional associations and unions it is to be expected that the character of these organisations will differ from unions with only working-class membership. To test this hypothesis Chapter 6 examines a number of organisations and details their major characteristics. It concludes that although their formal policies can be seen to differ from those unions organising primarily working-class members, these differences are not necessarily the most important. It is not the character of the union as determined by formal national policies that is most significant so much as the relationship of members to those policies and in particular the extent to which those policies actively intervene in the day-to-day relations between members and management at workplace level.

The approach adopted in this work has greatly benefited from the recent resurgence of interest in the areas of class analysis and the capitalist labour process. The first area, associated with the writings of Poulantzas, Carchedi and Olin Wright, has been concerned with emphasizing the complexity of class relations in capitalist societies.[13] In contrast to orthodox Marxist accounts that force all variations in class position on to one side or other of the capital – labour divide, these writers have all claimed the

5

continued and increased importance of a recognition of the position of what they variously term the new petty bourgeoisie, the new middle class and those occupying contradictory class locations. The second area of growth, that in work on the capitalist labour process, followed the publication of Harry Braverman's *Labor and Monopoly Capital* in 1974.[14] Subsequently much attention has been concentrated on managerial strategies and particularly the historical attempts to de-skill work.

These two areas of concern overlap in the recognition of the importance of changes in the capitalist production process and their effects on the class structure. However, the contributions to both areas have had crucial weaknesses. The debate on the class structure of the capitalist societies in particular has been marred by an abstruseness that has rendered it inaccessible to all but a small group of academics. This tendency has been reinforced by the lack of an historical dimension and an unwillingness to follow through the perspectives to an examination of class organisations in any given society. Whereas an historical account is central to theorists examining changes in the capitalist labour process, there has frequently been a failure to look at the implications for class analysis and to examine the concrete organisation of class interests.

This book has attempted to utilise the insights thrown up by structuralist theories of class and to integrate them with some of historical movement and change. In doing so an attempt has been made to avoid a formalistic account of class. Class is not simply a matter of definitions. Social groups do not move in and out of classes according to the reformulation of concepts but rather with their changing social relations with other groups. In such a perspective what real people think, feel and do is regarded not just as interesting, or as reflecting class relations, but as part of actively constructing class relations. This is not to belittle theoretical work, but merely to insist that it should also focus upon the practical relations of groups which ultimately prove or disprove theoretical speculation.

1 Sociology, Marxism and the class structure of capitalist societies

It is now almost conventional wisdom within the discipline to view much sociological theorising as a debate with the ghost of Marx.[1] This view is particularly appropriate when theories of class are being examined, for no other writer has placed class so centrally in their world view as Marx, nor done so with greater effect on subsequent thought.[2] It needs to be stressed, however, that the ghost that many sociologists have tried to exorcise is frequently not an apparition that Marx himself would recognise. What is taken for Marxism is often merely a dismembered fragment of his writings. Such is the case with Marx's approach to class and class structure. The impression is widely given that all that Marx had to say on the development of classes within capitalism was present in *Manifesto of the Communist Party*, 1848. It is claimed that Marx saw only two classes in capitalist societies and that subsequent developments in such societies have proved him wrong.

This extremely crude approach, while perhaps sufficient for those wishing to refute Marx at a popular level, does not capture the complexities of Marx's analysis of class. Furthermore, such approaches have continually been given credence by many sympathetic to Marxism, who have maintained the correctness of what were essentially polemical formulations and, perhaps more importantly, have published books on a wide range of aspects of Marxism without in any way regarding Marx's theory of class as problematic.[3] In these respects the gentle criticism offered by a leading member of the British Communist Party is worth noting:

> The analysis of class structure is a key starting point for a
> Marxist analysis of any society. Yet all too often in our analysis
> we rely on the over-simplified view that society is to be divided

7

solely between the working class on one side, and the capitalist class on the other.[4]

This version of Marxist class analysis I have termed orthodox Marxism, in spite of its simplistic interpretation of Marx. The consequence of this approach to class structure by Marxists is that until comparatively recently it was possible for both proponents and opponents of Marxism to talk of a Marxist class analysis with a degree of consensus about what was meant, if not about its validity.

Orthodox Marxism

The model of the class structure of capitalist societies embodied within orthodox Marxism either has been taken directly from, or at least coheres with, the picture of society sketched by Marx and Engels in *Manifesto of the Communist Party*. From this work it could be rightly concluded that they considered capitalism to be characterised by two classes only:

> Our epoch, the epoch of the bourgeoisie possesses, however, this distinct feature: it has simplified class antagonisms. Society as a whole is more and more splitting up into two great hostile camps, into two great classes directly facing each other: bourgeoisie and proletariat.[5]

These developments were explained by the constant need of the capitalists to expand their production and to revolutionise the means of production, causing increasing concentration of industry and the destruction of small-scale and independent production. As a consequence:

> The lower strata of the middle class — the small trades-people, shopkeepers, and retired tradesmen generally, the handicraftsmen and peasants — all these sink gradually into the proletariat, partly because their diminutive capital does not suffice for the scale on which Modern Industry is carried on, and is swamped in the competition with large capitalists, partly because their specialized skill is rendered worthless by new methods of production. Thus the proletariat is recruited from all classes of the population.[6]

Such a bold and sweeping picture opens up this analysis to a formidable criticism in that it can be argued that the actual course of development of capitalist societies has not been along this path. Marx, it is claimed, failed to foresee the expanding middle class that came with capitalist development and which has greatly increased social stability. To quote one of his critics, A.J.P. Taylor:

It is not true that everyone but a few capitalists is being forced into the ranks of the proletariat. Quite the contrary. The proletariat has tended to remain a static element in society, or even to decline. Marx in his analysis never seems to acknowledge the middle men and administrators who make capitalism work. The more capitalism flourishes, the more there are of them. Advanced capitalism has brought with it an increasing middle class.[7]

Even more sympathetic critics have expressed unease with Marx's account of the demise of the middle class. G.D.H. Cole, for instance, complained that:

Wherever Marxism won acceptance, the middle class ceased to be looked upon as a coherent and creative social group, and came to be thought of as merely a nuisance getting in the way of real historic conflict between the developed grande bourgeoisie and the proletariat.[8]

Anthony Giddens elaborated on this point, reducing Marx's treatment of the middle classes to two alternatives:

Middle classes are either of a transitional type, or they are segments of the major classes. Thus the bourgeoisie are a 'middle' class in feudalism, prior to their ascent to power; while the petty bourgeoisie, the small property owners, whose interests are partly divergent from those of large scale capital, formed what Marx sometimes explicitly refers to as the 'middle class' in capitalism.[9]

Giddens claimed that the dichotomous model that Marx employed was therefore unable to 'encompass that grouping, which has always escaped adequate analysis in Marxist terms, the new middle class'.[10]

These criticisms are somewhat harsh because the prognosis given for the lower strata of the middle class in *Manifesto of the Communist Party* has, if unevenly, been borne out. It is a less than adequate criticism, therefore, to claim that Marx's analysis of this class fails to explain a development that is separate from, though related to, the demise of this group, namely the growth of a new middle class that is constituted within the capitalist production process. Furthermore, it is, in fact, not correct that Marx made no reference to the growth of this new middle class. He was far from unaware of these developments. Indeed, commenting on David Ricardo in *Theories of Surplus Value*,

Marx stated:

> What he forgets to emphasize is the constantly growing number of the middle class, those who stand between the workmen on the one hand and the capitalist and the landlord on the other. The middle classes maintain themselves to an ever increasing extent directly out of revenue, they are a burden weighing heavily on the working base and increase the social security of the upper ten thousand.[11]

It is the case, however, that this awareness was not given any central importance by Marx and the passage itself remained unpublished during his lifetime. Moreover, the growth of the new middle class has subsequently not been considered by Marxists as altering the basic schema laid down by Marx in *Manifesto of the Communist Party*. Georg Lukács, for example, an important and original Marxist theorist in other areas, was solidly orthodox on this aspect of Marxism. In 1920, he stated that:

> Bourgeoisie and proletariat are the only broad classes in bourgeois society. They are the only classes whose existence and development are entirely dependent on the course taken by the modern evolution of production. . . . The outlook of other classes (petty bourgeois or peasants) is ambiguous or sterile because their existence is not based on their role in the capitalist system of production but is indissolubly linked with the vestiges of feudal society.[12]

Marxists, both inside and outside the Communist Parties, have continued to show a relatively common response to the rise of the salaried middle class that has grown with the expansion of capitalism. Whatever the term used by sociologists to describe this class, whether it be white-collar workers, non-manual workers, or the salariat, orthodox Marxists maintain that white-collar workers are either already objectively proletarian or are in the process of so becoming. This approach concentrates upon the relations of these groups to the means of production. It is argued that because they do not own the means of production they therefore need to sell their labour-power, and this is considered a sufficient criterion for their inclusion in the proletariat. It matters not whether they are workers by hand or brain, or whether they consider themselves to be so: they are proletarians.

There have been periodic attempts to argue from a more theoretical position that wage-labour, whatever its form, is the defining feature of the working class. Robert Schaeffer and James Weinstein, for instance, have argued that:

Marx's method of class analysis begins by abstracting people's common relation to capital (taken as a whole) and then demonstrates that the relation between capital and labor is based on abstract labor. . . . This relation is premised on the reduction of labor to a position of dependence on capital, which alone could provide it with a means of surviving.

This relationship is not based on what Marx called concrete heterogeneous labor (labor in all its complex and variegated forms) — labor with different skills performing different tasks within the capitalist division of labor. Marx insisted on the former, abstract labor, being the necessary tool of class analysis because capital continually puts living labor to different uses. And these uses change over time.[13]

The implication of the approach is that all those waged groups regarded as middle-class are in reality but part of a differentiated working class. They emphasise that: 'The particular kinds of labor, skills, and jobs employed by capital are always undergoing change. Capital is not tied to *any* particular kind of concrete labor.'[14]

When Marx was writing *Manifesto of the Communist Party* it was, of course, much clearer who was the wage labourer and who was not. A clear distinction is much more problematic today. The differentiation of functions within the productive process, complicated by the separation of legal ownership and control, has made the line between labour and capital much more difficult to discern. Schaeffer and Weinstein, in fact, recognise this in practice. When they considered certain categories of labour, such as scientists and engineers, which they regarded as charged with implementing strategies of control over the working class, Schaeffer and Weinstein maintained that these groups did so as 'representatives of capital'.[15] The implications of this designation for the class situation of these workers were, however, not explored. Having argued against the existence of a new middle class within the capitalist mode of production, Schaeffer and Weinstein were unable to resolve the problem of the location of the cleavage between their expanded working class and labour that acts as agents of capital.

Other orthodox Marxist accounts of class structure solve the difficult problem of the location of the line of cleavage between the two classes by admitting that intermediate strata blur the demarcation line, while at the same time stressing the validity of a two-class theory. The Communist Parties of Europe, in particular, have found this device convenient for maintaining their adherence to 'classical' Marxism in principle, while at the

11

same time attempting to come to terms with a changed reality. G. Ross, summarising the position of the French Communist Party (P.C.F.) in 1978 stated that:

> The P.C.F.'s general outlook is that in state monopoly capitalism there exist only two real classes, the bourgeoisie and proletariat. However, it is obvious that all social groups within the system cannot be subsumed within these two classes, since there are strata which do not fit into either basic category. Between two major classes exist a panoply of what the P.C.F. calls *couches intermédiaires*. . . . For the P.C.F. there are not only no 'new middle classes', there are no 'middle classes' at all, but rather a series of strata lying between bourgeoisie and proletariat. . . . The outer boundary at one extreme of the *couches intermédiaires* is participation in exploitation (either as a direct employer of labour or as a managerial functionary), which confers bourgeois class membership.[16]

Furthermore, the European Communist Parties were also able to uphold the basic dynamic of class development as outlined by Marx in *Manifesto of the Communist Party*:

> The general thrust of the P.C.F.'s analysis is to view all strata in society not immediately either bourgeois or proletarian as engaged in an historical process of becoming one or the other, as capitalism evolves . . . the general characteristic of the contemporary situation in France is that *all* of these groups have acquired deeper reasons to lean towards the working class.[17]

Similar perspectives are also held by the British Communist Party and can be summarised by the position outlined by Alan Hunt in his analysis of class structure in contemporary Britain. He argued that:

> it [the 'middle class'] certainly does not constitute a class in the Marxist use of that term, because its members do not share any objective unity of interests that separate them from the working class . . . it is necessary to reject the term middle class, and to insist on an analysis that examines the function of those who are neither employers nor manual workers. In particular it is necessary to concentrate on the functional relationship of the middle strata with the two main social classes in British society. That is, to distinguish between those whose primary economic activity is to carry out the functions of the capitalist, and are closely integrated with the success and failures of capitalism, and those whose primary position is the

selling of their labour power.[18]

He considered the distinction sufficiently clear to conclude that 'the vast majority of those in non-manual occupations, in that they sell their labour, and are exploited in the realisation of surplus value, are members of the working class'.[19] Once more the processes of history were firmly on the side of the proletariat. Of those middle strata not yet within the bounds of the working class, the major area of growth was at the lower income level, with the consequence that: 'Here people are employed at incomes not dissimilar from those in manual occupations. What is more important is that the style and nature of their work is increasingly similar to that of the manual working class.'[20] By emphasising the income levels of the middle strata and by simply asserting that the style and nature of their work was increasingly similar to that of the manual working class, Hunt formulated the problem in such a way as to minimise the differences between the middle strata and the working class. Conversely, the earlier insistence on the necessity to examine the functional relationship of the middle strata to the two main social classes is now absent. The middle strata can thus be collapsed into an expanded working class:

> The position of the middle strata is that we must underline their membership of the working class properly defined; the separation that exists is subjective and ideological in character, and its objective base is less stable. In this context it is important that in the definition of 'working class' emphasis must be placed upon the primary criterion, that of the sale of labour power for wages and salaries, rather than on the particular type of work done.[21]

The contradictions in this conclusion are rife. If the middle strata are part of the working class, then the concept of a middle strata is not necessary. On the other hand, an objective base for separation of this strata from the working class is recognised, stable or not. Finally, there are few people in the economy who do not appear to sell their labour-power for wages or salaries[22] and therefore Hunt fails in his aim, stated elsewhere, of finding a definition that avoids identifying 'the whole of the middle strata, particularly managers and higher professionals, with the working class'.[23]

The appeal to Marxists of analyses such as the above, which expand the working class, is obvious. But such analyses have brought serious problems in their train. In particular, the necessity arises to explain why numerous groups of workers

13

consistently fail to act in concert with other workers in their own class interests and exhibit no class consciousness. Attempts have been made to overcome this problem by accounting for the failure of white-collar workers to act in their own objective interests by subjective and ideological factors, the inhibitive nature of which will be overcome in the long-term. One example will suffice: 'As non-manual labour increases proportionately to manual, the likeness between the lower strata of the former and manual labour will increase both economically and status-wise. Class consciousness and trade unionism will increase.'[24]

The mechanical nature of such formulations has done little to convince the critics of Marxism that the entire analysis of the development of class structure is not simply based on wishful thinking rather than upon detailed observation of the actual development of capitalist societies. Frank Parkin, in particular, has revelled in the unconvincing nature of such a perspective:

> The awkwardness of this theoretical stance becomes evident whenever social groups act in blatant nonconformity with their assigned place in the formal scheme of things. Marxism in particular has been greatly exercised by the need to account for the well known tendency for the embodiments of labour to act politically in ways not altogether consistent with the stated opposition towards capital and its representatives.[25]

Having identified the key components of the orthodox Marxist class analysis and some of the problems arising from it, what have been the alternative conceptions established in contradistinction to it?

The challenge to orthodox Marxism in Germany

The most sustained attempts to formulate an alternative to the orthodox Marxist model of the class structure of capitalist societies took place in Germany in the period from the turn of this century to Hitler's seizure of power in 1933. During this period there was an extended debate on the social position of white-collar workers as competing theories claimed that this section of society belonged to first one class, then another. The reason for the greater interest in this group in Germany than elsewhere lay not in any difference in the role of white-collar workers in the economy, but rather their rate of development and the historical circumstances in which they grew. Despite later industrialisation, Germany was the most advanced industrial country in Europe by the early twentieth century, surpassing Britain and France in the key indices of pig iron, chemicals and

14

electrical power.[26] Indeed, Thorstein Veblen, in his *Imperial Germany and the Industrial Revolution*, 1915, argued that it was this very lateness in developing that enabled her to avoid 'the penalty of taking the lead'.[27] Germany, he pointed out, could borrow on a massive scale from the accumulated knowledge and technology of already industrialised societies. The result was, however, that when change did come to German society it was all the more abrupt and brutal. The balance between urban and rural areas changed rapidly. In 1871, two-thirds of the German population lived in the countryside; by 1910, almost two-thirds lived in towns. This change reflected both a decline in agricultural labour and the transformation of traditional trades: indeed, 'some trades even passed in a single generation through the three stages – independent handicraft, outwork and the factory system – an evolution which . . . had taken several centuries in earlier ages'.[28]

Simultaneously with these developments the German labour movement emerged as an important social force. Trade union membership doubled between 1891 and 1899, doubled again by 1904 to reach over one million members and once again doubled in the following six years.[29] The membership of the German unions had close ties with the Social Democratic Party of Germany (S.P.D.) and for a period their memberships were practically synonymous. The growth of the S.P.D., based on a seemingly Marxist programme,[30] was phenomenal, the Party becoming the first political mass organisation and the model for subsequent organisations. Founded in 1875, the membership of the Party grew steadily, reaching 384,000 in 1906. In the years up to 1912 the annual rate of increase was between 10 and 30 per cent, enabling the Party to achieve more than one million members by the outbreak of the First World War. In power, in size, and in theoretical influence the S.P.D. overshadowed every other socialist organisation in the world.

The growth of large-scale industry, the decline of independent and small-scale manufacturers and the growth of a politically organised proletariat all appeared to readily bear out the orthodox Marxist vision of an increasingly simplified class structure. There was, however, within these developments, a particular development at variance with the model that was in need of explanation: the salaried middle class grew at a faster rate than manual workers, giving Germany the highest ratio of salaried workers to manual workers in industry anywhere in Europe (Table 1.1).[31]

Instead of the decline of the social groups that Marx had indicated as swelling the ranks of the proletariat, they were being

15

TABLE 1.1 *Approximate number of salaried employees in industry per 1000 manual workers before and after the First World War*

	Pre-war		Post-war	
	Year	Number	Year	Number
Germany	1907	82	1925	154 *88*
Denmark	1911	77	1921	117 *52*
Great Britain	1907	74	1924	108 *46*
Norway	1910	73	1920	72 *1*
France	1906	66	1921	107 *62*
Belgium	1910	45	1920	39 *13*

reconstituted in salaried administrative, scientific and technical jobs within the productive process.[32] As a result of the growth of this *new* middle class the proportion of the proletariat in industry as compared with the labour force as a whole dropped from 56.8 per cent in 1895 to 45.1 per cent in 1925.[33]

Reformist and conservative social theorists alike seized upon the rise of the new middle class to refute the orthodox Marxist model and to provide alternative analyses of the development of the class structure. In this situation the future development of middle-class labour was considered a key issue in determining the balance of class forces by both Marxists and their opponents.

The German debate: a white-collar proletariat or a new middle class?

German Marxists were, of course, not unaware of the growth of white-collar labour. Indeed, Karl Kautsky (1854–1938) even asserted that he had been one of the first to discover this group. As the leading theoretician of German Social Democracy – he virtually founded and for thirty-five years edited *Die Neue Zeit*, the theoretical journal of the movement – his views were of considerable importance. Moreover, his prestige and influence spread far beyond Germany through the Socialist International. Having known both Marx and Engels in his youth, he became their principal literary executor on their deaths, and his writings on a whole range of subjects were regarded everywhere as classical statements of the socialist view. The fact that he is now better remembered for the polemics written against him by the Bolshevik leadership[34] should in no way be allowed to diminish the very real influence he had before the First World War.

The 'new middle class', Kautsky argued in 1899, was created by the desire of the top exploiters to slough off clerical duties. The growth in the size of enterprises, industries and state functions accelerated the process. He cautioned, however, that 'we would be committing a grave error if we merely added these people to the owning classes. The new middle class is based on entirely different foundations from the old, which is the firm bulwark of private property in the means of production.'[35] On the other hand, Kautsky did not believe that this new middle class could be treated by the socialist movement simply as proletarians because most of its members had been recruited from the bourgeoisie and many possessed educational privileges not enjoyed by workers. Kautsky considered this latter qualification to be of only temporary significance, however, and argued that the dominant trend was one of proletarianisation of the new middle class as part of a general process of growing polarisation. He stated that:

> As much as they cling to bourgeois appearances, the time will come for everyone of the proletarianized strata of the white collar groups at which they discover their proletarian heart. Then they will take an interest in the proletarian class struggle and finally they will participate in it actively.[36]

From the 1890s onwards this orthodox position came under increasing attack, not only from those who were openly hostile to the working-class movement, but also from the revisionist wing of the S.P.D. and particularly from its leading exponent, Eduard Bernstein (1850–1932). He held that Marxism needed to be revised, a view most succinctly stated in his *Evolutionary Socialism*, first published in 1899, which proclaimed his belief that socialism would come about through the gradual democratisation of capitalism.[37] He argued that the workers' movement, therefore, had to abandon the policy of class struggle for one of class collaboration with the 'progressive' bourgeoisie.

His views on the development of the class structure in capitalist society were a key component in his argument. Rejecting what he saw as the simplistic view of the orthodox Marxists, Bernstein insisted that the class structure of capitalism was highly complex: 'The structure of society has not become simplified. Far from it. Rather, both as far as income and economic activity are concerned, it has become further graduated and differentiated.'[38] Indeed, by so emphasising the complexities, the differences within classes, and the co-operation between classes, Bernstein came close to abandoning the concept of class altogether.

17

Although he nowhere gave a systematic treatment of the new middle class, it is of central importance to his overall argument, its growth underpinning his theory of gradualism and refuting Marxist claims of the polarisation of classes. This can clearly be seen in the following passage:

Social conditions have not reached the acute tension which the *Communist Manifesto* had predicted. Not only would it be useless, it would be the height of folly to conceal this from ourselves. The number of propertied people has not diminished but become larger. The enormous increase in social wealth is accompanied not by a shrinking number of capitalist magnates but by a growing number of capitalists of all ranges of wealth. The middle classes change their character, but they do not disappear from the social scale.[39]

The attention Bernstein paid to the spread of shareholding in corporations and growing income levels prefigured many subsequent attempts to refute Marxism. In addition to this empirical evidence, he also put forward a theoretical explanation for the growth of the new middle class, arguing that the vast increase in the productivity of labour and hence of the wealth produced meant that capitalists alone could not consume it all.[40] Nor could it all be exported:

Where does this mass of commodities go which is not consumed by the magnates and their stooges? If it does not go to the proletarians in one way or another, it must be absorbed by other classes. Either relative decrease in the number of capitalists and increasing wealth of the proletariat, or a numerous middle class − these are the only alternatives permitted by the continuous increase of productivity.[41]

The middle class that was growing within industry, however, was of a changed social character to the old middle class (as indicated above). Bernstein was confident that a large part of the increasing number of technical, office and sales personnel, as well as government employees would feel 'a strong community of interests with the workers'. He argued that 'the majority of them identify themselves more and more with the working class and should be added to it − along with their dependents'.[42]

Where Bernstein differed from the view put forward by Kautsky was in the nature of the process by which the identification of the middle class with the working class would take place. Bernstein argued against any idea that the unity of the two classes would be achieved by the acceptance of the new middle class that they were sinking to the low level of the

18

proletariat. Nor did he wish to see this outcome:

> Social Democracy does not wish to dissolve this society and to make proletarians of all its members. Rather, it labors incessantly at lifting the worker from the social position of the proletarian to that of a 'bourgeois' and thus to make 'bourgeoisie' — or citizenship — universal.[43]

The unification of interests was therefore to be achieved by the dual process of proletarianisation of parts of the new middle class and embourgeoisement of the working class, as well as through the intermarriage of the two classes. Moreover, these combined developments signalled a non-revolutionary outcome.

Outside the labour movement orthodox Marxism was confronted by more conservative and reactionary thinkers. In the years before the First World War, German writers and theorists such as Sombart, Salin and Spann emphasised the importance of peasants, artisans and shopkeepers and the old independent professions.[44] After 1918, however, this concern with non-proletarian elements focused increasingly on the position and roles of the middle class in salaried employment. Important in this change of emphasis were Oswald Spengler, Ernst Niekisch and numerous contributors to the periodical *Die Tat*.[45] The 'Tat' circle published numerous investigations into the position of the new middle class, including their relationship to fascism and to the working class.

What united the theorists of the right was their conception that the new middle class would serve as a check against the polarisation of society. They conceived of the class as independent of both capitalists and workers, as a 'third force', a notion which *Die Tat* was particularly active in advancing.[46] As such the new middle class would take upon itself certain social and cultural functions that the old middle classes could no longer perform because of their numerical weakness. Mediating between increasingly concentrated capital on the one hand and labour on the other, the new middle class would bring an end to the instability of the social system.

Within this perspective the position of the salaried worker was considered to be fundamentally different from that of the manual worker, because the former performed what were seen as delegated entrepreneurial functions. The influence of the theory was quite widespread, being held by large sections of salaried workers in Germany. The Deutschnationaler Handlungsgehilfen-Verband (D.H.V.), the strongest organisation of salaried employees in Germany, for example, was particularly active in propagating such a view.[47]

19

The controversy that surrounded the social position of salaried employees was reflected within German academic social theory, and some outstanding work on the subject was produced. Prominent amongst the published works was Emil Lederer's *Die Privatangestellten in der Modernen Wirtschaftsentwicklung*, 1912, chapters II and III of which were translated in 1937 as *The Problem of the Modern Salaried Employee*. [48] Lederer was editor of the influential journal *Archiv für Sozialwissenschaft und Sozialpolitik*. He held the positions of Professor of Economics at the Universities of Heidelberg and Berlin before leaving Germany for the United States after the rise of Hitler. He continued his academic work in the United States becoming the Dean of the Graduate Faculty of Political and Social Science in the New School for Social Research in New York. He was also a founding editor of the journal *Social Research*, established in 1934.

In *The Problem of the Modern Salaried Employee*, Lederer shared the revisionist judgment on Marxism that it oversimplified the stratification of classes. He argued that, 'the formula "capitalistic-proletarian" blurs all contrasts within the economic order and thus obscures all distinctions outside of and within the process of production'.[49] Although he acknowledged that there was a process of concentration of industry taking place which had the consequence of reducing the number of employers and increasing the number of workers, he emphasised that the process had other consequences as well:

> Above all, there emerges a class of technicians who, from a social point of view, cannot be categorically classified as either employers or workers. The importance of this class is heightened by the creation of a socially analogous strata in commerce and public service which make up an ever increasing portion of the population.[50]

In attempting to differentiate between salaried employees and workers, Lederer examined both technical and social differences between the two groups and concluded that no precise definition of the term 'salaried employee' was possible. He considered, however, that it was possible, by using two sets of criteria, to grasp the essential features of the salaried employee. Lederer designated a worker a salaried employee if:

> his work is exclusively manual, similar to that of a labourer, but concurrently assumes a special character on account of his intellectual contribution, or if his work is neither intellectual nor exclusively manual (i.e. only concerned with production).
> . . . Concretely expressed, the performance of the technical

employee is predominantly manual and, concomitantly, intellectual (e.g. the activities of a draftsman, a construction or chemical engineer); moreover, it is as a rule preparatory. The function of the commercial employee is frequently not intellectual (e.g. that of the store salesman or, even more, those of the stock room clerk); yet it is not merely manual like the work of the laborer engaged in production; within the stated boundaries are the absolutely intellectual functions, such as those of the accountant or factory manager.[51]

But it is not the case, as has been argued, that Lederer's distinctions were based solely upon a 'brain/brawn' dichotomy that might be inferred from the above.[52] Lederer goes on to insist that what unites salaried workers in contradistinction to manual workers was not their technical functions but their analogous social positions:

> In neither of these groups [i.e. technical and commercial employees] is social esteem, which determines their peculiar position, based upon the nature of their technical or economic work; on the contrary, their social valuation is chiefly decided by their relationship to the important classes, the employer and laborers. This middle position between the two classes − a negative characteristic − rather than definite technical functions, is the social mark of the salaried employees and establishes their social character on their own consciousness and in the estimation of the community. Hence, apart from their technical function, the social position of the salaried employees is of great significance.[53]

Lederer stressed that it was possible to speak of the 'same social position' of salaried workers only with many reservations, because the lower strata merge with the proletariat and the highest stratum with the class of employers. He maintained nevertheless that:

> uniformity may be established in a higher degree than at first seems possible by taking the relation of each group of employees to the employer and manual workers, between whom the employee group stands, as a criterion. Thus the foreman in a medium-sized enterprise stands between the employer and his help, i.e. in a position similar to that of a factory manager who stands between the large-scale employer and the industrial working class.[54]

As a consequence of the wide internal differentiation of

21

salaried employees, Lederer noted a tendency for both the capitalist and proletarian classes to absorb portions of salaried employees. He nevertheless believed that this in no way precluded the possibility that salaried employees would more and more become an independent group, not only on account of the increase in their numbers, but also as a consequence of a growing consciousness of their special interests.

The conclusions that Lederer drew can be compared with those in a later work 'Der Neue Mittelstand', 1926, which he undertook with Jacob Marschak.[55] In some respects this work closely resembled Lederer's earlier contribution. Their definition of salaried employees was almost identical to Lederer's 1912 definition. It stressed both their common social position between the major classes and their heterogeneity, and went on to again state that this heterogeneity did not prevent salaried employees from presenting a relatively united front. The work differed, therefore, not so much in its methodology, but in its description of the changes that had occurred in the allegiance of salaried employees.

In assessing the possible courses of action open to salaried employees, Lederer and Marschak noted that 'the rapid increase of the employees enhances their effective power and activity as a group'.[56] This enhanced power could be used in one of three ways. It could:

> offer a counterweight to the increasing numerical strength of the laboring class. In the social and political field, and elsewhere, the employees could adopt a policy aimed against the excessive concentration of business and against the elimination of the small independent from the economy − a policy which might be supported by various groups of employees in the whole national economy. Similarly, the employees could infinitely strengthen the position of the wage earner in the struggle between capital and labor, and considerably imperil the power of the entrepreneur.[57]

Had salaried employees adopted the course of supporting small business and maintained independence from both capital and labour, they would have acted in accordance with Lederer's earlier analysis. Indeed, Lederer and Marschak provided some reasons why at the time of the earlier study, such a perspective was a viable alternative:

> The employees, for the most part, come from the former independents or, at any rate, from 'bourgeois' strata. Before the collapse of 1918, their income was considerably higher than

the average income of wage-earners. Compared with the latter their work is characterised by definite qualifications; it enjoys higher social prestige and brings them in direct touch with the entrepreneur class. Moreover, [until] recently, it was possible for the salaried employee to attain a position consistent with his abilities or to become himself an independent. Such considerations foster among the employees those tendencies which seek to check the material and social degradation of their class and aim at the preservation of their middle-class standards of living and of their prestige.[58]

The move to organise as a new middle class meant that members of that class had to acknowledge that they were employees. The demands of the group had therefore taken the form of a labour policy, but, at the same time, Lederer and Marschak claimed that it could not be characterised as a proletarian policy, describing it as having 'an unmistakable middle-class character'.[59]

The common class interests of this group before 1918 were reflected in demands that were distinct from the social programme of wage-earners. According to Lederer and Marschak these included: the demand for employees' old age insurance; the abrogation of any clause in employment contracts which restrained the employee from entering the service of a rival concern; the safeguarding of employees' property rights to their inventions; the regulation of apprenticeships; and the establishment of uniform discharge notices. Their position as employees ensured that there were many aspects in common with labour's social programme, such as the demand for the unqualified right to organise and the extension of certain protective measures that at the time covered manual workers alone. As a whole, however, the policy was a middle-class one, modified by their dependency on employment.

Within this general characterisation of the policy of salaried employees, Lederer and Marschak noted variations, notably between commercial and technical employees. The former were strongly influenced by 'the traditional notion of one united mercantile class' and allowed employers to become members of many of their unions, which 'effectively precluded the adoption of all trade-union policies (strikes, collective bargaining, etc.)'. The technicians, in contrast, were 'strongly influenced by modern labor policies'. But even in the latter case radical employee organisations uncompromisingly rejected any co-operation with the manual workers' trade union movement, as well as rejecting its socialist ideology.[60]

The economic and social conditions that had underpinned such an independent course in the pre-war world changed dramatically in the post-war era. The attempted revolution in 1918; the reparations forced upon Germany by the victors of the war; the collapse of the mark on the international market; increasing domestic inflation and growing unemployment, placed huge strains on the fabric of German society. Consequently, according to Lederer and Marschak, a fundamental reorientation took place among salaried employees:

The 'middle-class' character of the salaried employee had to capitulate before the growing notion of the mere wage earner. Proletarianization of the middle-class strata, which went on at an unprecedented pace, and the raising of the social status of the 'manual worker', which brought him steadily closer to the employee, proved stronger than any class tradition. The economic conditions, the political changes, the recognition of trade unions and the abolition of all traditional conceptions of the social order forced the employee organisations to adopt the aims and methods of the labor unions. Consequently, numerous groups of employees rallied under the new banner.

The transformation of the whole employee movement after 1918 had the additional effect of shifting the balance of power to the more radical employee associations and of causing further changes in their policies. Such changes were the replacement, in associations, of the policy of 'harmony' by a trade union policy, and the infiltration of the formerly rejected socialistic doctrines into the radical organisations. . . . What is still more important, activities characteristic of the policy of labor unions − such as collective wage agreements and 'organised labor's last resort', the strike − were finally adopted and practiced in the manner of labor organisations.[61]

Lederer and Marschak concluded from these developments that the term 'new middle class', which they considered hardly appropriate when discussing the years before 1918, was even less appropriate after that date. Before the war, employees had in some respects attempted to secure for themselves the *economic security* of the old middle class. In other respects, they had exhibited a tendency to form a stratum *sui generis* and, as such, to remain independent of other social classes. But Lederer and Marschak claimed, 'even at this time it was apparent that, should they ever attach themselves to some social class, that could only be the class of organised labor. . . . As a result of the post-war collapse of the economy the alliance with labor has now become a fact'.[62]

Lederer and Marschak's conclusions were, therefore, radically different from those drawn by Lederer in his earlier work. Nor, it should be stressed, were the developments that they noted as a result of changed social conditions, regarded as temporary ones, lasting only as long as the new circumstances. Rather the allegiance of salaried employees to the working-class movement was regarded as part of a long-term historical process:

Urban society is constantly organising itself on the principle of group interests. . . . An intermediate position 'between the classes' is no longer possible and the fact of being employed in a dependent capacity triumphs over all class and traditional restraints. The adoption by the salaried employees and public officials of the aims and methods of labor (collective salary agreements), and the tendency among civil servants to change their relationship to the state from a subordinate one determined by public law [*Vertragsverhältnis*] are expressive of the fact that a single stratum of gainfully employed (if not a single organisation) is in the process of formation.[63]

This historical process, according to Lederer and Marschak, resulted in the simplification of the class structure. Echoing the commonplace view in orthodox Marxism, they claimed that the extensive pre-war stratification of social groups was based on ideological rather than economic differences. With the sweeping away of the last vestiges of the economic differentiation of salaried employees from the working class, the most serious objections to an organic alliance with the trade unions had been removed.

In concluding thus, they arrived at a position little different from the orthodox Marxism that Lederer had set out to attack fourteen years earlier. In so doing they ignored observations they themselves had made which provided evidence of a continuing differentiation among salaried employees and which made their allegiances far from unproblematic, stating, for example:

The radical turn in the movement of the great masses of 'the new middle class' prompted, on the other hand, a consolidation of the traditionally conservative tendencies in certain organisations of salaried employees and civil servants in the higher ranks . . . precisely because of the growing number of salaried employees and civil servants, certain groups with a higher social, intellectual and financial status sought to separate themselves from the masses and pursue their own aims independently. These groups endeavour for the most part to assure a privileged status to civil servants in higher ranks or

25

possessing academic training. Accordingly, these organisations of employees reveal a distinctly middle-class, conservative tendency. This explains why, after the revolution [i.e. 1918], the associations of higher salaried employees and public officials were practically the only ones that had nothing to do with a trade-unionist policy.[64]

What was more, Lederer and Marschak made it clear that the adoption of such a strategy stemmed not merely from different roles, but from ones that were also antagonistic to many other salaried employees: 'Sometimes the interests actually clash, as in the case of the executive salaried employees and higher public officials who in reality are called upon to perform a great many of the employers' functions.'[65] Lederer and Marschak failed to apply these observations to their analysis partly because their definition of salaried employees was too general, concentrating on those aspects that united the group rather than its heterogeneity. Thus, when they conceived of the changed positions and allegiances, they did so for salaried employees as a whole rather than seeing the possibility of contradictory tendencies amongst those employees. They therefore arrived at a view of salaried employees that was much too radical.

Given Lederer's failure to theorise correctly the nature of the new middle class and his tendency to characterise them by their level of activity and their identifications at a given time, it is not surprising that the collapse of employee radicalism should find him once again reverting to a position akin to his original one. Writing in *State of the Masses*, 1940, he again starkly refuted the orthodox Marxist view:

> The 'new middle classes' evolved rapidly; they were supposed to develop into a proletariat, according to orthodox socialist theory, while the conservatives expected them to become a stabilizing factor, a counterweight to the proletarianization of large masses. The new middle classes, in fact, formed a new layer of society, the size as well as the character of which was a new phenomenon. . . . They did not consider themselves as proletarians; they revolted against the idea that they should be of the same class. In fact there was a deep social cleavage, for neighbouring classes in a highly stratified society, with great emphasis on social differences, tend to deepen the gap between them, the more so the greater the potentiality that they merge.[66]

Not all German theorists, however, were as directly influenced by the ebb and flow of political positions adopted by salaried employees in Weimar Germany. Hans Speier, for example, continued to stress the specific nature of groups of salaried employees. Speier was a lecturer at the Deutsche Hochschule für Politik in Berlin and, like Lederer, was deeply involved in the *Archiv für Sozialwissenschaft und Sozialpolitik*. Again, like Lederer, he fled to the United States when Hitler seized power and joined the New School for Social Research, serving as Secretary for the journal *Social Research*.

In two works, 'The Salaried Employee in Modern Society', 1934, and *The Salaried Employee in German Society*, 1939, Speier continued to argue explicitly against the tendency to view groups of salaried employees from the vantage points of either capitalist or proletarian ideology.[67] Whilst acknowledging that salaried employees were a stratum within the working class whose economic and social interests were different from those of the entrepreneur, he argued that nevertheless their interests did not coincide with those of manual workers. The sociology of salaried employees, while accepting that salaried employees were wage-earners, should, he maintained, 'examine the difference between them and labor and evaluate its importance'.[68]

The relationship of salaried employees to employers Speier presented as a complex one. Originally brought into being to perform the planning, administrative and control functions previously performed by the capitalists themselves, these employees were regarded as socially superior to workers. Increasingly, however, these functions were performed by numerous relatively poorly paid and subordinate employees. Only a minority who held superior positions received higher pay than manual workers, the explanation for this being that 'the social level of the salaried employee sinks within the increasing extent of the group'.[69] Moreover, he concluded that 'to the employer the white collar workers are employees who burden the salary account. To this extent they are pushed down to the level of the manual workers'.[70] This tendency for salaried workers to be proletarianised was, he suggested also reflected in the increasing recruitment of employees from working-class origins into salaried positions.

At one and the same time, however, Speier argued that the very expansion of salaried employment which was depressing the social superiority of salaried employees presented new opportunities for existing employees, especially male employees from middle-class backgrounds. This resulted in a greater stratification within the salaried work-force which was based both on class background and sex.[71]

The division of salaried employees into different trade union

27

organisations according to the different political affiliations of those organisations had, therefore, an objective base, reflecting the different origins and roles of different groups of salaried workers within the workplace. Hence, in 1934, Speier could note that while, on the one hand, 12 per cent of salaried employees – chiefly technicians, employees in department stores and employees in the administration of social insurance – belonged to socialist organisations, on the other hand, a small minority of principal employees corresponded to the theory that salaried workers exercised delegated employer responsibility and supported the D.H.V.

This still left Speier with the major problem of explaining 'the peculiar position and consciousness' of the vast majority of salaried employees whose affiliations were with organisations 'adhering to a more or less prominent middle-class doctrine'.[72] This he attempted to do by maintaining that the character of work 'does not suffice to explain the superiority of salaried workers over manual workers, for the great majority of them perform only simple portions of a divided process and can easily be replaced'.[73] Rather their superiority was based upon a social valuation, based upon a 'pluralism of social esteem, which corresponds to various ideas of domination, various ideals of social rank, various potentialities for distinction'.[74]

The causes of the higher social valuation of white-collar workers in Germany were given by Speier as follows:

1 because of their share in the authority of those who rule the undertaking,
   (a) as assistants to the small entrepreneurs
   (b) as functionaries of the capitalists
2 because of their education: as co-bearers of the intelligence of scientific experience
3 because of their share in official authority as a result of their nationalistic sentiment.[75]

Speier recognised that certain of these principles were more applicable to particular groups of white-collar employees than others: 'Thus the possibility listed under (1) a is applicable only to white collar workers in small cities, who work in small establishments, while (1) b is predominantly operative in medium-sized establishments.'[76] While all white-collar workers could attain the esteem arising from education, this principle was also particularly relevant to salaried employees in medium-sized and large cities, where the expansion of modern specialised education had taken place. Finally, the third principle applied to all salaried workers, except those who tended to be in particular social positions and who supported socialist organisations.

Of these principles, Speier considered that (1) b and (3) were the most interesting. Without going into detail, Speier maintained that the former could be shown by an analysis of the social consequences of the hierarchy within an establishment. Such hierarchical organisation caused the salaried employee to be subordinate to those above him but superior to those below him. If the Marxian analysis of there being two main classes was accepted, Speier argued, then the class affiliation of the white-collar workers was hidden.

Speier thus presented a much more balanced analysis of salaried employees than did Lederer and Marschak. In his model the social level of the great majority of this group was sinking, but only a small minority had affiliations with the working class: the great majority continued, despite this downward movement, to display distinctly middle-class characteristics. What was more, their social valuation continued to be higher than manual workers despite their growing proletarianisation. The suggestion was clear that the vast majority of white-collar workers would seek 'to maintain the social distance between them and manual workers'[77] even if the eventual cost was National Socialism. It is not possible to deny that this was partly the explanation for the rise of German fascism. What must be challenged, however, is that such a development was historically inevitable because of the nature of salaried employees.

To explain the reactions of middle-class labour and their support for fascism it is not sufficient to centre upon the nature of their position and their self-conceptions alone. It is also necessary to examine the balance of forces between the two major classes and to examine the effect that this has upon the psychology of middle-class labour. Writing contemporaneously with Speier, Leon Trotsky provided a more dynamic framework within which to understand the path taken by German white-collar workers. In a series of pamphlets and articles written between 1930 and 1933, Trotsky provided an unparalleled analysis of the unfolding of German fascism.[78]

Speier acknowledged that the social crisis had caused salaried employees to look for solutions through various allegiances. Indeed, he stated at one point that 'they have supported a different party at almost every election'.[79] Nevertheless, the possibility of contradictory tendencies both within the group and over time was not emphasised. For Trotsky, however, these contradictory tendencies were central to his evaluation of the role of middle-class labour. The new petty bourgeoisie, along with the old, was essentially a vacillating social force and the failure to

29

attract it to the revolutionary pole was part of a general failure to attract the vast majority of workers. As Ernest Mandel commented in his introduction to Trotsky's works on the growth of German fascism:

> At first the fascist bands organize only the most resolute and desperate parts of the petty bourgeoisie (the part 'gone mad'). The petty bourgeois masses, as well as the unconscious and unorganized part of the wage workers — especially young workers and white-collar youth — will normally waver back and forth between the two camps. They will be inclined to join the side that demonstrates the greater boldness and decisiveness. They want to bet on the winning horse.[80]

Few would accuse the German Communist Party in the 1930s of such boldness and decisiveness, and Trotsky concluded that even as far as the rank and file workers were concerned, 'the policy of the Communist Party does not inspire them with confidence, not because the Communist Party is a revolutionary party, but because they do not believe in its ability to gain a revolutionary victory, and do not wish to risk their heads in vain'.[81] Trotsky, in some detail, noted what he described as the 'mistakes, defects, fictions, and direct deception of the masses' from 1923 to 1930. As a consequence of these, he believed that: 'Without internal confidence in itself, the party will not conquer the class. Not to conquer the proletariat means not to break the petty bourgeois masses away from fascism. One is inextricably bound up with the other.'[82]

A similar 'Trotskyite' analysis of the vacillations of the middle classes was made by Daniel Guérin in his *Fascism and Big Business* first published in 1939. Guérin, a French journalist, concluded after his study of German fascism that:

> The working class disappoints the middle classes by showing itself incapable of finding a way out of the crisis. In addition, it exasperates the middle classes by its day-to-day economic struggles, which are too fragmentary and timid to even maintain past gains, but which are sufficient to maintain a state of instability without curing any of the ills of society as a whole. So the middle classes do an about face and blame not only the trusts, but also the workers for their economic stagnation.[83]

It may well be, therefore, as a matter of historical fact, that in the words of a much more recent commentator 'the answer given by the new middle class, when the centre and liberal parties collapsed, was by and large to shift their support to the Nazis rather than the working-class parties'.[84] But the analysis of writers like Trotsky and Guérin serve to remind us that it should not be implied from such a movement that this direction is the only one that could have been taken. In their view, the politics and organisation of the working class at particular points in history have a crucial part to play in influencing the direction of the politics of the new middle class.

The debate extended

Other theorists, writing after this period and in some cases about countries other than Germany, stand firmly within the traditions of this debate. This does not mean, of course, that they were unaffected by the changed social conditions after the Second World War. The pre-war identification of white-collar workers with fascism, together with the post-war stabilisation and expansion of capitalism, served to lessen the credibility of theories stressing rapid polarisation of classes and the proletarianisation of white-collar workers. The post-war world was, therefore, fertile ground for further refutations of the orthodox Marxist view.

A personal link with the earlier debate was provided by Karl Renner (1870–1950), the sole post-war survivor of the so-called 'Austro-Marxist' group.[85] On the reformist wing of the Austrian Social Democratic Party before the war, he became President of the Second Austrian Republic in 1945. His earlier work had maintained the need to revise Marx's theory of classes, but by 1953, when he published *Wandlungen der modernen Gesellschaft*,[86] the break between his own theory and that of Marx was complete. According to Renner, the post-war world had consolidated a new class – the service class – which arose from the growing sub-division of the functions of capitalists. As he saw it: 'These aids are neither capitalists nor workers, they are not owners of capital, they do not create value by their work, but they do control the values created by others'.[87] Renner considered that this new social stratum had traditionally been a caste opposed to the working class. Before the Second World War, 'the service class was on the borderline between caste and class. Fascism was able to gain support . . . from these castes by flattering their caste pride and promising to maintain their position of superiority'.[88] In the post-war world, however, they ceased to be a caste and became a class, the majority of whom were propertyless. This development produced the material base for the possibility of a democratic advance to socialism, as 'the service class is closer to the rising working class in its life style, and at its boundaries tends to merge with it'.[89] Renner's analysis, therefore, closely replicated that of Bernstein.

The voices of pre-war conservative critics of Marxism were also to be echoed by Fritz Croner. In his *Die Angestellten in der modernen Gesellschaft*, 1954, Croner claimed that the twentieth century had witnessed a social revolution and the emergence of a new class:[90]

> Everywhere the social revolution with which we are dealing here has changed the face of society fundamentally. . . . Its product and its bearer is a new social class: white collar.
>
> Capitalist order created in its beginning the social space for a new class: the class of salaried employees. . . . This process is the real cause why society today appears in an entirely different light than society 50 years ago: this social process is the real substance of the 'social revolution' of our time.[91]

The growth of this new class, and its parameters, Croner explained by the historic delegation to it of the original functions of employers. What distinguished white-collar workers was that they performed certain functions that were formerly carried out by the employers. These functions were broadly stated as administrative; design, analysis and planning; supervisory and managerial; and commercial. As the size and complexity of industrial organisations grew, it became, according to Croner, increasingly necessary for the employer to delegate some or all of these functions to subordinates. As the enterprise grew, so did the chain of managerial authority within it. No matter how routine or unskilled the work at the bottom of the hierarchy of command became, however, Croner maintained that it continued to be white-collar employment by nature of it having previously been performed by the employer. This functional approach, while appearing disarmingly simple and logical, was, in fact, difficult to apply. It incorrectly assumed that jobs could simply be defined as either supervisory, administrative or commercial, though Croner himself avoided this problem − or rather obscured its existence − by including whole industrial sectors in his functional areas.

The second element of Croner's theory − that certain functions were delegated by employers to white-collar workers − was also seriously limited in its understanding of the formation of white-collar occupational roles. The historical model that Croner employed was that of the artisan initially delegating manual work and thus establishing himself as an employer. The functions of the employer were then later delegated to white-collar workers. This was, however, only one route to capitalist development which overall was a more complicated process. In England in the eighteenth century the first step in 'delegation' within many small businesses was not to an operative but to a clerk[92] or, in many cases, to the wife of the owner who acted as 'mistress of the managing part of it', while her husband continued to work at his craft or trade.[93] In the second half of the eighteenth century administrative, managerial, craft and design functions began to be delegated more or less simultaneously as master craftsmen such as furniture-makers expanded both the size and scope of their firms.[94] Croner's original employer, therefore, was a hypothetical rather than an historical construct. In concentrating on the delegation of the employer functions, he completely ignored what was an equally important historical shift of responsibility: much of the separation of supervisory, administrative and commercial tasks has not been from employers to white-collar workers, but from one group of workers to other groups, including white-collar ones, by the continuing process of the division of labour.

However, expanding capitalist economies, rising working-class affluence and relative social stability throughout the 1950s and 1960s meant that considerations of white-collar workers as part of the working class were few and far between. C. Wright Mills's *White Collar*, first published in 1951, is exceptional in this respect, as well as for the knowledge it displays of the earlier German debate on white-collar workers and the breadth of empirical material used. Mills considered that objectively

the white collar mass is becoming more and more similar to that of wage earners. . . . All factors in their status position, which have enabled white collar workers to set themselves apart from wage workers, are now subject to definite decline. . . . In the course of the next generation, a "social class" between lower white collar and wage workers will probably be formed.[95]

But this did not imply that white-collar workers would automatically support the labour movement, nor would they lead any independent political movement. 'The political question of the new middle class is, Of what bloc or movement will they be most likely to stay at the tail? And the answer is, the bloc or movement that most obviously seems to be winning.'[96] Mills, in short, shared a similar view of white-collar workers as Trotsky, characterising their affiliations as follows: 'They hesitate, confused and vacillating in their opinions, unfocused and discontinuous in their actions.'[97]

There remains one more contribution to this extended debate

which needs examination and fittingly enough it returns us to our starting point – Germany. Ralf Dahrendorf, while fully conversant with the historical controversies surrounding the new middle class, attempted, in an influential work, *Soziale Klassen und Klassenkonflikt in der industriellen Gesellschaft*, 1957, published in England in 1959 as *Class and Class Conflict in an Industrial Society*, to re-conceptualise the position of white-collar workers from a 'conflict theory' perspective. Such a perspective, Dahrendorf stated, recognised only two possible positions: white-collar workers were either part of the capitalist class or part of the working class. On this he was quite explicit – 'in a situation of conflict, whether defined in a Marxian way or in some other way, this kind of intermediate position just does not exist, or, at least, exists only as a negative position of non-participation'.[98]

On the other hand, Dahrendorf recognised that the heterogeneity of white-collar positions and the wide discrepancies in their authority made both theories that maintained white-collar workers were part of the ruling class and theories maintaining they were part of the working class, equally unsatisfactory. He concurred with C. Wright Mills that 'because of the vastly different "definitions" of the "new middle class" the two theories not only may peacefully co-exist but even both be correct'.[99] In other words, Dahrendorf concluded that no single new middle class existed, but rather two separate classes each of which were part of the two major classes:

> Instead of asking which of two apparently conflicting theories applies to the 'new middle class', we can, so to speak, reverse our question and ask whether there is any criterion that would allow us to distinguish between those sectors of the 'new middle class' to which one theory applies and those to which the other theory applies. . . . It seems to me that a fairly clear as well as significant line can be drawn between salaried employees that are part of a bureaucratic hierarchy and salaried employees in positions that are not. . . . I suggest the ruling-class theory applies without exception to the social position of bureaucrats, and the working-class theory equally generally to the social position of white collar workers.[100]

It should not be imagined, however, that Marx and Engels's view in *Manifesto of the Communist Party* of two hostile camps directly facing each other was validated by Dahrendorf. His argument ran directly counter to this. He claimed that

> both classes have become, by these extensions, even more complex and heterogeneous than their decomposition had

made them in any case. By gaining new elements, their unity has become a highly doubtful and precarious feature . . . it is highly doubtful whether the concept of class is still applicable to the conflict groups of post-capitalist societies.[101]

In so far as Dahrendorf retained the concept of class he made it clear that it was not defined in the original Marxist sense. He argued that rather than class being defined in terms of ownership of private property, the tie between private property and authority should be seen as only a specific instance of authoritative rights of control more generally. For Dahrendorf, authority relations were pre-eminent. Class membership was based upon possession of or exclusion from authority:

> in every social organisation some positions are entrusted with a right to exercise control over other positions in order to ensure effective coercion . . . in other words . . . there is a differential distribution of power and authority . . . this differential distribution of authority invariably becomes the determining factor of systematic social conflicts of a type that is germane to class conflicts in the traditional (Marxian) sense of the term. The structural origin of such conflicts must be sought in the arrangement of social roles endowed with expectations of domination and subjection.[102]

Dahrendorf's attempt to resolve the problem of the class position of white-collar workers was less than successful. His division between those white-collar employees who were part of a bureaucratic hierarchy and those who were not was arbitrary. Furthermore, he failed to show that there was such a division in society and that even were it to exist, that it would be a significant line of social cleavage. It is difficult to accept Dahrendorf's major premise that authority divisions can be readily analysed in terms of a dichotomous division between a 'dominant' and a 'subordinate' group. It was on just these grounds that orthodox Marxism was so unconvincing and, Dahrendorf's modifications to Marx's theory notwithstanding, he remains equally unconvincing. He underestimated the extent to which conflict between groups *within* the bureaucratic hierarchy could take place. Certainly the inclusion of the lowest clerical officer in government employment in the ranks of the ruling class indicates Dahrendorf's searching for solutions through definitions rather than through an examination of the actual relationship of employees in this group with those who control state power.

Both the work of Dahrendorf and that of C. Wright Mills introduced to Britain, if only in an indirect fashion, the

35

alternatives to orthodox Marxism thrown up in Germany in the course of academic and political conflicts. It would be wrong, however, to over-emphasise the impact that this introduction had on British perspectives on the position of middle-class labour. The dominant alternative to orthodox Marxism does have its roots in German theory, but that alternative is primarily associated with the writings of Max Weber. The dissemination and adoption of Weber's perspectives have been part of an independent and much broader process.

The British challenge to orthodox Marxism

Judged by the attention paid to the history, growth and function of middle-class labour in Britain social theorists have regarded this social group as a force of little significance. F.D. Klingender advanced an orthodox Marxist analysis of clerical labour in Britain in 1935, in which he argued that clerks had been objectively proletarianised.[103] Despite this proletarianisation, he maintained that a number of factors conspired to keep the majority of clerical workers aloof from the trade union movement. These factors included the continued petty bourgeois ideology of clerks, the employers' success in steering them towards professionalism, and the sabotage of the building of a clerks' union by reformist trade union leaders. Apart from this exception, however, there was a silence from both Marxists and their opponents on the social class position of white-collar labour. This lack of concern with the nature and behaviour of white-collar workers, in contrast to the importance accorded to their counterparts in Germany, is largely explained by the different historical circumstances of Britain. Middle class labour in Britain formed a much lower percentage of the employed population (Table 1.2).[104]

TABLE 1.2 *Approximate number of salaried employees in industry per 1000 manual workers before and after the First World War*

| | Pre-war | | Post-war | |
	Year	Number	Year	Number
Germany	1907	82	1925	154
Britain	1907	74	1924	108

The growth of this section of labour was significant but its impact was not as dramatic as in Germany. In addition, and perhaps more importantly, the lower level of social conflict in Britain ensured that middle-class labour was not pulled between two sharply competing poles. The role of middle-class labour was therefore never as problematic and it never felt itself as vulnerable to changes as did its counterpart in Germany. It was concerned about the aggressive trade unionism of the unskilled and the rise of independent labour politics in the late nineteenth and early twentieth centuries, as well as its own unsecurity. Such fears were accommodated within mainstream party politics, however, and produced little in the way of independent middle-class political organisation. As Geoffrey Crossick noted,

> there were organisations of a militantly right-wing complexion, such as the Liberty and Property Defence League and the Anti-Socialist Union, yet both were backed by large-scale business interests to counter socialism and state intervention, and neither were the kind of extra-parliamentary organisation to mobilise the small man or appeal to his interests or fears.[105]

There was, however, one organisation that displayed the kind of 'third force' perspective that characterised German middle-class organisations. After 1918 the Middle Class Union appeared with a perspective that could not simply be subsumed by capital: the chairman of the Union told his members, 'If you are properly organised . . . you can possibly hold up all the workers, you could hold up the capitalists, or you could even hold up the Government. You must see to it that you are not crushed or squeezed.'[106] But such a statement emanating from the middle classes was rare and the lack of impact of the union emphasises the lack of political and economic anxiety of this group. The lack of social conflict on the scale that took place in Germany was also one reason why the influence of Marxism on the British labour movement was relatively weak. The ideological challenge to the viability of British capitalism was therefore weaker, and sociology also remained relatively under-developed, failing to provide a significant 'father' or 'fathers' of the discipline.[107]

The growth of British sociology has been a largely post-Second World War phenomenon, coinciding with a period of rising living standards and free from major social conflict. Orthodox Marxism, while rarely being an explicit target for refutations, has nevertheless been the object of implicit ones. Since the 1950s, British sociology has offered its own view of the class structure largely by adopting the perspectives that Max Weber fashioned against Marxism in an earlier period. The place of the new middle class in these neo-Weberian perspectives is not un-

37

important, the picture of the class structure being made up of a shrinking working class on the one hand and a vast, differentiated middle class on the other. Frequently, therefore, as has recently been pointed out, 'middle class' covers the whole span above 'working class' (itself usually conceived as embracing only the mass of manual workers): nonsensically 'middle' between a lower group and a vacuum.[108] In this model the nature and role of the middle class is seen as central but not regarded as problematic. The model precludes the question of possible vacillations by the salaried middle class because, having distinguished the middle class from the working class, it allows no alternative pole to which that class might be attracted.

The influence of Weber, however, has been far from monolithic. As in the case of Marx, Weber's work has been open to conflicting interpretations. Anthony Giddens, for instance, has commented that:

> in the English-speaking world, the real import of Weber's analysis has frequently been misrepresented. The customary procedure has been to contrast Weber's discussion of 'Class, status and party', a fragment of *Economy and Society*, with the conception of class supposedly taken by Marx, to the detriment of the latter. Marx, so it is argued, treated 'class' as a purely economic phenomenon and, moreover, regarded class conflicts as in some way the 'inevitable' outcome of clashes of material interests. He failed to realise, according to this argument, that the divisions of economic interest which create classes do not necessarily correspond to sentiments of communal identity which constitute differential 'status'. Thus status, which depends upon subjective evaluation, is a separate 'dimension of stratification' from class, and the two may vary independently.[109]

Such an interpretation of Weber, which counterposes status to class, encouraged the development of subjective theories of class. According to such theories, harsh economic realities can be overcome by will power. This subjectivism is well illustrated by Moeller van den Bruck's statement that: 'He is a proletariat who wants to think of himself as one. The proletarian consciousness makes man a proletariat, not the machine, not the mechanization of labor, not wage-dependency on the capitalist mode of production'.[110] British sociologists have rarely gone so far, but much of their work has been concerned with status rather than social class. Nichols noted two aspects of this approach:

> Two broad tendencies can be distinguished. The one relates to

the granting of status in the sense of *esteem*. Apt to figure here are those interviewer's probes that seek to elicit the interviewee's own estimation of his or her class membership and that of other 'classes'. Never far away is that out-and-out psychologism, according to which classes do not exist if people say they do not. The other way in which status enters in is evidenced by attempts to categorise by *status group*, that is by actual style of life.[111]

Whatever the proponents of the first tendency may claim such an approach can only be based upon a serious misreading of Weber. An examination of his work illustrates both this and the weakness of the latter approach, which has a more serious claim to be derived from Weber's work.

There can be no doubt that the distinction between class and status was for Weber fundamental to the understanding of social stratification. Class for Weber was an objective relationship ultimately determined by a person's position in the market. But he recognised no necessary correspondence between objective place in the class structure and communal class consciousness:

> In our terminology, 'classes' are not communities; they merely represent possible, and frequent bases for communal action. We may speak of a 'class' when (1) a number of people having in common a specific causal component of their life chances, in so far as (2) this component is represented exclusively by economic interests in the possession of goods and opportunities for income, and (3) is represented under the conditions of the commodity of labor markets.[112]

The differential distribution of control over material property created different life chances. Property, therefore, played a central role in the determination of classes: according to Weber, ' "Property" and "lack of property" are, therefore, the basic categories of all class situations'.[113]

The class situations within these two basic categories were not, however, homogeneous, but were differentiated according to, on the one hand, the kind of property that was possessed, and, on the other, the kind of services that could be offered on the market. There was no necessary coherence, therefore, amongst the ownership classes:

> Ownership of domestic buildings, productive establishments; warehouses; stores; agriculturally usable land, large and small holdings − quantitative differences with possibly qualitative consequences − ownership of mines; cattle, men (slaves); disposition over mobile instruments of production or capital

39

goods of all sorts, especially money or objects that can be exchanged for money easily and at any time; disposition over products of one's own labor or of others' labor differing according to their various distances from consumability; disposition over transferable monopolies of any kind — all these distinctions differentiate the class situation of the propertied.[114]

Similarly, the class situations of those who have no property were also differentiated according to the types of services they could offer in the market. Particularly important in this respect was the degree of monopolisation of marketable skills.

In addition to these internal differentiations, the dichotomous model implied by the basic categories of property ownership and non-property ownership was further modified by the recognition of various types of 'middle class' which stood between them. While the middle-class groupings were all nominally propertyless, those with highly marketable skills had different life chances and were in a different class situation from those who possessed skills with little or no market value. Because, for Weber, class situation was ultimately market situation, groups which had no access to the market were logically not class groups, but status groups, and he cited slaves as just such a group.

Weber's concept of class was reduced to a narrow economic relationship that existed independent of particular individuals' or groups' conceptions of their class positions. More importantly, because of its subsequent influence, the corollary was also the case — a common class position did not necessarily give rise to communal action. People's conceptions of their roles and positions in society were not tied directly to their class position and there was an alternative base for social stratification. Weber framed this alternative basis around the concept of status groups:

> In contrast to classes, status groups are normally communities. They are, however, often of an amorphous kind. In contrast to the purely economically determined 'class situation' we wish to designate as 'status situation' every typical component of the life fate of men that is determined by a specific, positive or negative, social estimation of honor.[115]

Status honour, although conceptually distinct from class as a basis for stratification, was, however, related in a complex manner to class position in concrete situations:

> Class distinctions are linked in the most varied ways with status distinctions. Property as such is not always recognised as a status qualification, but in the long run it is, and with

extraordinary regularity.

Both propertied and propertyless people can belong to the same status group, and frequently they do with tangible consequences. This 'equality' of social esteem may, however, in the long run become quite precarious.[116]

Status groups were distinguished by particular styles of life. A concomitant part of this style of life was restriction on social intercourse which in turn led to social closure.

The distinction between class and status was, therefore, for Weber, one partly between economic and communal identification, partly between objective and subjective identification, and partly between production and consumption. But such a formulation led Weber into a number of difficulties. His narrow definition of class positions as market situation created the possibility of an almost unlimited number of classes. As Giddens remarked:

the range of 'goods and capabilities' possessed by individuals is highly variable, and one could push the view to its *reductio ad absurdum* by supposing that every individual brings a slightly different combination of possessions or skills to the market, and hence there are as many 'classes' as there are concrete individuals participating in market relationships. In practice, of course, it is only the more glaring differences between market situations of individuals which are likely to be worth terming 'class differentials'. But even then we are likely to be left with a very large number of 'classes'.[117]

Weber must certainly have recognised such a problem because he later modified his model by talking of 'social classes' in such a way as to confound adherents to his earlier clear distinction between class and status. In his empirical work, moreover, he never attempted to operationalise this concept of class. When he did use the term class in his writings it tended to take on a straightforward Marxian sense, as when he talked of the 'bourgeoisie', the 'peasantry' and the 'working-class'.

The other major criticism of Weber's approach is that his narrowing of class to market situation seriously limits this understanding of relationships in capitalist society by concentrating on distributional rewards rather than relationships within the production process. It is these very relations in production that in some measure explain the market situations, whereas Weber treated the relations between market situation and relations in production as unproblematic. As two recent critics of Weber stated:

41

We would raise the question as to *why* skills and resources have assumed this marketable, commodity-like quality. We would argue that these 'commodities' have emerged as commodities because of the development of capitalist relations of production. Such a mode of production requires both freely transferable property and readily available labour.[118]

These two major problems of the Weberian analysis of class — (i) the difficulty in drawing class boundaries because of multifarious market situations, and (ii) the concentration on market relations to the detriment of examining relations in production — can be seen recurring in much contemporary work on social stratification. In this respect David Lockwood's influential *The Blackcoated Worker*, 1958, can be seen as not only an attempt to overcome the orthodox Marxist position that because clerical workers are propertyless they are therefore working-class, but also the absence within the Weberian framework of an examination of relations inside the productive process. Lockwood attempted to synthesise the analyses of Marx and Weber in the following manner:

> Under 'class position' will be included the following factors. First, 'market situation' that is to say the economic position narrowly conceived, consisting of source and size of income, degree of job-security, and opportunity for upward occupational mobility. Secondly, 'work situation', the set of social relationships in which the individual is involved at work by virtue of his position in the social division of labour. And finally, 'status situation' or the position of the individual in the hierarchy of prestige in the society at large. . . . 'Market situation' and 'work situation' comprise what Marx essentially understood as 'class position'; 'status situation' derives from another branch of social stratification theory.[119]

The issue of whether 'market situation' and 'work situation' combined adequately encompass Marx's analysis of class is not of major concern here. What is important is the extent to which the addition of the dimension of 'work situation' modifies the Weberian emphasis on market and status. Lockwood's description of the extent of discretion and responsibility within clerical work, the extent to which clerical workers are physically concentrated in their work and the authority relations in which they are involved, cannot be challenged. But the work remained on a descriptive level. The features Lockwood described were seen to be a consequence of growing size and technical complexity, but the dynamic behind these developments was not examined. As a result the structure of workplace relationships appeared simply as part of the order of things. Just as the market determines different rewards, so does the work situation determine different experiences.

Whatever the weaknesses of Lockwood's approach in explaining the dynamic aspects of capitalism, there is no doubt about its superiority to both orthodox Marxism and purely subjectivist accounts of class. Nor can there be any doubting its influence. Similar perspectives were adopted by Anthony Giddens in *The Class Structure of Capitalist Societies*, 1973. Giddens emphasised the difficulty of constructing a general theory of white-collar labour. The market situation of professional, technical and managerial workers is not only varied but markedly different from that of routine clerical and sales workers. Furthermore, these latter groups, Giddens noted, are primarily composed of female workers. Most male white-collar workers, he maintained, are part of a privileged managerial hierarchy. Where Giddens departed from Lockwood's analysis was in his insistence on the separation of what he termed paratechnical relations (relations arising from a given technique of production) from authority relations, which he claimed had been conflated by Lockwood. Taking this distinction into account, Giddens claimed that it is possible to further differentiate between white-collar groups which are similarly placed in labour market terms, thus reinforcing his claim as to the difficulty of trying to identify any one class position for white-collar occupations.[120]

Lockwood's approach to class analysis was not restricted to studies of white-collar labour. It also formed the basis for Lockwood and Goldthorpe's criticisms of other sociologists' far from rigorous attempts to come to terms with the British class structure. In particular, they attacked those writers who saw in rising working-class affluence a process of embourgeoisement.[121] Lockwood's methodology, framed against orthodox Marxism, was admirably suited to this task, for the embourgeoisement theory was orthodox Marxism's mirror image: not only were white-collar workers not being proletarianised, manual workers were entering the middle class.

The question of the embourgeoisement of the working class dominated discussions on the British class structure throughout the 1950s and 1960s. Proponents of this thesis, while seldom explicitly acknowledging Weber, shared much in common with his approach. Embourgeoisement was predicated on a view that the working class was highly differentiated in respect of levels of skill; that increasing specialisation of occupations had created a far more complex status system, as well as a multiplicity of

43

sectional interests; that far greater social mobility had undermined the solidarity of the working class and had led to a swelling middle class.

Certainly, the rising living standards could not be denied, nor the effects that this had upon working-class culture and lifestyle. The central problem was, however, the significance placed upon such changes. Those such as Anthony Crosland,[122] who argued the embourgeoisement thesis, saw in them the eclipse of the capitalist class structure. As Goldthorpe and Lockwood noted:

> a picture has been built up — and it is one that would be generally accepted — of a system of stratification becoming increasingly fine in its gradations and at the same time somewhat less extreme and rigid. Of late, however, still further economic progress has resulted in a new factor entering into the discussion — that of working class 'affluence'. . . . It has been argued by a number of writers that the working class, or at least a more prosperous section of it, is losing its identity as a social stratum and is becoming more merged into the middle class.[123]

Goldthorpe and Lockwood were extremely critical of this thesis and maintained that such changes that had taken place within the working class had to be examined in what they termed their economic, relational and normative aspects. Examination of those aspects shows, however, that while Goldthorpe and Lockwood's approach was incomparably more sophisticated than the work they criticised, it remained, itself, firmly within the Weberian perspective.

Their argument was that while the working class had undoubtedly made some economic progress, this had been exaggerated because insufficient account had been taken of such factors as economic security, opportunities for promotion, and fringe benefits of various kinds. With regard to the relational aspects (i.e. the extent to which manual workers were accepted on terms of equality by middle-class people in formal and informal social relationships), and the normative (i.e. the extent to which manual workers had adopted a new outlook and new standards of behaviour which resembled those of the middle class), Goldthorpe and Lockwood claimed that what evidence there was suggested that the gulf remained very wide. Their subsequent works, *The Affluent Worker* studies, confirmed these conclusions, arguing, amongst other things, that the affluent worker was not integrated into middle-class circles and tended to display a privatised lifestyle.[124]

In adopting such a framework the overwhelming concentration

was still on distribution and consumption patterns rather than on the value-creating process within production. Moreover, although rejecting subjectivism in its cruder manifestations, Goldthorpe and Lockwood made substantial concessions to it. This is not to suggest that people's reactions to and thoughts about their situations are unimportant, only that they are necessarily limited. Answers to questions concerning unemployment give indications as to what people feel about unemployment, not necessarily what causes it. Furthermore, Goldthorpe and Lockwood's work was heavily predicated upon the existence of relatively homogeneous and discrete social images that were held to reflect various locations, both geographical and in the class structure.[125] In giving these images such weight and coherence the impression is given that the economic situation and the social relations of workers are much less problematic and contain fewer contradictions than is the case.

The attempt to develop a solution to the problems thrown up within the Weberian perspective can also be seen in the work of Frank Parkin. In his *Class, Inequality and Political Order*, 1972, Parkin set out to criticise, and offer an alternative to, the multidimensional view of class which he maintained had its origin in Weber's work. Nevertheless, he went on to adopt a Weberian framework himself, believing that one of Weber's major contributions was 'to broaden Marx's concept of class position by defining it not simply in terms of property ownership but of market advantages in general'.[126] By accepting this framework and by thus regarding the occupational order as 'the backbone of the class structure, and indeed the entire reward system of modern Western society', Parkin similarly encountered the problem of where to place meaningful class boundaries.

> The picture of the reward system . . . is one marked out by a hierarchy of broad occupational categories each representing a different position in the scale of material and non material benefits. Although it is possible to demarcate these categories from one another in some approximate fashion, we cannot usefully regard them as each forming a distinct social class. This is partly because the reward hierarchy does not exhibit sharp discontinuities, or cut-off points, between each major occupational grouping. For the most part, the flow of rewards takes the form of a graduated continuum, rather than a series of sharply defined steps.[127]

Parkin solved this problem, like many before him, by claiming that there was a significant break in the reward hierarchy between manual and non-manual occupational categories. This division did not rest solely on differences of income; indeed, Parkin recognised that there was a good deal of overlap in the actual earnings of groups that clustered at the margins of the class-dividing line. Rather, the differences in rewards encompassed the wider advantages enjoyed by white-collar workers which included better promotion and career opportunities; greater long-term economic security; guaranteed annual salary increases on an incremental scale; a cleaner, less noisy, less dangerous, and generally more comfortable work environment; greater freedom of movement and less supervision.

Parkin's principal line of cleavage, that between manual and non-manual workers, corresponded to one that has dominated much social thought and indeed the conceptions of white-collar and manual workers themselves. In doing so it turned attention away from those white-collar jobs where the advantages outlined by Parkin are not generally available, such as lower grade clerks and shop assistants. More importantly, it gave no explanation as to why the market determined that certain jobs did accrue such advantages. The market, in other words, was again simply accepted as a fact of life.

Parkin, however, was obviously far from happy with his essentially arbitrary resolution of the problem of class structuration, and in two later works, 'Strategies of Social Closure in Class Formation',[128] and *Marxism and Class Theory*, 1979, he turned specifically to the problem of social closure. Re-examining Weber's work, Parkin believed that by modifying the concept of 'social closure' he could overcome the problems associated with, on the one hand, the necessary emphasis on dichotomy for conflict purposes, and on the other, the inability of a dichotomous model to deal with intra-class conflict.

Social closure as specified by Weber referred to the process by which social collectivities sought to maximise rewards by restricting access to them to a limited circle of eligibles. This action could be taken by any group located at any level in the stratification order, although the criteria adopted for exclusion purposes by any one group were likely to depend on the group's general location in the distributive system. Parkin's contribution was to give equal emphasis to the strategies adopted by the excluded groups. He was thus able to delineate two major types of social closure: that based upon the power of exclusion and that based upon the threat of usurpation.[129] While the former was always used in a downward direction in that it created subordinate groups, in the latter power was always used in an upward direction against dominant groups.

This modification to Weber, Parkin considered, allowed the

concept of social closure to be directly connected to social stratification. For Parkin, classes were defined 'not specifically in relation to the productive processes but in relation to their prevalent modes of closure, exclusion and usurpation'.[130] This conceptual schema allowed the retention of a dichotomous model: 'it is possible to visualize the fundamental cleavage in the stratification order as the point where one set of closure strategies gives way to a radically different one'.[131]

At one and the same time the schema could also encompass the adoption by social collectivities of both strategies: 'Indeed, the apparent anomalies of class may be seen to arise from this tendency of certain groups to resort to the practices of both solidarism and exclusion.'[132] Such, maintained Parkin, was the case with the 'white collar proletariat'. By focusing on social closure practices, he argued, it would be possible to study the changing fortunes and character of such groups through a time in which their non-manual status had remained constant.

By regarding property as only 'one form of exclusionary relationship' and as only one form of exploitative relationship, Parkin maintained that the exclusion/usurpation dichotomy could be used to conceptualise as class relations, ethnic, sexual and communal conflicts. All such areas of conflict were in principle potentially exploitative, autonomous and co-equal. White workers in South Africa, for example, were, according to Parkin, part of the dominant class, not because of their part in the productive process or division of labour, but because 'exclusion is their chief mode of operation'.[133]

These later works represent a break with Parkin's earlier analysis. Having attempted in *Class Inequality and Political Order* to solve the Weberian problem of class structuration by maintaining that inequalities stemming from different positions in the market produce the major line of social cleavage (and hence social closure), Parkin recognised the essentially arbitrary nature of the solution. He therefore inverted the relationship: rather than market position determining social closure, modes of social closure (exclusion and usurpation) now determine market and other (communal, sexual, ethnic) inequalities.

Parkin's inversion only succeeds, however, in solving the problem of social closure at the level of typologies. Some groups adopt both strategies. Nevertheless, he maintained that they fall into the dominant or subordinate class according to which strategy was primary. The determination of primary strategies, however, cannot be arrived at in an *a priori* fashion. It is by no means guaranteed that groups can be objectively allocated into their appropriate class.

There is another sense also in which the problem is solved only at the definitional level. Parkin, having recognised the difficulties that arise from lack of correspondence between positions allocated in formally defined class structures and the consciousness and political actions of those allocated, simply avoids rather than confronts the difficulties:

> If the mode of collective action is itself taken to be the defining feature of class, as proposed by the closure model, it follows that problems of this kind do not arise. There is no independently defined structure of positions for class action to be discrepant with.[134]

The idea of an objective determinant of class, outlined by Weber and adopted earlier by Parkin, has been totally abandoned: class is coterminous with action.

Parkin's formulation is open to a further criticism. The adoption of one or other of the strategies of closure will itself be influenced by prior location in the structure of relations. Parkin treats as primary what, in fact, is determined. Parkin foresaw such criticism, however, and he attempted to pre-empt it by characterising the Marxist position as one in which closure strategies are seen as mere responses to the material pressures and forces set in play by the capitalist mode of production, i.e. not mediated by the historical situation and peculiarities of any specific society. This 'Marxist' position would, he claims, carry considerable weight but for the fact that exclusionary social closure is found in all large-scale societies regardless of a particular set of productive relations or material factors. While it cannot be denied that such practices have been present in a variety of different types of society, what has to be contested is Parkin's implication that this ubiquitous form of social closure is the key to understanding the dynamics of these societies, rather than the way these societies produce and reproduce their material life. If, as Parkin proposes, modes of social closure define classes, and the same modes of closure have been dominant throughout the ages, he comes close to suggesting that the characterisation of societies as capitalist, socialist or feudal is misleading in that to do so deflects attention from the principal determinant of cleavage and class formation.

At this point, however, it is necessary to reassert a general point made already, though this time in the context of Britain. This is that the retention of a simple two-class model by Marxists has given much credibility to their critics and weakened their own ability to describe society with their own concepts. The consequences for Marxist sociologists have been noted by one of them:

> we rely on the oversimplified view that society is to be divided
> solely between the working class on one side, and the capitalist
> class on the other. For any deeper analysis we tend to utilise
> the categories of bourgeois vote predictors, such as 'middle
> class', 'lower middle class', etc. which have little or no
> connection with a *class* analysis.[135]

The weakness of the orthodox Marxist position is acknowledged by the appropriation, albeit eclectic, of Weberian
perspectives. Frankel, for example, comes close to the very
Weberian tendencies, that he himself had earlier criticised, when
writing

> The 'middle class' consists of strata based mainly on criteria of
> occupation, income and way of life. The occupations are
> mainly non-manual, but their incomes, way of life and working
> behaviour are spread over a very broad branch indeed. At the
> lower-end they overlap the upper working-class, at the top
> they reach into the ruling class. The bulk of the middle strata
> are near the working class on the more objective criteria,
> nearer the ruling class on subjective behaviour.[136]

Likewise, Westergaard and Resler, the authors of a major
Marxist account of the British class structure, are far from
consistent on the primary determinants of class. While stating, on
the one hand, that they start 'with an assumption that property
and property relations play the key part in forming the contours
of inequality',[137] they had difficulty in relating ownership and
lack of ownership to the differentiation amongst those whose
principal or only income is from wages or salaries. Westergaard
and Resler therefore in practice relied upon market relations to
explain the differentiation of labour:

> The existence of an intermediate cluster of people between
> wage earners and directors, managers, high officials and
> members of the established professions is . . . of crucial
> significance. . . . The people in these intermediate jobs depend
> no less essentially than rank-and-file earners on the sale of
> their labour. But they sell their labour at a premium which puts
> their earnings some way above those of ordinary workers.
> They share, if only on a modest scale, some of the fringe
> benefits enjoyed as a matter of course by their economic
> superiors. Their life cycles follow at least in part an upward,
> incremental curve, rather than the low hump and downward
> slope of most manual and other routine workers. For these

49

reasons there is some element to their lives of security, predictability and opportunity for individual 'investment' in the future which are much more firmly established among those above them in the hierarchy. These as well as other features of their situation — their prospects of promotion in addition to increments of salary, for example, and the share in minor authority which many members of the intermediate strata enjoy *modify the nature of their dependence on the sale of* their labour.[138] (my emphasis)

This reliance upon differences in the *market situation* of different groups was further illustrated by Westergaard and Resler's treatment of clerical workers:

Routine-grade clerks and sales workers, though they used to be part of this intermediate cluster, at least at its lower margin, are no longer so. They retain some of the special advantages that went with that position. A line drawn by criteria relating to access to moderate fringe benefits, relative security of employment, regularity of earnings and hours of work, will still separate most clerical workers — shop assistants not so clearly — from manual workers. But in terms of earnings — sheer cash as well as its distribution over the life cycle — male clerks and shopworkers are now firmly among the broad mass of ordinary labour; and indeed often well towards the bottom of the pile.[139]

Using this modified Weberian perspective, whereby market situation was primarily reduced to income level, Westergaard and Resler were able to reclaim on behalf of the working class sections of clerical workers, only then to question the identification of clerical workers as working class because of their traditionally higher promotion prospects.

Conclusion

This survey of various approaches to class structure and the position of middle-class labour has outlined significant weaknesses in both orthodox Marxism and the responses to it in Germany and Britain. By utilising ownership and non-ownership of the means of production as the primary determinant of class membership, the orthodox Marxist approach encourages a passive, formalistic definition of class. It fails, therefore, to differentiate between those in the swelling ranks of the propertyless. The necessity to make distinctions within the propertyless group became particularly apparent in Germany with the active part played in politics by the middle class. As first radicalisation and then reaction took sections of white-collar workers first one way and then the other, competing theories attempted to explain these movements. Although particular periods gave credibility to particular theories this was, in part, a measure of the weakness of the theories – they could explain why the tide went with them, but they were stranded when it turned. The vacillating nature of the new middle class is the lesson to be learnt from an examination of its historical relationships. No theory can determine in an *a priori* fashion in which direction they will turn.

The rising affluence and relative stability of post-Second World War Britain has encouraged and given credence to analyses within the Weberian tradition, with a concentration on the differentiation of white-collar workers from manual ones, through higher incomes, greater security, and lack of identification with the labour movement. This tradition has treated these differences as essential rather than as historically conditioned. As the conditions which gave rise to these features change and as recession, unemployment and instability loom larger, however, such a perspective appears increasingly outmoded.

A theory explaining the contradictory tendencies of middle-class labour needs to:

(i)   locate the new middle class within the capitalist productive process that gave rise to it

(ii)   specify the basis of identification with and differentiation from the working class

(iii) specify the basis of identification with and differentiation from the bourgeoisie

(iv)   relate differences in ideology to differences in their day to day practices and experiences.

It is the contention here that such a theory can be constructed on the basis of Marxism – but of a kind that goes beyond the simplistic schema of the orthodox school.

2 Marx, Marxism and the new middle class

An elaboration of Marx's theory of class is faced with a number of difficulties. Marx wrote about class and class struggles in all his major works. Having different purposes, however, the works differed in degrees of abstraction and specificity. The conceptualisations of class differed, therefore, according to Marx's different projects. In consequence, it is not possible to tear out these conceptualisations from the contexts in which they are discussed, place them end to end and declare a Marxist theory of class.[1] The different usages of the term 'class' − Marx wrote about 'ideological etc. classes', 'unproductive classes', 'serving class', 'educated classes', the class of 'professional conspirators', the 'servile class of lawyers' and others[2] − confound any such attempt.

The absence of consistent usage of the concept of class in his works is explained, in part, by its very centrality. If all 'history . . . is the history of class struggles'[3] with the relationships between different groups in societies taking on different forms according to definite stages in the development of those societies, it becomes impossible to capture those diverse relationships within a definition. Marx faced a similar problem with the concept of property and commented:

> In each historical epoch, property has developed differently and under a set of entirely different social relations. Thus to define bourgeois property is nothing else than to give an exposition of all the social relations of bourgeois production.
> To try to give a definition of property as if an independent relation, a category apart, an abstract and eternal idea, can be nothing but an illusion or metaphysics of jurisprudence.[4]

In order to examine classes the actual relationships between

52

groups in particular societies have to be examined. This relational aspect of class is of paramount importance. Classes are not entities in themselves but come into being through social relations with others. E.P. Thompson is correct in complaining that:

> There is today an ever present temptation to suppose that class is a thing. . . . 'It', the working class, is assumed to have a real existence, which can be defined almost mathematically − so many men who stand in a certain relationship to the means of production.[5]

The relationship to the means of production, which, for the working class in capitalist society means non-ownership of the means of production, is an important determinant, but it is not the only one. The development of structurally differentiated classes is predicated upon the development of societies with a surplus product. Classes are defined not only in terms of their relationships to the means of production, or their role in the labour process which produces that surplus, but also in terms of their relationship to the surplus product. The form that these relationships took were, for Marx, of fundamental importance in determining the nature of the society:

> The specific economic form, in which unpaid surplus-labour is pumped out of direct producers, determines the relationship of rulers and ruled, as it grows directly out of production itself and, in turn, reacts upon it as a determining element. Upon this, however, is founded the entire formation of the economic community, which grows up out of the production relations themselves, thereby simultaneously its specific political form. It is always the direct relationship of the owners of the conditions of production to the direct producers . . . which reveals the innermost secret, the hidden basis of the entire social structure.[6]

The fundamental divisions of any class society were, for Marx, those between direct producers and the ruling class. It was this central relationship that was 'the hidden basis of the entire social structure' and on it was built the rest of the class structure. The exact nature of this central relationship and how other classes relate to the two polar classes were matters for investigation. As Hal Draper succinctly stated:

> The way in which a given society divides into classes is specific to its own social relations. Thus there are warlord elements in many societies, but a warlord becomes a *feudal* lord or baron

only when specific social relations become dominant. There is no rule-of-thumb definition which decides whether the chief of an armed band who resides in a stronghold and lives off the surplus labor of the unfree producers, etc. is or is not a member of a *feudal* class. The point can be settled not by a glossary but only by a concrete examination of the actual social relations of the society.[7]

There are thus two centrally important points when considering Marx's writings on class: firstly, the primacy given to the relations between rulers and direct producers and, secondly, the specificity of particular class configurations.

Marx's analysis of classes in capitalist societies

The common misconception that Marx considered capitalism to be characterised by only two classes can be traced to two main works by Marx. The influence of *Manifesto of the Communist Party* has already been noted. It is worth reiterating, however, that this work was a political tract written in the heat of struggle and contains simplifications and overstatements. Historically important as it is, too much emphasis should not be placed upon this work. It contains throughout an unmodified sense of historical inevitability, in which classes are the subjects of history transposing, with no mediations, struggles from the economic to the political level.[8] More pertinently, Marx did not deal with the increasingly complex relations that were to arise within the wage-labour/capital relationship. The second major source of the misconception is the failure to understand the method of *Capital*. This work, representing the culmination of Marx's endeavours, is of fundamental importance. If there is not an adequate basis for understanding the position and roles of the new middle class within it, then the harsher judgments upon Marxism will have been fully justified.

The method of 'Capital'

Marxists have paid scant attention to the analysis of the new middle class. The political reasons why this is so have been discussed in Chapter 1[9] but the precedent was set by Marx himself. The new middle class has grown considerably since Marx died in 1883, however, and it is necessary to establish whether, despite Marx's lack of focus on the new middle class as such, his methodology can be fruitfully applied to explain the origins and functions of this group.

It is becoming widely recognised that in *Capital* Marx was concerned with handling a model of 'pure capitalism'.[10] His aim was to follow through the logic of capitalist development unimpeded by mediations and competing and contradictory tendencies. As Marx himself wrote, 'in theory it is custom to assume that the laws of capitalist production evolve in their pure form'.[11] On the other hand, Marx was well aware that these laws would not evolve in their pure form, but would be modified by the historical circumstances in which they worked themselves out, and through the intervention of human agencies. As he stated elsewhere, 'Men make their own history, but not of their own free will; not under circumstances they themselves have chosen.'[12] In the third volume of *Capital*, Marx began to examine some of the countervailing tendencies that affect the operation of the laws of motion of capital in concrete societies. Present in *Capital* as a whole therefore were two schemata. This methodological device has important implications for Marx's analysis of class. In the first schema, i.e. the model of pure capitalism, the paramount importance that he already attached to the bourgeoisie and the proletariat was reinforced by his methodology. Society was assumed to be constituted solely around the wage-labour/capital relationship; all labour was assumed to be wage-labour, divorced from ownership of property, and all property was assumed to be capital. Within the second schema, the actual constitution of society was acknowledged to be more highly complex:

> In England, modern society is indisputably most highly and classically developed in economic structure. Nevertheless even here the stratification of classes does not appear in its pure form − middle and intermediate strata even here obliterate lines of demarcation everywhere (although incomparably less in rural districts than in the cities).[13]

The analysis using schema one envisaged the complete supremacy of the capitalist mode of production. As a consequence of this assumption, Marx recognised 'no other class except the working class' apart from the capitalist class:[14] all third persons were excluded. The middle class disappeared from Marx's schema, as did others. Most obviously excluded were the traditional petty bourgeoisie – the independent handicraftsfolk and small farmers − or, in other words, those whose demise had already been signalled in *Manifesto of the Communist Party*. The existence of these groups was a consequence of an earlier mode of production. With the advent of the capitalist mode of production they functioned outside the dominant mode. Nevertheless, despite being outside capitalist relations of production, they still bore the imprint of capitalist society:

> in line with the dominant mode of production even those kinds of labour which have not been subjugated by capitalism in reality are so in thought. For example, the self-employing worker is his own wage-labourer; his own means of production appear to him in his own mind as capital. As his own capitalist he puts himself to work as wage-labourer.[15]

The consequences of such an exclusion from schema one are not very serious. To understand such groups it is necessary to look first not at them but at the dominant mode of production. Furthermore, as has already been noted, their significance in the social structure of developed capitalist societies has greatly lessened.

A second major exclusion was those performing unproductive labour, i.e. labour that did not create surplus-value, and fell outside the capitalist production process. Such labour was typified by certain kinds of service work. This was considered as relatively unimportant by Marx, who commented that:

> On the whole types of work that are consumed as services and not in products separable from the worker and hence not capable of existing as commodities independently of him, but which are capable of being directly exploited in *capitalist* terms, are of microscopic significance when compared with the mass of capitalist production. They may be entirely neglected therefore and can be dealt with under the category of wage-labour that is not at the same time productive labour.[16]

Two points emerge from this passage. Firstly, that services which are directly consumed and in which labour is therefore not objectified, are normally unproductive. Secondly, however, it is claimed that certain services can be directly exploited even when of this nature. Marx conflated both types of services purely for convenience not because the externalisation of labour into material commodities was a necessary criterion for productive labour.[17]

The unproductive labourers of this type were, for Marx, insignificant in comparison with the other classes because their fate was bound up with the fate of those other classes:

> All members of society who do not figure directly in the reproduction process, whether as workers or not, can receive their share of the annual commodity product − i.e. their means of consumption − in the first instance only from the hands of

those classes to whom this product firstly accrues – productive workers, industrial capitalists and landlords. To this extent, their revenues are, in a material sense, derived from wages (the wages of productive workers), profit, and ground-rent, and hence appear, in contrast to these original revenues, as derivative.[18]

Marx also excluded from his analysis a third group which could not be considered external to the dominant mode of production, the functionaries in trade and marketing. This group comprised wholesale merchants, middle men, brokers, speculators and commercial labourers who were essential under the capitalist mode of production. He considered, however, that the intervention of this group obscured the essential relations between capital and labour and commented that:

> As the capitalist mode of production presupposes production on a large scale, so it also necessarily presupposes large-scale sale; sale to the merchant, not to the individual consumer. . . . Commodity trade is presupposed, as a function of merchant's capital, and this develops even further with the development of capitalist production. Thus we occasionally take its existence for granted in illustrating particular aspects of the capitalist circulation process; but in this general analysis we assume direct sale without the intervention of the merchant, since this intervention conceals various moments of the movement.[19]

This notwithstanding, Marx detailed the class position of particular groups within this category. It is not the case, as Abram L. Harris implies, that Marx, by excluding this group, was excluding a uniform middle class.[20] On the one hand, merchants were clearly identified by Marx as commercial capitalists:

> The conversion of commodities (products) into money, and of money into commodities (means of production) is a necessary function of industrial capital. . . . But these functions neither create value, nor produce surplus value. By performing these operations and by carrying on the function of capital in the sphere of circulation after productive capital has ceased to be involved the merchant merely takes the place of the industrial capitalist.[21]

On the other hand, the commercial clerks are, at least on an economic level, clearly identified as wage workers:

> The commercial worker produces no surplus-value directly. But the price of his labour is determined by the value of his labour-power, its exertion, expenditure of energy, and wear

and tear, is as in the case of every other wage-labourer by no means limited by its value. His wage, therefore, is not necessarily proportionate to the mass of profit which he helps the capitalist to realise. What he costs the capitalist and what he brings in are two different things. He creates no direct surplus-value, but adds to the capitalist's income by helping him reduce the cost of realising surplus-value, inasmuch as he performs partly unpaid labour. The commercial worker in the strict sense of the term, belongs to the better paid class of wage-workers − to those whose labour is classed as skilled and stands above average labour.[22]

Strictly speaking, therefore, neither group were considered by Marx to belong to the new middle class, but were extensions of the two main classes into the unproductive spheres of capitalism. They were excluded from detailed analysis because circulation was a subordinate moment in the capitalist production process. As stated earlier, the real composition of this sector in no way corresponds to a division into only two classes. However, for the very reasons that Marx omitted detailed consideration of the sphere of circulation − because it reflected, in a less clear form, the relationships expressed in the production process itself − consideration of the new middle class in the sphere of circulation will be examined after the new middle class in the sphere of production has been discussed.

The fourth and most important section that was excluded under Marx's schema one were the groups who obscured the relations between capitalists and workers in the capitalist production process. Marx commented upon their growth and function but before this is examined it is necessary to consider in greater detail the functions and characteristics of the two main classes because, in part, the character of the new middle class is stamped with features of both major classes.

Capital and labour

The capitalist production process was perceived by Marx as being the unity of two analytically distinct processes. The first process he termed 'the real labour process', by which he referred to the process whereby the labourer 'creates new use-value by performing useful labour with existing use-values'.[23] The worker makes use of the means of production in the course of his work to objectify his labour in new use-values. This real labour process is a labour process in general, in the abstract. Marx stated that, 'As such its elements, its conceptually specific components, are those of the labour process itself, of any *labour process*, irrespective of the mode of production or the stage of economic development in which they find themselves'.[24] He went on to point out, however, that labour processes never occur in the abstract, but only under definite social relations in concrete societies. Under capitalism the production process is also a surplus-value producing process. Viewed from this vantage point, Marx stated:

> Here it is not the worker who makes use of the means of production, but the means of production that makes use of the worker. . . . It is precisely as *value-creating* that living labour is continually being absorbed into the valorisation process of objectified labour. In terms of effort, of the expenditure of life's energies, work is the personal activity of the worker. But as something that *creates value* as something involved in the process of objectifying labour, the worker's labour becomes one of the *modes of existence* of capital, it is incorporated into capital as soon as it enters the production process.[25]

Although the process of production was the unity of the labour process and the valorisation process, the two processes, for Marx, were not simply fused. The valorisation process was the 'determining dominating and overriding' one.[26] Marx believed that 'the labour process itself is no more than an instrument of the valorisation process, just as the use-value of the product is nothing but a repository of its exchange-value'.[27]

The two main classes in Marx's pure model of capitalism had diametrically opposed relationships with this production process. The capitalist owned the means of production (owner), did not produce value (non-labourer), appropriated surplus-value (exploiter) or surplus-labour (oppressor). The worker, on the other hand, did not own the means of production (non-owner), produced surplus-value or surplus-labour (labourer) and had surplus-value or surplus-labour expropriated (exploited or oppressed).

These features of class relationships within capitalism were, for Marx, paramount. He was concerned to examine classes not for their personal characteristics but as embodiments, personifications of capital and wage-labour.[28] When Marx asked, 'What makes wage-labourers, capitalists and landlords constitute the three great social classes?',[29] there could be only one answer as far as workers and capitalists were concerned: it was primarily their relations within this production process.

The dominance of the surplus-value producing process revolutionised the relationship of labour to the production process as the capitalist production process proper was established. Marx described a change from what he termed 'the formal subsumption of labour under capital' to 'a real subsumption of labour under capital'. The formal subsumption denoted a stage whereby labour was transformed into wage-labour. According to Marx, however:

> The change itself does not imply a fundamental modification in the real nature of the labour process, the actual process of production. On the contrary, the fact is that capital subsumes the labour process as it finds it, that is to say it takes over an *existing labour process*, developed by different more archaic modes of production.[30]

Work might have become more intensive, its duration extended, and made more continuous by supervision of the capitalist, but it did not change its nature. Under these conditions additional surplus-value could only be created by lengthening the time at work, that is, by increasing absolute surplus-value.

This position contrasts with the development of the real subsumption of labour under capital:

> the development of the specifically capitalist mode of production (large scale industry, etc.) . . . transforms the situations of various agents of production, it also revolutionises their actual mode of labour and the real nature of the labour process as a whole.[31]

As the transition from formal to real subsumption of labour under capital took place, so too was there a corresponding transition from the extraction of absolute surplus-value to the extraction of relative surplus-value.

The function of the collective worker

These changes had, Marx believed, fundamental repercussions for social relations within the labour process. In the earlier stages of production the individual worker was the producer, but as the capitalist mode of production took hold, less and less could an individual be said to be the direct producer, and increasingly products were the result of socialised, collective labour.

> The product is transformed from the direct product of the individual producer into a social product, the joint product of a collective labourer, i.e. a combination of workers, each of whom stands at a different distance from the actual manipulation of the object of labour. With the progressive accentuation of the co-operative character of the labour

process, there necessarily occurs a progressive extension of the concept of productive labour, and of the concept of the bearer of that labour, the productive worker. In order to work productively, it is no longer necessary for the individual himself to put his hand on the object, it is sufficient for him to be an organ of the collective labourer, and to perform any one of its subordinate functions.[32]

Elsewhere, Marx gave an indication of those groups drawn inside the concept of the collective worker:

Some work better with their hands, others with their heads, one as manager, engineer, technologist etc. the other as overseer, the third as manual labourer or even drudge. An ever increasing number of types of labour are included in the immediate concept of *productive labour* and those who perform it are classed as *productive workers*, workers directly exploited by capital and *subordinated* to its process of production and expansion.[33]

The function of the worker became a collective function. The engineer, manager and technologist became part of the collective worker, but only in so far as they produced surplus-value or, in non-productive spheres, surplus-labour. It could also be said, therefore, that engineers, managers and technologists, while not producing surplus-value or surplus-labour, were not carrying out the function of labour, and for that duration were not part of the collective worker.[34]

The function of capital

The capitalist was characterised by Marx as merely an agent of capital, its representative in the valorisation process. He stated this explicitly:

The *functions* fulfilled by the capitalist are no more than the functions of capital − viz. the valorization of value by absorbing living labour − executed *consciously* and *willingly*. The capitalist functions only as personified capital, capital as a person.[35]

He went on to detail the reponsibilities assumed by the capitalist in order to ensure the successful valorisation of capital. It is worth noting these at some length since attention has rarely focused upon the functions of the capitalist:

it is the task of the capitalist to see to it when purchasing these means of production that their use-values have no more than the average quality needed to manufacture the product. This applies both to raw materials and to machinery. They must all function with average quality and not present labour, the living factor, with any abnormal obstacles . . . however, if the value of constant capital is not to be eroded, it must as far as possible be consumed productively and not squandered, since in that case the product would contain a greater amount of objectified labour within it than is *socially necessary*. In part this depends on the workers themselves, and it is here that the *supervisory responsibility of the capitalist* enters. (He secures his position here through piece-work, deductions from wages, etc.) He must also see to it that work is performed in an orderly and methodical fashion and that the use-value he has in mind emerges *successfully* at the end of the process. At this point too the capitalist's ability to *supervise* and enforce *discipline* is vital. Lastly, he must make sure that the process of production is not interrupted or disturbed and that it really does proceed to the creation of the product within the time allowed for by the particular labour process and its objective requirements.[36]

The capitalist therefore functioned within the production process, and this, according to Marx, affected the ideology of the capitalist. The profits of the enterprise appeared to the capitalist as being independent of his ownership of capital and the result of his function as a non-proprietor, a 'labourer'. Profits, therefore, appeared to the capitalist as the 'wages of superintendence of labour'.[37] Thus, to the capitalist the process of exploitation appeared as a simple labour process (as opposed to a surplus-value producing process) in which the capitalist merely performed a different kind of labour from the labourer. The conception of the profit of the enterprise as the wages of supervision was further strengthened by the fact that, according to Marx, 'a portion of wages appears under capitalist production as [an] integral part of profit'.[38] He argued that a part of what appeared to the capitalist to be 'wages of supervision and management' was indeed wages. This concealment of a part of wages as profit occurred because of the double nature of the work of supervision and management within the capitalist production process. One component part of the work the capitalist performed was part of the labour process and would be necessary in any system of social production:

> On the one hand, all labour in which many individuals cooperate necessarily requires a commanding will to coordinate and unify the process, and functions which apply not to partial operations but to the total activity of the workshop, much as

that of an orchestra conductor. This is a productive job, which must be performed in every combined mode of operation.[39]

For that portion of their time that the capitalist (or, by extension, anyone else) spends on this kind of work they are productive workers, part of the collective worker. They therefore produce value and, if not paid in full, surplus-value (or surplus-labour). Furthermore, if they are not paid a wage for such work it appears in the form of profit. But this was not the only labour that comprised supervision and management. Marx maintained that the work of the capitalist was also central to the surplus-value producing process:

> On the other hand . . . this supervision work necessarily arises in all modes of production based on the antithesis between the labourer, as the direct producer, and the owner of the means of production. The greater the antagonism, the greater the role played by supervision. Hence it reaches its peak in the slave system. But it is indispensable also in the capitalist mode of production, since the production process in it is simultaneously a process by which the capitalist consumes labour power.[40]

In other words, 'the wage-labourer, like the slave, must have a master who puts him to work and rules over him'.[41] For such 'work', part of the function of capital, they were 'paid' out of surplus-value.

The work of management and supervision therefore contained two functions that were analytically separate. The capitalist functioned as both worker — when unifying and co-ordinating the labour process — and as capital personified — when controlling and surveilling the work-force. Marx quoted from Hodgskin's *Labour Defended Against the Claims of Capital, etc., 1825*, to this effect:

> Masters are labourers as well as their journeymen. In this character their interest is precisely the same as that of their men. But they are also either capitalists or agents of the capitalists, and in this respect their interest is decidedly opposed to the interests of the workmen.[42]

The capitalists did not, of course, experience these analytically distinct roles as distinct in practice. They were 'directly and inseparably connected'.[43] Nor were contradictions experienced; the capitalist's overriding purpose was the creation of surplus-value. The dominant function within the complex of activities performed by the capitalist was therefore the function of capital. This function was not one of productive labour. Nor, it must be stressed, was it unproductive labour, as it fell outside the labour process entirely and was located within the valorisation process, i.e. it produced neither surplus-value nor surplus-labour. The payment for the function of labour came not out of variable capital but out of profit. While the function of capital was non-labour, being outside the labour process, however, it was nevertheless inside the capitalist production process.

It is in this latter sense that Marx talks of the productive capitalist, asserting that the capitalist was essential in the valorisation process.

> As the representative of *productive capital* engaged in the process of self-expansion, the capitalist performs a *productive* function. It consists in the direction and exploitation of productive labour. In contrast to his fellow consumers of *surplus-value* who stand in no such immediate and active relationship in their production, his class is the *productive* class par excellence.[44]

He was clear that this function was not a function of labour, contrasting the above function of the capitalist with that inside the labour process: 'As the director of the labour process the capitalist performs *productive labour* in the sense that his labour is involved in the total process that is realised in the product.'[45]

The function of capital, like the function of labour, has, however, been transformed from an individual to a collective one, and is no longer embodied in the individual capitalist. Marx noted that at a certain stage in the development of capitalism, and particularly with the growth of joint stock companies based upon credit, the function of capital was placed in the hands of 'a special kind of wage-labourer'.[46] With this development, he claimed that:

> the mere manager who has no title whatever to capital . . . performs all the real functions pertaining to the functioning capitalist as such, only the functionary remains and the capitalist disappears as superfluous from the production process.[47]

The capitalist no longer played a role in the production process and Marx was clearly aware therefore of the separation of ownership from management. The function of capital, however, continued through an increasingly complicated managerial structure. The function of capital was collectivised and with that collectivisation grew the new middle class.

The new middle class

According to Marx, the changing nature of capitalism had two profound affects on the two main classes. On the one hand, it altered the relationship of labour to capital, increasingly subordinating it through changes in the division of labour. This process brought within the bounds of productive labour an increasing number of types of labour, including managers, engineers and technologists. On the other hand, there were also transformations in the representatives of capital at the workplace. Increasingly, the capitalist withdrew from the workplace and abandoned supervision of the productive process, choosing to leave his previous functions to hired employees. As a consequence of these changes, the social structure of the factory has become far more complex. While it is still analytically possible to distinguish the function of capital and the function of labour within the production process, fewer occupations correspond with one function or the other in a pure way. An increasing number of people perform jobs the composition of which is made up of part function of capital, part function of labour. People performing such jobs make up the new middle class. As a consequence of these changes, it is even less credible to view the capitalist class structure as being composed of two classes defined by a unity of oppositions — owner/non-owner, labourer-non-labourer, exploiter/exploited or oppressor/oppressed. There now exists a relatively large group of employees who share characteristics on both sides of the oppositions. Foremen, for instance, while not owning the means of production nor having any control over strategic decisions, nevertheless carry out control functions on behalf of capital.

The parameters of this new middle class cannot be delineated in any mechanical fashion. Their position can, however, be differentiated from those of the two major classes. The fact that such employees either perform supervisory or control functions, or are seen by workers to be active in worsening their conditions of labour by, for instance, work-studies or time and motion-studies, gives an objective basis for the antagonism that many workers feel towards such groups. The degree to which employees perform these roles as opposed to ones inside the labour process will further condition both their attitudes towards workers and vice versa.

On the other hand, there is an objective basis for the antagonism of the new middle class towards the owners and controllers of the means of production. The new middle class is controlled from above and the more their roles are those of the collective worker, the greater the likelihood of direct supervision. At one and the same time, however, the greater their participation inside the labour process, the greater degree of confidence and independence from capital are members of the new middle class likely to exhibit. Conversely, where they perform only the function of capital, or where such a function gives them substantial control over aspects of production, their identification with those above them is more likely to be closer. Indeed, in many instances, those exercising substantial control can be considered as having merged with the ruling class.

With regard to this latter tendency for certain managers to merge with the ruling class, the distinctions drawn by the French Marxist, Charles Bettelheim, are pertinent. In *Economic Calculation and Forms of Property* he stated that one should distinguish three sets of relationships, each referring to a different level of control; possession, ownership as a relation of production (or economic ownership), and legal ownership.[48] Possession designated the ability to put the means of production to work and referred to the management of factories. For Bettelheim, economic ownership consisted of the power to assign to specific uses objects under its control, particularly the means of production, and to dispose of the products so obtained through these means of production. This latter concept was distinguished from legal ownership which, while entitling participation in decisions over assignment and disposition, did not entitle assignment and disposition as such.

The relevance of such distinctions here is that the difference between possession and ownership as a relation of production coincides with, and furthermore underpins, the distinction between new middle class employees performing the function of capital (at the level of possession) but not having strategic control (economic ownership) and those managers who belong to the bourgeoisie because of their economic ownership.

It is possible, following Guglielmo Carchedi, the Italian Marxist, to summarise the main characteristics of the new middle class:

1 They have neither the legal nor the real ownership of the means of production.
2 They perform both the global function of capital and the function of the collective worker.
3 Since they do not have the real ownership of the means of production, the global function of capital is not necessarily the dominant one. This role can also revert to the function of the

collective worker.

4 When they perform the function of the collective worker, they are either the exploited or the economically oppressed; when they perform the global function of capital, they are either the exploiters or oppressors. However, since they do not have the real ownership of the means of production, when they perform the latter function they are also economically oppressed.

5 Since they are not the real owners, and since therefore the global function of capital is not necessarily dominant, their fundamental role is not necessarily that of exploiters or oppressors.

6 On the basis of points mentioned above, they are partly on the side of capital and partly on the side of labour. This is the contradiction inherent in their position. Moreover, even when they are on the side of capital, they are both exploiters (or oppressors) and oppressed. This is an element of further contradiction inherent in their position.[49]

Such an analysis has advantages in that it can account for the vacillation of the new middle class and is radically different from those analyses that rely on the simple dichotomy of ownership/ non-ownership of the means of production. It allows for a recognition of the differentiation of waged employees while explaining the differentiation with an analysis that is directly connected to the labour theory of value. It forms part of a coherent Marxist approach, in contrast to the 'orthodox' Marxists who resorted to Weberian concepts.[50]

In so far as the new middle class perform as part of the collective worker, producing surplus-value or surplus-labour, they are paid from variable capital. In so far as they perform as agents of capital, they are paid out of revenue, as part of what Marx called the *faux frais de production*.[51] If, as has been the case, the salaries of many new middle-class employees fall relative to average wages, this could indicate either of two tendencies. Firstly, that the wage part of income is reduced relative to average wages due to de-skilling and fragmentation of the collective worker function. A senior draughtsman, for instance, the repository of skills and experience, might see these devalued by the introduction of computer-aided design. Secondly, that the proportion of income received as revenue falls due to the reconstitution of jobs and the progressive elimination of the role of capital within them: the same senior draughtsman might find his supervisory role reduced by the introduction of computer-aided design as control is objectified into the computer (by the utilisation of standard times and the recording of work rates).

This proletarianisation process is a constant tendency, but it is, it should be stressed, only one side of a relationship. As authority is removed from certain personnel it is not simply abolished but is reconstituted in the hands of others. The centralisation of authority concentrates the function of capital into fewer positions. Any overall account of the restructuring of middle-class employment has therefore to deal with both tendencies and not simply argue the one-sided case of proletarianisation.

All this is equally applicable to the new middle class in the unproductive spheres of the capitalist production process. It has already been established that there is an identifiable commercial wage-worker, who, while not producing surplus-value, never-theless does provide surplus-labour, in that he reduces the cost of realising surplus-value. In order to ensure that the commercial wage-worker performs this work in no more than the average socially necessary labour time the capitalist himself originally supervised the work. This function of capital has also been fragmented and is now performed by a hierarchy of people functioning as agents of capital. These agents may combine this function with the function of the collective worker. In the case of selling, for example, a supervisor or manager of a supermarket performs the function of capital by ensuring that no more than the average socially necessary time is taken to sell goods. He may also take part in the labour process itself either by selling directly or by his knowledge of particular aspects of the work such as hygiene, or butchery. He will also be responsible for co-ordinating the labour process, ordering stock and ensuring the maintenance of buildings and machinery. The extent to which these latter responsibilities can be separated from the function of capital is open to doubt, but it is clear that employees in this situation are certainly not in charge of strategic decisions such as closure, pricing, wages and staffing levels, and are therefore, while not workers, differentiated from capital.

Carchedi and his critics *1977*

The general similarity of the approach outlined to that of Carchedi has already been noted.[52] Carchedi's work has been subjected to several criticisms even though he acknowledged the limitations of his work in *On the Economic Identification of the New Middle Class* and outlined them as follows:

> It should be kept in mind . . . that the analysis given here is

limited to the economic aspects of the new middle class . . .
and that very little attention has been paid to the ideological
and political instances. Yet no class, when analysing concrete
society, can ever be defined only on the economic level: its
economic identification . . . is, however, a necessary although
not a sufficient step.[53]

Any analysis of classes in a particular social formation
therefore needs to go beyond this economic identification. This
necessitates the examination of political and ideological relations
and the role of groups in the class struggle, which changes the
preliminary definition of class given at the economic level. It
would appear that Carchedi recognised this when he stated:

Therefore, we have also a *direct overdetermination* of the
identification of class, the change the definition of class
undergoes due to the class struggle and superstructure, the
change which writes off an automatic identity between the
economic identification of a class and its definition, since the
definition must be given in economic, political, and ideological
terms.[54]

Carchedi's position has been criticised by Terry Johnson, who
has argued that 'if there is no theorized or necessary relationship
between class . . . identification and the class struggle in the . . .
concrete society then class determination has no known relevance
for specifying actual class alliances'.[55] Johnson also maintained
that if it is claimed that class determinations are expressed in
actual class relations then Carchedi's analysis would simply be a
return to economic determinism.[56] Johnson's attempt to
represent Carchedi's analysis as either irrelevant or reductionist is
mistaken. The prime criticism that Johnson made was not
concerned with the consistency and coherence of the analysis but
rather with the fact that it did not deal with 'the relationships of
the economic, political and ideological within *specific* capitalist
processes which occur within the parameters of *actual institutions
and organisations*'.[57] This point is beyond dispute. It does not
follow, however, that Carchedi's perspectives are incapable of
highlighting relationships within particular capitalist processes
and institutional contexts, nor that they are so framed as not to
permit modification in the light of actual ideological and political
relations.

Johnson made a further criticism of Carchedi's analysis, one
reiterated by both Fairbrother and Urry.[58] It is that Carchedi's
identification of new middle-class positions rests on the
distinction between functions of co-ordination and unity on the

one hand and control and surveillance on the other – dual functions which rest on the distinct processes of labour and surplus-value production. It is claimed that, because Carchedi identified the new middle class as performing both these functions, the inability to distinguish which work tasks were composed of which functions suggests that the new middle class 'is merely a creature of Carchedi's dubious logic of abstraction'.[59]

It must be conceded that Carchedi's claim that members of the new middle class can perform collective worker functions and functions of capital, but not both simultaneously, cannot be empirically verified. A production engineer, for instance, designing new plant performs the two functions in that not only is new plant necessary for the labour process, but also it will have work tasks and objectified control in-built. Too much can be made of this particular aspect of Carchedi's formulation, however, and certainly it is not superseded by attempts to construct a new middle class who perform solely the function of capital. Johnson's formulation, for example, stated that 'the new petty bourgeoisie are characterized by positions within the social division of labour (as structured within the process of realization) which operationalize a function of capital but do so as part of an increasingly fragmented and routinized labour process'.[60] This formulation conflates the valorisation process and the labour process.

Whatever the empirical difficulties in distinguishing the two processes within the work of management (surveillance and control/unity and co-ordination), the distinction is nevertheless central to class relations. If the function of capital is part of the labour process, then those performing it become direct producers. Surplus-value would disappear from the conceptual schema because profit of enterprise would indeed comprise the wages of supervision. This point is not central to Johnson's work because he only considered new middle-class employees removed from the labour process proper. There is no possibility, therefore, of them performing dual functions and Johnson gives no indication as to how to locate in the class structure employees such as professional engineers who have both necessary skills *and* supervisory functions. Moreover, as a classification of a particular group of people within the global function of capital, Johnson's formulation can be subsumed into Carchedi's view that 'even when they find themselves on the side of capital, they are both exploiters (or oppressors) and oppressed'.[61] The 'wages' of the agents of capital, as Marx remarked, find their 'definite level and definite market-price, on the one hand, with the development of a numerous class of industrial and commercial managers and . . .

on the other, . . . with the general development which reduces the cost of production of specially trained labour-power'.[62]

Poulantzas 19 75

Undoubtedly the most influential attempt to construct a Marxist theory of the new middle class is that of the Greek Marxist Nicos Poulantzas. His *Classes in Contemporary Capitalism*, 1975, can be viewed as an implied criticism of the approach of Carchedi. While Carchedi conceived of the relations of production at the level of the pure capitalist mode of production as economic, Poulantzas presented a radical reformulation of the role of the economic:

> The relations of production and the relations that comprise them (economic ownership/possession) are expressed in the form of powers which derive from them, in other words class powers; these powers are constitutively tied to the political and ideological relations which sanction and legitimize them. These relations are '*not simply added on to the relations of production that are already there*', but are themselves present in the form specific to each mode of production, in the constitution of the relations of production. The process of production and exploitation is at the same time a process of reproduction of the relations of political and ideological domination and subordination.[63] (my emphasis)

It is one of the merits of Poulantzas's work that it focuses closely on the ideological and political relations within the workplace attendant upon a given division of labour. It highlights the problem that although certain workers perform productive labour and are thus members of the proletariat at an economic level, the same division of labour within the enterprise has political and ideological repercussions. Regarded in another way, certain identical technical functions would have to be performed in a socialist society just as they are in a capitalist one, but they would not necessarily be done in combination with other functions that presently make up the occupations of particular employees. Engineering skills are necessary, but not necessarily embodied exclusively in professional engineers as they are today.

The propositions and general framework elaborated by Poulantzas can be summarised as follows:
(i)   Social classes are defined 'principally but not exclusively by their place in the production process'. The economic has the determinant role in a mode of production or a social formation, but 'the political and the ideological (the superstructure) also

have a very important role'.

(ii)   Classes cannot be defined outside of class struggle, that is to say 'social classes do not firstly exist as such, and only then enter into a class struggle. Social classes coincide with class practices, i.e. the class struggle, and are only defined in mutual opposition'. Classes are defined by the antagonistic nature of the relationships into which they enter, and not simply at the level of consciousness.

(iii)   Classes designate certain objective places in the social division of labour, which are independent of the will of the agents occupying those places. This structural determination of class includes, not only places in the relations of production, but also in the political and ideological relations of domination and subordination.

(iv)   The structural determination of classes does not necessarily correspond to the positions that various groups and agents adopt in specific circumstances. That is to say that as a particular group's ideology and actions change it does not necessarily indicate a change in its class place.[64]

Poulantzas, having outlined these basic premises, turns specifically to the economic, political and ideological criteria in the determination of class boundaries.

Economic criteria

The dividing line between the working class and the new middle class at the economic level is defined for Poulantzas by the performance of productive or unproductive labour: 'The working class is not defined by a simple and intrinsic negative criterion, but by productive labour'.[65] Moreover, Poulantzas feels it necessary to amend Marx's conception of productive labour because, he claims, Marx's unsystematic treatment has given rise to ambiguities. Poulantzas, therefore, uses a definition of productive labour in the capitalist mode of production, which includes only labour which 'produces surplus-value while *directly reproducing the material elements that serve as the substratum of the relation of exploitation: labour that is involved in material production by producing use-values that increase material wealth*'.[66]

Using the amended concept of productive labour as the criterion for membership of the working class, Poulantzas thus excludes from membership all service workers, workers in the sphere of circulation and all state employees (other than those directly productive workers in the nationalised industries and public transport).[67]

Political criteria

Poulantzas stresses that the economic criteria are insufficient in themselves structurally to determine class membership. Classes are also determined by their role in the political relationships of domination/subordination.[68] Following Marx, Poulantzas acknowledges that those performing the work of management and supervision play a role in the labour process, by co-ordinating and unifying the production process, but maintains that the social division of labour gives dominance to roles stemming from the relations of production. Hence supervisors and foremen belong to the new middle class because of the dominance of the political role they play. They ensure the extraction of surplus-value from direct producers, while they themselves are politically dominated by capital.

Ideological criteria

The working class are not only economically exploited and politically dominated, but are also dominated ideologically. The chief source of the ideological domination is the separation of direct producers from knowledge of the production process. Poulantzas characterises this separation as the split between mental and manual labour.[69] This division is not simply a technical one but also a social one. Neither does it correspond to the division between 'brain' and 'hand' work. Engineers and technicians may be part of the collective worker in that they may perform productive work. They should not, however, be considered as working-class, because their place as 'experts' in the social division of labour excludes the direct producers from such knowledge and thus they are complicit in the ideological domination of the working class.

Those on the mental labour side of this divide are dominated ideologically and politically by capital. Their work is controlled and fragmented. Furthermore, the division between mental and manual work continually makes its appearance on the mental side of the divide, causing a polarisation of labour within the mental side.[70]

Economic determination

Poulantzas's economic criteria construct a double disqualification of agents in the production process from membership of the working class. Firstly, he defines as working class only those wage workers who perform productive labour. There is no justification for such a restrictive definition, however, in the writings of Marx, which point to a much wider conception of the working class. As already noted, Marx discussed the commercial worker as belonging to 'the better paid class of wage workers – to those whose labour is classified as skilled and stands above average labour'.[71] There is no indication that the related concepts were to be the dividing line between classes. Where Marx discussed productive and unproductive capital, for instance, it was to define function, not to suggest that commercial and industrial capital represented two hostile classes.[72] The real significance of the concepts is in their relation to the accumulation process.

Poulantzas restricts the concept of productive labour, and hence the working class, to those workers producing surplus-value while involved in the production of material commodities. He attempts to establish that this is consistent with the views of Marx by using highly selective quotations.[73] Marx, however, was consistent and explicit in stating that labour is productive if it directly creates surplus-value and that for such labour to be designated productive, 'qualities are required which are utterly unconnected with the specific content of labour, with the particular utility or use-value in which it is objectified'.[74] A singer, for example, who does not produce material commodities, can be a productive worker if 'engaged by an entrepreneur, who makes her sing to make money'.[75]

Poulantzas's definition forces him to exclude all service workers from being productive labourers, even when they are wage-earners producing surplus-value. To avoid this problem he considers only services that are provided outside the wage-labour/capital relation, use-values purchased from revenue. Thus, he ignores services such as gardening, tailoring and cleaning which can be performed by the same person either in the service of an industrial capitalist or on behalf of the immediate consumer. According to Marx, 'He is a wage-labourer or day labourer in either situation, only he is a productive worker in the one case and unproductive in the other, because in one he produces capital and in the other not.'[76]

Perhaps more importantly, given his general propositions, Poulantzas acknowledges that unproductive workers still have surplus-labour extracted from them and are thus 'exploited'.[77] This does not suggest that Poulantzas regards their class interests as being in any way separate from those of productive workers. Yet classes are defined for Poulantzas by class struggle, by opposition to other classes. Consequently, there is a contradiction between his general proposition and its fulfilment at the economic level.

Political determination

Poulantzas maintains that agents who perform productive work will not necessarily be working-class because the distinction between productive and unproductive labour is not sufficient to delimit class boundaries. This is the case, for instance, with supervisors who are directly involved in the process of material production. Poulantzas claims that their political role within the productive process always dominates their economic one, and he makes reference to Marx's contention that the valorisation process dominates the labour process, or, in other words, the social relations of production and the social division of labour dominate the technical division of labour. But when Poulantzas examines the double nature of the work of management (co-ordination and unity/control and supervision) instead of the division being represented as part of a social division of labour (collective worker/function of capital), Poulantzas represents it as a position in the technical division of labour (co-ordination) which is dominated by the social division of labour (function of capital). The way is thus open for Poulantzas simply to assert that the principal function of foremen and supervisors is the extraction of surplus-value whether or not they are engaged in productive labour or to whatever extent they are so engaged.

It is the case, as noted above, that Marx considered the valorisation process as dominant, but this dominance affected different groups in different ways. It caused the capitalist to identify with this process despite performing, in part, as a labourer:

> At the same time the process of production is a real labour process and to the extent to which that is the case and the capitalist has a definite function to perform within it as *supervisor* and *director*, his activity acquires a specific many-sided content. But the *labour process itself* is not more than the *instrument* of the valorization process. . . . The self-valorization of capital — the creation of surplus value — is therefore the determining, dominating and overriding purpose of the capitalist; it is the absolute motive and content of his activity.[78]

It does not follow, however, that as the capitalist's role has become fragmented people having no real ownership of the means of production and performing minimal tasks of supervision and major collective worker tasks are, as Poulantzas decrees, automatically dominated by the global function of capital. Their

75

class determination cannot be allocated in this *a priori* manner. To understand their position it is necessary to examine their complex and many-sided relationships.

Ideological determination

Poulantzas further delimits the extent of the working class by distinguishing between mental and manual labour. Thus engineers and technicians are members of the new middle class despite the fact that they perform productive work because they are the bearers of relationships of ideological domination. The distinction between mental and manual work, as noted earlier, is not for Poulantzas that between 'brain' and 'hand' work, but rather:

> every form of work that takes the form of knowledge from which the *direct* producers are excluded, falls on the mental side of the capitalist production process, irrespective of its empirical natural content, and that this is so whether the direct producers actually do know how to perform the work but do not do so (again not by chance) or whether they in fact do not know how to perform it (since they are systematically kept away from it), or whether *there quite simply is nothing to be known*.[79] (my emphasis)

Having attacked 'the incongruities of empirical definitions of types of labour',[80] Poulantzas substitutes a definition that has no content or determining features. It is its very vagueness that gives the formulation credibility; indeed, there is a tendency on the part of the reader to make the distinctions more concrete by using exactly the same empirical/natural distinctions, 'brain' work and 'hand' work, that the definition is formally ranged against. That this void left by the definition tends to be filled by subjective judgments is itself reflected within Poulantzas's work.

He places labour on the mental side of the divide when it is popularly associated with secrecy and domination even though it may not possess these qualities. Poulantzas maintains that office workers, although increasingly dependent upon and subordinated to capital and the enterprise management, often find themselves involved in legitimating the power that management exercises over the work-force. His sole evidence for this, however, is Lockwood's statement that:

> it is no exaggeration to say that 'management', *from the point of view of the manual worker, ends* with the lowest grade of routine clerk. The office worker is associated with managerial

authority, although he does not usually stand in an authoritarian relationship to the manual worker, the orders governing the labour force being transmitted from management through the foreman rather than through the clerical staff . . . the administrative separation of the office worker . . . is based primarily on the conception of the secret and confidential nature of office work.[81]

Poulantzas thus relies on manual worker prejudice on the one hand and managerial conceptions of confidentiality on the other. There is no objective assessment of the nature of their work. The earlier insistence that the distinction between mental and manual labour was based upon objective ideological relations has been replaced by a concept of ideology that consists of no more than the ideas in people's hands, with no necessary relation to reality.

This is not to suggest that the divisions between sections of the work-force which Poulantzas attempts to capture and analyse do not exist and are not important. There is hostility and suspicion towards 'experts' amongst other sections of the work-force. There is also a corresponding elitism amongst sections of 'knowledge' workers even where they do not carry out the function of capital. But Poulantzas fails to establish that these divisions are more than a reflection of a differentiation within the working class; that the divisions are qualitatively different from divisions between skilled and non-skilled workers. The alienation felt by workers does not arise simply because they are dominated by experts who exclude them from knowledge. The very organisation of the productive process, the fragmentation of knowledge between workers, is a sufficient basis. Marx commented upon such alienation:

Subsumed under capital the workers become components of these social formations, but these social formations do not belong to them and so rise up against them as the *forms* of capital itself, as if they belonged to capital, as if they arose from it, in opposition to the isolated labour-power of the workers.[82]

The division seized upon by Poulantzas as a separate and determining one is part of a much wider and complex problem. If ideological determination is sufficient to produce class boundaries then the choice of mental/manual work is quite arbitrary: boundaries could equally be drawn around sexual and racial divisions as they manifest themselves in production, divisions which also reflect hostility and exclusion.

Far from presenting a systematic and coherent theory of class determination, Poulantzas's work reveals a number of imprecise formulations and internal contradictions.

(i) The role of the 'economic' is highly ambiguous and is not the principal determinant. It is, in fact, over-ruled by the political and ideological determinations.

(ii) Despite the proposition that classes are defined by mutual antagonism, by class struggle, Poulantzas fails to elaborate on the irreconcilable interests of productive and unproductive labourers.

(iii) The distinction drawn by Poulantzas between social class as defined by *place* in the ensemble of social practices, and class position of groups in any specific conjuncture is formulated in such a way as to negate the overall determinacy of class struggle in the formation of classes. This is because, although there are transformations within the new petty bourgeoisie that produce cleavages which, in turn, present objective preconditions for the adoption by certain groups of proletarian class positions, the groups remain, nevertheless, petty bourgeois.[83] The groups with 'an objectively proletarian polarization' will never become proletarian in Poulantzas's schema because they remain 'marked by their place in the politico-ideological relations of the enterprise'.[84] Nor is this mark merely conjunctural, it is continually reproduced:

> But accentuating the reproduction of the mental/manual labour division within mental labour, these transformations bring certain fractions of the new petty bourgeoisie close to the barrier which separates them from manual labour and from the working class. *But these transformations do not undermine the basic barrier between mental and manual labour, since they simultaneously reproduce it in a new form.*[85] (my emphasis)

Poulantzas's work is both characterized and marred by his formalism. Classes are defined in an *a priori* fashion and the boundaries between them are considered immutable. The primacy Poulantzas gives to their determination in struggle is thus purely ritualistic. His mechanical separation of the complex relations within the production process into economic, political and ideological leaves insuperable problems in integrating them into a coherent theory.

Erik Olin Wright 1978

Some of the criticisms of Poulantzas made above are similar to ones raised by E.O. Wright. In his *Class, Crisis and the State*, Wright advances an alternative conceptualisation of groups that Poulantzas has characterised as a new petty bourgeoisie. These groups, Wright insists, should not be forced into one class or another, but rather the ambiguities in the class structure should be recognised. He argues that these ambiguities mean that certain groups occupy 'objectively contradictory relations within class relations', i.e. they are torn between the basic classes of capitalist society. This approach has the advantage, Wright claimed, of being more sensitive to the actual relations present under capitalism:

> The concept of contradictory locations within class relations . . . does not refer to the problem of pigeon-holing people within an abstract typology; rather it refers to the objective contradictions among the real processes of class relations.[86]

Wright established three clusters of positions within the social division of labour which can be characterised as occupying such a position. He claimed that managers and supervisors occupy a contradictory location between the bourgeoisie and the proletariat, that certain categories of semi-autonomous employees who retain relatively high levels of control over their immediate labour process occupy a contradictory location between the working class and the petty bourgeoisie, and that small employers occupy a contradictory location between the bourgeoisie and petty bourgeoisie. Wright represented these relations in the way shown in Figure 2.1.[87]

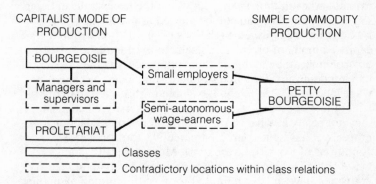

Figure *2.1*

Class polarisation in capitalist societies takes place for Wright around three central processes underlying the basic capital– labour relationship. They are control over the physical means of production, control over labour power, and control over new investment and resource-allocation.[88] Capitalists have basic control of all three processes and, conversely, workers are excluded from control of all three. The combination of these respective positions constitute for Wright the two basic antagonistic class locations within the capitalist mode of production.[89]

The class structure of any given social formation is, however, recognised by Wright as being more complex, for two reasons. Firstly, capitalist societies always contain subordinate modes of production, such as petty commodity production, other than the capitalist mode itself. Secondly, the combination of relations that form the two basic class positions within capitalism do not always coincide. A foreman, for instance, has neither control over accumulation and investment, nor over the physical means of production, but he is not a proletarian if he has control over the labour power of others.[90]

Had Wright's analysis been restricted to the locations between the bourgeoisie and the proletariat it would have been less open to challenge. His treatment of 'semi-autonomous employees', located between the proletariat and the petty bourgeoisie, however, is less than satisfactory. Categories of employees who have a certain degree of autonomy over their own immediate conditions of work, over their immediate labour process, are not considered proletarian by Wright:

> even though such employees work for the self-expansion of capital and even though they have lost the legal status of being self-employed, they can still be viewed as occupying residual islands of petty-bourgeois relations of production within the capitalist mode of production itself. In their immediate work environment, they maintain the work process of the independent outsider while still being employed by capital as wage labourers. . . . A good example of this is a researcher in a laboratory or a professor in an élite university. Such positions may not really involve control over other people's labour power, yet have considerable immediate control over conditions of work (i.e. research). More generally, many white-collar technical employees and certain highly skilled craftsmen have at least a limited form of this autonomy in their immediate labour process. Such minimal control over the physical means of production by employees *outside* of the authority hierarchy constitutes the basic contradictory location between the petty bourgeoisie and the proletariat.[91] (my emphasis)

There are a number of weaknesses and inconsistencies in such a formulation. In posing the contradiction of the position as that between the proletariat and the petty bourgeoisie, the impression is given that such employees are torn between two independent poles, one located inside the capitalist mode of production and the other outside it. In practice, however, the active relations of such groups are entirely within the capitalist mode of production, between them and the proletariat on the one hand and the capitalists on the other. In order to maintain that these groups constitute 'residual islands of petty-bourgeois relations of production within the capitalist mode of production', Wright greatly reduces the characteristics of the petty bourgeois mode of production and simultaneously expands the autonomy of the categories inside the capitalist mode of production. An important feature of the traditional petty bourgeoisie thereby minimised by Wright is the ownership of the means of production. On the other hand, researchers and technicians may have a limited control over how they perform their tasks but there is no doubt about who defines their ends. It is not the case that they act as free-floating individuals outside the authority structure. The fact that they are considered to have sufficiently internalised the values and orientations of the enterprise for authority not to be imposed upon them directly in no way dissolves that authority, as would readily become apparent were they to deviate from the expectations placed on them by employers. Similarly, their control over their conditions of work is likely to be directly connected to their own control over the labour of other people, placing the contradictions in their location, once again, primarily between bourgeoisie and proletariat, rather than proletariat and petty bourgeoisie.

Barbara and John Ehrenreich *1979*

A different approach, but one containing similarities to that of Poulantzas, has been put forward by Barbara and John Ehrenreich. Their interest centres upon what they term the professional and managerial class (PMC), defined rather loosely as consisting of 'salaried mental workers who do not own the means of production and whose major function in the social division of labour may be described broadly as the reproduction of capitalist culture and capitalist class relations'.[92] This class, they maintain, in contradistinction to Poulantzas, is not part of any wider petty bourgeois class, being specific to the capitalist mode of production. They do not, however, examine the relationship of the PMC to the labour process in any detail and the implication is that the reproduction of capitalist culture and capitalist class relations – the defining function of the PMC – is counterposed

81

to a role in the production process. The impression is therefore given that there are specific occupations that exist solely to reproduce the culture, defined as the 'total repertory of solutions and responses to everyday problems and situations' and capitalist class relations.[93] The working class, on the one hand, and capitalists, on the other, are either at most *post facto* objectors to the products of this process, or, more normally, passive spectators.

Their definition leads the Ehrenreichs to another serious problem. It is relatively simple for them to establish 'an objectively antagonistic relationship'[94] between the PMC and the working class, but they have a much greater difficulty in establishing the basis of antagonism between the PMC and the capitalist class. The PMC grew, they claim, as the process of Taylorisation of major industries saw specialists expropriate the skills and knowledge of the working class. This process was also mirrored in the wider society where the skills and culture of working-class communities were expropriated and then fed back to them as commodities and services designed to socially control the communities. Such a presentation makes it clear that the aim of the PMC, the production of a 'rational' reproducible social order 'was ultimately in accord with capitalism'.[95] What, therefore, is the evidence of antagonism between the PMC and capital? It does not consist of the production by the PMC of an anti-capitalist ideology of technocracy, for, despite maintaining its independence, the Ehrenreichs claim that such an ideology would have 'smacked too overtly of self interest'.[96] The Ehrenreichs are therefore forced to distinguish the PMC from the capitalist class by asserting its increasing social and cultural coherence, despite having elsewhere insisted on its heterogeneity.

Conclusion

It is worth reiterating that the absence of a formal definition of class in Marx's work was not an oversight but stemmed from the impossibility of capturing the manifold and diverse relations of groups in particular societies without at one and the same time examining the whole society. As Braverman has noted, 'difficulties arise, in the last analysis, from the fact that classes, the class structure, the social structure as a whole, are not fixed entities but rather on-going processes, rich in change, transition, variation, and incapable of being encapsulated in formulas, no matter how analytically proper such formulas may be'.[97] Attempts at a definition, therefore, are unavoidably schematic and cannot serve other than as guide-posts to important relationships. Definitions cannot articulate the actual relations between the economic, the political and the ideological. If class is determined by the practical relations of different groups in society through class struggle, then location of new middle-class groupings must necessarily be tentative because the nature and resolution of conflicts, the ways in which particular groups are accommodated or defeated, cannot *a priori* be known. Any insistence to the contrary places theorists in the place of alchemists, searching for magical formulations that will reconcile as yet irreconcilable contradictions.

This study therefore attempts to put alchemy to one side. Although the theoretical understanding of the new middle class broadly coincides with Carchedi's analysis, it is in no way to be regarded as a formally articulated 'truth', the essence of which is then revealed in particular situations. Rather, it is a starting point from which to examine the class relations of actual groups of workers, including their political and ideological relations, and how these are affected by the ebb and flow of class struggle. The historical dimension is therefore a vital component of the perspective. The next two chapters examine the rise of the new middle class in both the private and public sector of the economy and their changing relations with both capital and labour.

3 Monopoly capitalism and the rise of the new middle class

The rise of managerial work, and the development of a specific social and occupational group to perform it, is closely tied to changes in the organisation of capitalist production. The history of the development of capitalism is also the history of the growth of the management function. As areas of autonomous activity were progressively integrated and harnessed to the production of profit in the eighteenth and nineteenth centuries, management ceased to be the relatively underdeveloped function of the individual owner of an enterprise and emerged as a function divorced from both the legal owners and the direct producers.

Today capitalism is almost synonymous with factory production. Historically, however, the capitalist era was established long before the spread of factory production, developing with the growth of merchant capital from the sixteenth century. Initially, merchant capital had a purely external relationship to the mode of production which continued to be independent and untouched by capital. The merchant was simply 'the man who "removes" the goods produced by the guilds or peasants'[1] in order to profit from price differentials in different productive areas. Later, merchant capital began to seize hold of the mode of production and a section of producers themselves accumulated capital, took to trade, and began to organise production on a capitalist basis free from the handicraft restrictions of the guilds.

By the seventeenth century merchants had concentrated producers under one roof in large 'manufactures'. What distinguished these from factories was that there was as yet no change in the instruments of production, which could still be purchased by craftsmen of modest means and used individually in their own homes. As Dobb states, 'the only difference between manufacturing and domestic production was that in the former a number of looms were set up side by side in the same building instead of being scattered in the workers' homes'.[2] The concentration of production under one roof, however, did enable greater supervision and hence an increase in productivity and the curtailment of theft of materials.

The subordination of domestic production to capital and the dependence of the producer upon the capitalist was a critical step on the road to fully capitalist production. Capital had ceased to be external to the production process and could no longer be considered simply parasitic. Capitalist domestic industry was able to effect significant changes in production: the division of labour was extended between successive stages of production, time was saved in passing material from stage to stage, and a more balanced and integrated process was secured.

The essence of the further transformation, the 'industrial revolution', was the change in the character of production associated with the harnessing of machines to new sources of power. This not only led to workers being concentrated in a single place of work but it imposed upon the productive process a collective character. This collective character was reinforced by a further division of labour to an extent never hitherto experienced, increasing the dependence of labour on capital. These changes also signalled a growing management function, though one performed at this stage by the capitalists themselves. In place of the old mercantile capitalist 'a role was created for a new type of capitalist, no longer simply as usurer or trader in his counting house or warehouse, but as a capitain of industry, organiser and planner of the operations of the production-unit, embodiment of an authoritarian discipline over a labour army'.[3]

Not all sections of merchant capital preferred to take this road. The new social relations established under the factory system produced dangers as well as opportunities. The Committee on the Woollen Manufactures of 1806, for example, argued against the establishment of large factories, claiming that by the continuation of outwork merchants would not only save on capital investment but would also not need 'to submit to the constant trouble and solicitude of watching over a numerous body of workmen'.[4] Andrew Ure, writing in 1835, also noted that the early establishment of capitalist factories presented entrepreneurs with serious labour problems:

> If the factory Briareus could have been created by mechanical genius alone, it should have come into being thirty years sooner; for upwards of ninety years have now elapsed since John Wyatt, of Birmingham, not only invented the series of

85

fluted rollers (the spinning fingers usually ascribed to Arkwright) but obtained a patent for the invention, and erected 'a spinning engine without hands' in his native town. . . . Wyatt was a man of good education, in a respectable walk of life, much esteemed by his superiors, and therefore favourably placed, in a mechanical point of view, for maturing his admirable scheme. But he was of a gentle and passive spirit, little qualified to cope with the hardships of a new manufacturing enterprise. It required, in fact, a man of a Napoleon nerve and ambition, to subdue the refractory tempers of work-people accustomed to irregular paroxysms of diligence, and to urge on his multifarious and intricate constructions in the face of prejudice, passion, and envy. Such was Arkwright.[5]

The role of the entrepreneur within the production process, however, should not at this stage be exaggerated. The increasingly successful establishment of factories was a result less of a series of victories for Napoleon-type nerve and ambition than the adaptation of old systems of organisation and control to new conditions. The traditional lack of involvement of many capitalists in the process of production, the customs of workforces whose skills pre-dated factory organisation, and the lack of necessary technical and administrative advances, meant that while capitalist control was enhanced by factory production, it had yet to be exercised within a coherent management system. Many tasks associated with modern management were in the early nineteenth century delegated to sub-contractors. Eric Hobsbawm comments on this feature thus,

Capitalism in its early stages expands, and to some extent operates, not so much by directly subordinating large bodies of workers to employers, but by subcontracting exploitation and management. The characteristic structure of an archaic industry such as that of Britain in the early nineteenth century is one in which all grades except the lowest labourers contain men or women who have some sort of 'profit incentive'.[6]

It is difficult, if not impossible, to ascertain the extent of this subcontracting but Littler, who has produced the most recent study of the subject, argues that 'it seems difficult to exaggerate the extent of some form of subcontracting'.[7]

The specific form of the 'profit incentive' offered to certain employees varied from industry to industry[8] as did the length of its survival. Nevertheless, it seems that as late as 1870 'the immediate employer of many workers was not the large capitalist but the intermediate subcontractor who was both an employee and a small employer of labour'.[9] Such organisation prevailed for a period because it had certain advantages:

It enabled small-scale enterprises to expand operations without raising unmanageably-great masses of circulating capital, it provided 'incentives' to all groups of workers worth humouring, and it enabled industry to meet sharp fluctuations in demand without having to carry a permanent burden of overhead expenditure.[10]

Whatever its advantages as a system, however, historically it was 'a method of evading management'[11] until the necessary organisational and administrative advances had been made. It was a transitional form of organisation that capital replaced with 'direct management, direct employment of all grades, and the provision of "incentives" by various forms of payment by results'.[12] This replacement cleared the way for modern management practice. But its evolution was not automatic. Indeed it can be argued that modern management practice was largely imported to Britain from America where in the late nineteenth and early twentieth centuries the greater size of factories and the earlier formation of giant corporations encouraged more systematic solutions to the problems of capitalist control.

Management in America

After the establishment of factory production many American capitalists, like their British counterparts, left the tasks of workplace control and the organisation of production to semi-independent subcontractors, known in the United States as inside contractors. Dan Clawson argues that in the 1860s and 1870s inside contracting was one of the most important ways of organising and controlling the work process.[13] Inside contractors negotiated a price with the company to produce a certain product. They then set wages and hired and fired their own employees, whom they disciplined at will. The inside contractors also controlled the methods of production and frequently introduced technological changes. They remained, however, employees of the company, using only company machines, equipment and raw material and selling their entire output to the company.

A consequence of this system of organisation was that inside contractors were the only effective controllers of labour. Workers were necessarily afforded a great deal of autonomy, especially in relation to methods of work, because, whatever the formal responsibilities of the inside contractor, no managerial organisation existed to supervise the details of work and impose effective, overall discipline. This was the case in some of the largest and most technically advanced firms of the mid to late nineteenth century, including the Singer Sewing Machine Company, which produced nearly half a million sewing machines in 1879,[14] as well as in small and more technologically backward businesses.

Factory production in 1880 displayed an underlying continuity with earlier workshop production. As a result of the day-to-day running of the factory being left not only to inside contractors, but also to foremen and skilled workers themselves, the factory remained 'congeries of craftsmen's shops rather than an integrated plant'.[15] This was due in some part to the relatively small size of the pre-1880 factory, to the manufacturer's preoccupation with financial and other entrepreneurial problems, and the failure to recognise the need for effective control of the labour process itself – control that would have called for the creation of supervision and personnel relations as distinct administrative functions.

Despite its apparent compatability with capitalism, the inside contractor system was, like its British variants, a transitional form of factory organisation. The reasons for its demise are various. Although the system did not discourage technical innovation, in that it allowed inside contractors to retain any savings in production costs brought about by improvements, top company officials became increasingly concerned that improvements were being held back each year until after contract prices had been fixed: 'The management sees the contractor, in spite of the yearly cut in prices, constantly drawing larger pay than he could obtain as a foreman, because he seems always able to impose his methods so as to reduce the cost of his product to himself.'[16]

If savings were there to be made, employers became increasingly anxious to retain them within the company. They aimed, therefore, at a redistribution of surplus value from the inside contractors to themselves. In order to achieve this they were forced to take upon themselves managerial functions that they had previously been happy to delegate and to integrate them within a unified system of factory administration. The processes of unification and concentration of the function of capital proceeded, however, in an uneven and piecemeal fashion.

The concern of the employers, however, was not limited to the degree of surplus-value retained by inside contractors. As important for employers was the fact that the system rested upon a delegation of decision-making and control to the work-force itself and especially to skilled workers. Workers had considerable autonomy in deciding how to do their work and this ensured that their initiative and goodwill were necessary to smooth production. The inside contractors constituted a barrier between the owners and top officials on the one hand and the actual process of production on the other. Companies therefore began to keep a more comprehensive set of records in order to begin fully to comprehend the processes that went on within their factories and to enable them to be in a position to encroach upon the functions of inside contractors. At the Singer Company, for instance, the first step was that management took over responsibility for the payment of all workers and were thus able to calculate the profit of the contractor and whether or not the rates they paid to him were in need of adjustment.[17] A later development was the loss of the inside contractor's right to hire and fire which went to the factory superintendents. Where the functions of inside contractors were taken over by foremen (and even where foremen had historically performed those functions) there were still major barriers to unified managerial control. Until the very end of the nineteenth century the foreman himself appeared to wield considerable power. His role, and sometimes his status, approached that of inside contractors. As undisputed ruler of his department, he determined the manner and timing of production, the cost and quality of the work and had virtually complete authority over the men or women in his department. The considerable personal power of the foreman was also indicated by the absence of any clearly defined relationship with higher management. Certainly the foreman was not merely a subordinate part of a bureaucratic hierarchy. It was not the replacement of inside contractors by foremen which was, therefore, particularly significant, but rather the fact that this heralded a movement towards a radical attack on traditional workplace practice.[18]

This attack was perceived as necessary by employers because, despite the apparent power of the foreman in a particular department, there were real limitations to the extent of foremen's control of production. Nowhere was this clearer than in the social limitation of output. Writing in 1911, Frederick Taylor noted that:

> As usual then, and in fact still usual in most of the shops in this country, the shop was really run by the workmen, and not by the bosses. The workmen together had carefully planned just how fast each job should be done, and they had set a pace

for each machine throughout the shop, which was limited to about one-third of a good day's work. Every new workman who came into the shop was told by the other men exactly how much of each kind of work he was to do, and unless he obeyed these instructions he was sure before long to be driven out of the place by the men.[19]

This social limitation of output, or rather the realisation of this limitation, encouraged management to take new directions. However, the growing size of plants and the increasing complexity of manufacturing operations, together with the growing recruitment of trained engineers to managerial positions, also gave increased impetus to the need to adopt systematic management practices. A more elaborate hierarchy began to emerge within the factory as administrative systems were implemented and *ad hoc* responsibilities, such as production and cost control, were transferred from foremen to staff department. These developments crystallised in the philosophy of scientific management which represented a concerted attack on shopfloor practice and traditions. Fundamental to this attack was the establishment of a planning office, the centralisation of knowledge of the work process and the issuing of instructions to the work-force on the methods and details of work.[20] In order to achieve this control a managerial hierarchy needed to be established within workplaces.

The emergence of the giant corporation

The growth of the size of factories, which made workplace control such a pertinent issue, was also paralleled by the emergence of companies controlling numerous plants and operations. Whereas the former gave rise to the well-studied changes in management brought about by the philosophy of scientific management, the latter also required a fundamental restructuring of management above the level of the factory if companies were to be successful. These changes have received rather less attention and yet the growth of extended, company-wide hierarchies of managers are as significant for an assessment of the class relations of managers as the changes at factory-level.

Large corporations first began to appear in significant numbers in the United States in the 1880s, but it was in the following decade that this form of organisation became increasingly popular and a wave of mergers occurred, from which were formed many of the giant corporations, such as US Steel,

American Tobacco and International Harvester, that still today wield massive economic power. In 1899 alone, there were 1,028 mergers creating combined assets of over 2,262 million dollars.[21] Many of the mergers were not soundly based, however, and few were successful. One of the major reasons for the high failure rate, moreover, was the fact that many corporations did not establish a managerial hierarchy to control and direct the new organisation. They failed to secure the full utilisation of economies of scale and maximum use of resources that give large corporations their economic advantage.

The large corporations that succeeded initially tended to be those which were vertically integrated, having expanded by extending their marketing and purchasing organisations, rather than those that expanded by merger. Their very success presented their entrepreneur-owners with numerous problems associated with producing, marketing and purchasing a massive volume of goods for national and international markets. One of the responses to the problems of growth was the rapid creation of a large number of middle and lower management posts, with certain companies employing hundreds of managerial staff.[22]

In those companies that remained owner-controlled despite their size, advances tended to be restricted to middle and lower management levels and were not reflected in the development of management systems at a higher level. This was less the case in corporations formed by merger. The process of merger often ensured that no single family held all the voting stock and frequently stock was sold to assist the reorganisation of the new company. It could no longer, therefore, be treated as a personal possession. Moreover, the corporate structure was much more problematic. The detailed planning needed to carry out the vertical integration of the component companies posed much more complex administrative problems. This led to the central-isation of administration and the adoption of uniform accounting and statistical controls:

> A combination became administratively a consolidation only after its executive office began to do more than merely set price and production schedules. It remained a combination as long as decisions on how to produce or market and how to allocate resources for the present and in the future were left to constituent enterprises. It became administratively consolidated when the small executive office became transformed into a centralised headquarters that determined nearly all the activities of the enterprise's plants or marketing units. The factories or sales offices, formerly managed by the

91

heads of member firms, became operated by salaried plant managers or sales representatives.[23]

The model of organisation adopted by these consolidations was the centralised, functionally departmentalised structure. Superior as it was to the non-integrated, unconsolidated combinations, it too had its own weaknesses. In particular, it forced a small number of people to take important decisions in areas about which they frequently had only remote knowledge and little sympathy. As competition between the giant firms became increasingly systematic and success more dependent upon the quality of decisions arrived at collectively within the managerial hierarchy, the centralised, functionally departmentalised structure could not utilise and integrate the wide range of information needed. While a firm was involved in a stable market and no major long-term decisions appeared urgent, the weakness of the structure was not necessarily apparent but, in conditions of rapid change such as those after the First World War, mistakes were easily made and opportunities lost.

In response to the problems emerging from over-centralisation, companies were, by 1917 already beginning to set up semi-autonomous, integrated divisions to co-ordinate the flow of goods to different markets. In none of these companies, however, had the relations between subsidiaries or divisions and the general office, between middle and top management respectively, been clearly defined. In consciously adopting a multi-divisional, decentralised structure a few firms, most notably General Motors and Du Pont, clarified these relations.[24] Top managers in the general office were relieved of all day-to-day operating responsibilities thus eroding their loyalties to particular functions. At the same time, they took over responsibility for monitoring the performance of the various divisions. The task of day-to-day management therefore fell more clearly on divisional managers. The results of these changes were that 'policy and planning were no longer made through negotiations between the senior managers of powerful operating departments or divisions. Policy was formulated by general executives who had the time, information, and psychological commitment to the enterprise as a whole, rather than to one of its parts'.[25]

As already stated, relatively few firms followed this example until after the First World War and thereafter the adoption of such a system was slowed down, if not postponed, by the Depression. Few companies felt that, with the uncertainty of the market, they could risk the capital expenditure or administrative effort involved in what appeared to be a very complicated system. It was the massive post-Second World War expansion of the economy which saw the multi-divisional, decentralised structure become the accepted form of management for the most complex and diverse of American industrial enterprises.

Management in Britain

Companies in Britain adopted modern organisational forms somewhat later than their American counterparts. The British equivalent of the merger mania of the 1890s took place between about 1916 and 1930, when modern corporations such as ICI, Unilever and English Electric (now part of GEC) were formed. There had been earlier mergers, of course, but this period saw much more 'rationalisation' of production and distribution facilities and the creation of a more extensive managerial hierarchy. Nevertheless, by the 1930s the looser holding company arrangement with only an embryonic managerial hierarchy was still dominant in Britain.[26] This is no longer the case. Today, the concentration of British industry is greater than that in America and this, together with the relatively high number of American-owned subsidiaries, using imported management techniques and sometimes managers, has led to a convergence of organisational forms and managerial practices. Derek Channon, surveying 92 out of the top 100 manufacturing companies in 1970, found that more than half were multi-product concerns with a modern multi-divisional management structure, compared with less than a quarter in 1956.[27]

The sociology of managers

There has been no authoritative study of managers in British society. A notable study has been produced on the development of British managerial thought[28] and the social background of managers has been the subject of periodic reviews. There has, however, been no systematic study of what managers do, the social significance of their day-to-day relations and how changes in their functions relate to their growing tendency to organise. In short, while studies acknowledge that there are different levels of management carrying out different functions, there has been no attempt to view the internal relations of management within the wider perspectives of a theory of social class.

This lack of consistent theoretical concern with managerial roles does not mean that a discussion of managers has not featured in major sociological controversies. Indeed, within the extensive debate on the divorce of ownership from control in industrial enterprises, the position and role of managers, albeit top managers, was a central issue. Despite this centrality, little concrete evidence emerged as to the managers' functions inside the enterprises in which they worked. This discrepancy is explained by the fact that while the debate apparently centred upon the extent to which ownership was divorced from control, in reality the major concern was whether or not it was possible to talk about the continued existence of capitalism. Nevertheless, this debate raises important questions crucial to the under-standing of the changing class position of sections of managers.

It was the contention of the proponents of the thesis that ownership and control had been separated and that this separation had fundamentally altered the dynamics of business. The profit motive, so central to capitalism, had, the managerial-ists claimed, been superseded, ushering in a new type of society. This approach was clearly exemplified by Anthony Crosland when he wrote in *The Conservative Enemy*, 1962, that:

> the new managers do not have the same relationship to private property as the old owners (though also for other reasons),
> there are significant differences in the nature of the profit goal and the degree of responsibility with which economic power is exercised. These differences constitute one feature of present-day, as opposed to capitalist, society.[29]

Similarly, Ralph Dahrendorf in *Class and Class Conflict in an Industrial Society* (English edn, 1959), argued that managers had replaced the old owner-managers and that these new managers, being different by social background, training and experience, acted differently from the old capitalists. It followed, he claimed, that it was necessary to talk of a new social order, a post-capitalist society.[30]

Although the managerialists did not openly defend capitalism as a system, there were many critics who saw their work as an apologia for it: despite the attempts of the managerialists to obscure the fact, the critics insisted that capitalism continued unabated. While these critics set about attacking such views they did so, however, very much within the framework established by the managerialists, because they too accepted the logic that, had the separation indeed taken place, then it would truly have signified the transformation of capitalism.[31] A great deal of effort was therefore expended in an attempt to demonstrate that ownership was still sufficiently concentrated and reinforced by inter-locking directorships to ensure control. Furthermore, it was maintained that whatever power managers did wield was used directly in the interests of owners. By accepting this framework, both sides of the debate predicated the continuation of capitalism on the existence of a clearly identifiable shareholding elite.

It is not, however, necessary to be trapped within this framework to accept that capitalism still flourishes. Such a framework places great importance on voluntarism and assumes that whoever is formally in control has great freedom to make decisions and is thus crucially important for the nature of decisions taken. In contrast to this, Marx viewed the constraints placed upon enterprises by capitalism as objective ones. The law of competition has no regard for whether the enterprise is controlled by owner or manager. In *Capital* he argued that:

> What appears in the miser as the mania of an individual is in the capitalist the effect of a social mechanism in which he is merely a cog. Moreover, the development of capitalist production makes it necessary constantly to increase the amount of capital laid out in a given industrial undertaking, and competition subordinates every individual capitalist to the immanent laws of capitalist production, as *external and coercive laws*.[32] (my emphasis)

It was in this sense, emphasising the impersonal nature of capitalism, that Marx went on to talk of the capitalist as 'a mere function of capital' and to recognise that the capitalist was 'just as enslaved by the relationships of capitalism as his opposite number, albeit in a quite different manner'.[33] Marx was well aware that the functions of the capitalist were being fragmented. Indeed, he drew attention to the fact that, at a certain stage, the capitalist hands over the work of direct and constant supervision of individuals and groups to 'a special kind of wage-labourer'.[34] This, however, in no way caused him to doubt the viability of capitalism as such.

More recently, Stuart Holland has emphasised that 'the rise of "managerial" capitalism has not diluted the power of capitalism as a mode of production',[35] and has even suggested that managers are more likely to follow the 'logic of capital' than owner-controllers, knowing that failure to do so would result in their removal from office.[36] An insistence on the pre-eminence of external constraints as opposed to the motivations of individual controllers of enterprises is not meant to suggest that the growth of managerial labour is not without significance. Not only does this growth signify changes in the degree of concentration of capital and its socialisation, but it also has implications for the class structure of capitalism. This latter point was seen by the managerialists, although in a quite mistaken fashion.

James Burnham, the most extreme of the managerialists, in his

The Managerial Revolution, first published in 1941, interpreted these changes as having given rise to a new ruling class.[37] The majority of the managerialists, however, were not prepared to follow Burnham to the same conclusion. They commonly differentiated managers from capitalists as a separate and dominant interest group, but not as a ruling class. No emphasis was placed upon the subordinate position of managers as employees, and, because they were considered a dominant interest group, it was not felt necessary to consider their need to join trade unions. One study, noting the lack of progress of trade unions amongst managerial employees expressed precisely this point, 'if managers are increasingly the controllers rather than the controlled, such membership may appear superfluous'.[38] The critics of managerialism, intent on identifying the actions of managers with the interests of the owners, similarly placed no importance on the employment relations of managers. The critics saw managers only as standing in the place of employers. Because of the lack of precision as to exactly who was a manager, the fact that the line of command within enterprises had grown extremely long was obscured by both sides in the debate.[39]

Managerial work and class divisions

When managers first emerged, their class position was close to that of the capitalist. As Sidney Pollard commented of the manager in his *The Genesis of Modern Management*:

> The social differentiation downwards became much more pronounced than that upwards, towards the capitalist owner, and, in fact the line between the manager, the managing partner, and the managed-partner was increasingly difficult to draw, as mobility between these categories remained high and helped to determine the status of the manager himself.[40]

In the earlier decades of this century managers were generally responsible for running a single enterprise on behalf of an owner or group of owners. The vast majority of firms were simple organisations with few managers. There was specialisation but the division between jobs was often fluid with jobs tailor-made to the particular individuals available. Relations within management were usually informal: the foreman could go direct to the managing director with a problem. In consequence, managers not only had a degree of autonomy unknown to present-day managers, but the job of management was also 'an easier, more intuitive job than it is today. . . . Rules were few. Decisions were made by hunch based on experience'.[41]

The growing size of companies since the Second World War has transformed management structures and the more informal organisation, granting managers more power and autonomy, is increasingly rare. Changes in the structure of ownership have undermined the traditional roles and class position of managers by subordinating them to a managerial hierarchy. According to one estimate, by 1975 one in five industrial workers was employed by a company structured in the form of a hierarchy with at least six levels.[42] The implication of this development for the majority of managers is that instead of standing in the place of the owner at the factory, as the embodiment of capital on the ground, they have had their class position reduced to that of the new middle class. In Bettelheim's terminology, they have lost the real ownership of the means of production and now stand only in a relationship of partial or minimal possession, i.e. they have a limited amount of authority to run the factory within fixed parameters. All strategic decision-making powers now reside at higher levels of the corporate structure. Other developments, which introduce or extend tasks performed by managers which are part of the collective labour process, change the nature of certain managers' jobs and lead to a section of managers being proletarianised.

One side of the relationship of managers to capital is revealed when companies expand by acquisition or merger. Frequently the process involves the shedding of some managerial labour, albeit often on better terms than manual workers receive. Some of the more spectacular mergers, such as that between GEC and AEI in 1968, have attracted attention to the problem,[43] but on the whole the problem has escaped serious consideration. In general, managers have greater job security than manual workers and this reflects their special relationship with capital. One study estimated that in 1977, 4 per cent of all professionals and executives became unemployed in the course of a full year and that if this rate continued the average professional or executive could expect to experience between one and two periods of unemployment in a 40-year career.[44] By contrast, the same data showed that 24 per cent of manual workers became unemployed in 1977 and that if this rate was projected over a 45-year working life, the average worker would experience not one or two periods of unemployment, but more than ten.

The relative protection of managers from the uncertainties of wage-labour is not, however, the whole story. Managers are seldom guaranteed to be unaffected by mergers or acquisitions. As companies are integrated, parallel posts are frequently subordinated or eliminated and managers find themselves more

97

distant from centres of decision-making with their areas of authority further reduced. Just as 'one capitalist always strikes down many others',[45] so, in merger situations, does one manager subordinate many others. This was shown in a study of management during mergers which revealed that displaced managers show great reluctance to accept that they are 'no longer the final arbiters'.[46] Demotions weaken any claim to economic ownership that they may have had, although they may still perform the function of capital.

An examination of projected future mergers and acquisitions of manufacturing industry indicates that the full effects of these developments on managerial authority at factory level have still to be felt. In 1950 the top 100 manufacturing firms in Britain controlled one-fifth of all manufacturing output but this had risen to one-half by 1970, with the National Institute for Economic and Social Research estimating that it would reach two-thirds of all manufacturing output by 1985. Elsewhere, it has been suggested that in the foreseeable future just twenty-one companies could control as much as three-quarters of manufacturing output if counter-measures are not taken.[47]

With the development of more complex managerial structures, new techniques have been introduced to integrate, monitor and control middle and lower management. These are now a feature of company life, with or without mergers. The multi-divisional management structure of modern corporations, for example, that appears by its decentralisation to offer more power and autonomy to divisional managers, developed hand in hand with the spread of management techniques for the effective monitoring of performance. A.P. Sloan, former head of General Motors and a pioneer of such changes, for instance, declared that decentralisation places 'each operation on its own foundation . . . assuming its own responsibility and contributing its share to the final result . . . [each section] develops statistics correctly reflecting the relationship between the net return and the invested capital of each operating division − the true measure of efficiency'.[48] Decentralisation has not meant less accountability, but more. Furthermore, decision-making now tends to be decentralised only where standard procedures have been evolved to regulate and record behaviour,[49] thus robbing the manager of a 'creative' aspect of management.

The changing internal relations of management are reflected in part by the change in the functions of accountants and their greater prominence within British boardrooms.[50] Modern accountancy has its origin in the needs of corporations for both internal financial controls and the assessment of external market possibilities. The role of the accountant developed from that of the counting-house clerk, who kept the books, into an advisor to the directors. The internal control function became more sophisticated and effective by the addition of budgetry control and standard costing to the older techniques of double-entry bookkeeping. In Britain additional developments have placed accountants in a pivotal position in the managerial hierarchy. In particular, certain accountants have managed to appropriate from other specialists 'those responsibilities whose successful exercise required *inter alia* a knowledge of accounting'.[51] The accountant has gradually come to assume responsibility for the way in which a company utilises computer systems as well as newer areas of managerial expertise such as corporate and taxation planning and operational research.[52]

It can be argued that these developments have brought the minority of accountants, who frame and supervise the systems of financial control, much closer to effective power within companies. Terry Johnson, examining the relationship between accountancy and capital, concluded that:

> Such accountants fulfil a special function in relation to large-scale organisations which, while not necessarily involving them directly in a system of 'line' authority, does include the creation of those systems of surveillance and control which are fundamental to the process of surplus value production. . . . Thus, the conventional distinction between 'line' and 'staff' becomes meaningless, for specialist knowledge functions as an instrument of 'line' authority; as a mechanism of control.[53]

If a minority of accountants are increasingly identified with the global function of capital, the systems which they devise have the opposite effect on other managerial employees. While some managerial tasks have become more routine and devoid of decision-making, others have become subject to more effective monitoring. The flexibility of modern control systems can place great pressure on persons identified as responsible for particular areas, thus avoiding the inertia and lack of initiative shown by some bureaucratic organisations. Managers have to log key indices that monitor their own effectiveness. This feature of managerial behaviour was noted by Nichols and Beynon, who, after observing a large multi-national chemical company, stated that:

> the performance records which today's manager keeps on his subordinates are a further source of control. By means of these bureaucratic devices the manager himself can ultimately be further exposed to the chill wind of the market. Each manager

99

has a job description and formally specified objectives. Such predefined expectations of performance make failure all the more glaring and cost consciousness all the more important. Moreover, just as each manager holds regular reviews of progress with his foreman, and the foreman with his works, so he too is subject to regular reviews of progress, about his performance with his boss.[54]

Both budget control and management by objectives are now standard control mechanisms exercised by higher managements over their representatives on the ground. Neither are necessarily arbitrarily imposed upon managers: indeed, they are likely to be more effective as means of control when mutually agreed. Peter Drucker illustrates this latter point in his account of management by objectives:

> Management by objectives and self control makes the interests of the enterprise the aim of every manager. It substitutes for control from the outside more exacting and more effective control from the inside. It motivates managers to action not because someone tells them to do something or talks them into doing it, but because the objective task demands it. They act not because somebody wants them to, but because they decide themselves that they have to − they act, in other words, as free men and women.[55]

Drucker's vision of the freedom of today's managers is illusory. The control system portrayed is simply so effective that the need for disciplinary action is not envisaged. This control is achieved not by abolishing authority relations as Drucker implies, but by representing them as internalised in managers and reified in tasks. The real relationships would be clarified in the event of managers' inabilities or failures. One practising top manager made it brutally clear:

> Well, you have to take a hard line sometimes. And you know we can measure performance without much difficulty. It's not too hard with modern methods for us to have a fairly good hold of what is going on. If our bids for contracts are widely out, or if performance is not up to what it ought to be we have a change in management. As I said you have to take a hard line sometimes. Management is a profession and if someone is no good at it or, for some reason or another he isn't suited to it, he should get out.[56]

That there are fundamental divisions opening up within management by the processes of corporate restructuring has been the contention of writers on management for some time. As early as 1958, Leavitt and Whisler made the following sweeping claims about the effects of the introduction of computer information technology. They claimed that it would:

1. Move the boundary between planning and performance upward, so that many middle management jobs would lose much of their discretionary elements as operating decisions were laid down governing day to day decisions.
2. Lead to recentralisation in large companies as top managers take on even more of the planning and innovating functions.
3. Result in the reorganisation of middle management with some jobs moving downward in pay and prestige because they will require less discretion and skill, and others moving up into top management, because, like research and development, they become of increased importance.
4. Make for a sharper line between top and middle management and one which is difficult to pass.[57]

Some of these claims were substantiated by Rosemary Stewart in 1963 when she noted the trend towards the centralisation of decision-making: 'We can already see the decline in autonomy in some management jobs. The factory manager in some companies, for instance, is much less important than he used to be, as what the factory will produce, in what quantities and when, will be decided by head office.'[58] She argued that the tendency to reduce the responsibilities of some middle-management jobs would 'be accentuated as more of the discretionary elements in a manager's job were made unnecessary by the better flow of information.' The recent advances in information technology, due to micro-processor technology, promise to give these tendencies an added impetus, but not, it should be stressed, through any technological imperative. It is simply that organisations tend to adopt systems that reinforce their own characteristics. Computer technology is therefore used to 'concentrate organisational power and decision making into fewer and fewer hands, by presenting information more concisely and extending the range of operations which each manager can control'.[59] The scope for increased control by top management and even the elimination of middle management posts has greatly increased, causing one psychologist employed by General Motors to remark that 'the computer may be to middle management what the assembly line is to the hourly paid worker'.[60] The new information technology, therefore, can be added to the arsenal of control mechanisms already aimed at middle management.

Despite all the recent developments affecting managers,

empirical work on these questions has been negligible. Peter Fairbrother has detailed a situation in which the restructuring of management had the effect of increasing divisions amongst the managers to the extent that while power increased at one pole, certain managerial posts were subject to a degree of proletarianisation at the other. The status of the personnel department of the factory studied was so enhanced that it became the central department of management, responsible for recruitment, deployment of labour, training and labour relations. Fairbrother, unlike most other writers in the field, does not treat these changes simply as rational administrative ones, but recognises that they have repercussions throughout the management structure. He argued that not only did the changes lessen the power of the majority of managerial employees within the managerial hierarchy, it also accelerated a trend towards an increase in the performance of some managers of tasks that were necessary to the labour process and hence that the changes were part of a proletarianisation process. He concluded that:

> The routinisation of tasks and the specialisation of tasks was evident. Moreover, the areas of discretionary activity had become more restricted and increasingly subject to order and control. However, while some staff workers had become more or less exclusively concerned with the administration of people, performing a variety of tasks from supervision to the coordination of activities, the number of these workers as a proportion of the staff workforce had been declining relative to the technically specialised staff workers. The industrial staffworkers — the engineers, the designers, the metallurgists, the technicians — and administrative staffworkers — the schedulers, the controllers and administrative staff — had become relatively more numerous.[61]

Not surprisingly, these changes in the structure of managerial control have brought about changed promotion and recruitment policies within companies and such policies are establishing a major break within the management hierarchy. It was common in the recent past for scientific and technical personnel to transfer from their disciplines to more general management work. They were promoted from staff to line: Kornhauser noted in his study of scientists made in 1962 that 'having seen the larger rewards go to managers, and having themselves experienced some upward mobility on the basis of assuming administrative responsibilities, they are likely to make administration their personal goal.'[62] This was, no doubt, a realistic strategy for personal advancement, but such advancement is becoming increasingly outmoded. The path to senior management *via* a technical career that progressively adopts more and more managerial responsibility is being increasingly eclipsed by the direct recruitment of graduates as management trainees. As early as 1970 a common fear amongst middle managers was that their career prospects were being threatened by such recruitment, fearing that the graduates whom they were then supervising would, within two or three years, be their status equals and perhaps in another two or three years be their supervisors.[63]

The very skills of middle managers that had been their strength in the past were the very features inhibiting their progression. Before the introduction of graduates, a person's knowledge of the detail of the job was his greatest asset. That knowledge was developed and protected. But the older managers found themselves asked to train the graduates and then saw the latter promoted over their heads. For the graduate management trainees, emphasis was placed on broad familiarity with the work while others were expected to know it in detail. To many older managers, 'the route to the top was no longer clear'.[64]

This lessening of the possibilities of internal promotion has been paralleled by the increasingly restricted mobility between firms. Managers are aware that at a certain stage in their career they become dependent upon their firm for employment. Nichols and Beynon recorded the typical anxiety of one manager:

> I'm 48 years old. I joined ChemCo at the age of 24. I've got 24 years service too. Say I go for an interview. 'Ah! Mr Smith, you're a chemist', they say. 'A chemist are you?' And there I am, I took my degree in 1947 . . . there are young people, just taken their degrees, 25 to 30 years old, can ask for a much lower salary than I'm used to. 'Ah' they say, 'well you're a Manager are you, Mr Smith? and what do you manage?' And I say, 'Well, I've managed this plant now for seven years.' 'Ah' they say, 'well, where have you managed your plant?' 'At ChemCo I say.' Now I know the ChemCo system but what about modern innovations they think.[65]

This conclusion was confirmed by W. Robins who, in his study of the treatment of scientists, technologists and engineers in industry, claimed that once over the age of forty, often without realising it, 'the individual is frequently specialised, institutionalised, expensive and pension tied'.[66]

This growing barrier between levels of management, reflected in the recruitment of graduate management trainees, also appears *within* graduate recruitment. The Unit of Manpower Studies, reporting in 1978, identified three general categories of demand

103

for graduates: management trainees who are recruited for their potential as senior manager (sometimes against the long-term needs of the employer) and who usually follow well-designed training and career development schemes; specialists who are appointed to specific jobs within a short period of joining a company, often in response to more short-term needs of particular departments or functions; and general intake graduates who are recruited against shorter-term needs and who are seen as potential junior and middle managers. The Unit found that firms recruited 'high flyers' with good academic qualifications and suitable personalities as management trainees ultimately to fill important senior posts within management. At the same time, firms also recruited graduates to fill vacancies in middle management and technical functions that were 'formerly filled by school leavers'.[67] However, at the same time as these latter posts were being transformed into graduate occupations, the remunerations paid to those who filled them were declining relative to those of other members of the working population.

The growth of extended managerial hierarchies makes obvious nonsense of the contention that managers as such stand in the place of capital. The majority of managers have, to return to Bettelheim's categories, neither legal nor economic ownership of the means of production. Indeed, because of the bureaucratisation of the managerial process, for many the relationship of possession is extremely limited. Within the broader context of this book, they constitute not a bourgeois class but part of a new middle class. This change in the class position of managers is reflected within the shifts of managerial ideology: managers have now become the objects of managerial theory rather than simply implementing it.

The philosophy of management

The main component of the philosophy of management during the 1930s and 1940s was, according to John Child's systematic study, *British Management Thought*, 1969, the human relations perspective. This perspective viewed the enterprise as a closed system, underplayed the economic needs of employees, and concentrated on workers' needs for belonging, satisfaction and self-esteem, which were to be generated by the factory social system. The perspective consequently regarded economic conflict as irrational, having its basis in misunderstandings. Trade unions, as outside bodies exploiting domestic misunderstandings, were not therefore seen as legitimate vehicles of representation. This perspective, however, did not survive the changes of the post-war years intact. The growth and consolidation of trade union influence from its low-point in the 1930s rendered any perspective based upon the factory as a closed social system, and the company as the primary objective of employee identification, naive in the extreme. The manipulative paternalism of the approach therefore gave way to a pluralistic one in which trade unions represented one of a number of interests that make up the company and society.

Nevertheless, in spite of these changes, there was also a growth in what has been called the new human relations approach, characterised by the works of Herzberg, Maslow, McGregor and Argyris.[68] This approach also sees trade unions as obstructions, but it is primarily a response to the belief that the costs of traditional methods of industrial control have become disproportionately high.[69] It is therefore regarded as a sounder strategy to rely not on external and authoritarian modes of discipline, but upon what its proponents consider are the innate needs of people to extend themselves by 'self-actualisation'.[70] Based upon narrow psychological theories, the new human relations approach aims explicitly at tapping the 'wasted' energy of worker resistance and turning it into creative and productive work. This may mean attempting to restructure and extend some jobs, in order to curtail craft control. More frequently, it is simply a response to an unorganised lack of motivation associated with lack of trade union control.[71]

The most significant difference between the new human relations approach and earlier versions is that it has as its object not only the restructuring of shopfloor jobs but also managerial ones. At one level, the concern with managerial jobs has centred upon the dissatisfaction which has resulted from the processes of fragmentation and routinisation of those jobs. But the concern of the new human relations theorists is not entirely benign because there is a clear awareness of the inefficiency and lack of initiative that such dissatisfaction brings. Managerial practices have also, therefore, become the object of critical scrutiny:

> it is in our management structure where much of the
> inefficiency lies . . . it is management's demarcations which
> restrict initiative and management attitudes which form a
> barrier to change. If we want flexibility and a sense of
> responsibility from our workforce, we must create a climate in
> which such things flourish.[72]

The quest for productivity, which lies behind attacks on shopfloor control and defences is now being directed towards management itself. Middle managers find themselves attacked from two sides:

responsibility for relatively minor matters is taken from them and given to the work-force, while the internal demarcations of management are removed making the already flattened hierarchy less stable.

Neither the human relations ideology of the 1930s and 1940s nor the new human relations movement of the 1960s and 70s had strong organic links with management practice. Nevertheless, the move amongst managerial ideologists from one to the other reflects changes in the real world and confirms a movement in managerial preoccupations from the assumption of managerial unity and professionalism to a concern over the utilisation and control of managerial labour.

The school of scientific management, which developed from the work of Frederick W. Taylor, and its status within managerial ideology contrasts with that of the human relations approach. The former did not formally constitute part of managerial ideology in the 1930s and 1940s and today its adherents are few. Nevertheless, the practical importance of scientific management was, and still is, immense. As Harry Braverman has argued:

> the successors to Taylor are to be found in engineering and
> work design, and in top management; the successors to
> Münsterberg and Mayo are to be found in personnel
> departments and schools of industrial psychology and sociology
> . . . if Taylorism does not exist as a separate school today, that
> is because, apart from the bad odour of the name, it is no
> longer the property of a faction, since its fundamental
> teachings have become the bedrock of all work design.[73]

Its importance is not restricted to the struggle between capital and labour, because it also has serious implications for relations within the function of capital. As the relation of sections of managers to real control of the enterprise has weakened, the principles of scientific management have increasingly been turned upon them, as an examination of the work of Taylor and his adherents shows.

Frederick W. Taylor (1856–1917), an American, was the leading propagandist of scientific management. Taylor put forward three principles of management: the gathering in of all knowledge from the work-force, its concentration exclusively within management, and the use of this monopoly of knowledge to control the way in which workers carry out their tasks.[74] This doctrine has received much attention from those quite rightly concerned with the use of aspects of this philosophy to attack shopfloor control of the labour process.[75] What has received much less attention is the consequences of Taylor's perspectives for managerial employees, although their implementation required a revolution in managerial practices.

Taylor himself claimed that his methods met even greater resistance from managements than from workers. These managerial objections were of two kinds. Managers objected to the increase in managerial responsibilities, but more importantly, objections were also raised to the principle of functional organisation. As Littler commented:

> This principle is usually lost sight of because it was rarely put directly into practice. Even the early acolytes had reservations about functional foremanship. . . . Functional organisation is important as a prescription because it represents the idea of a *division* of management: a movement away from a single hierarchy.[76]

Once managements assumed the wider responsibilities advocated by Taylor, then the separation of conception and execution, so central to Taylor's method, acted as a dynamic *within* the management hierarchy, causing concentration of decision-making responsibilities at one pole and loss of responsibility at the other.

The potential influence of Taylor's methods on managerial jobs can clearly be seen in the work of the influential management theorist, Peter F. Drucker. Reflecting on the collectivisation and fragmentation of the managerial function and the consequent difficulty in determining who, in fact, was a manager, Drucker maintained in 1979 that it was possible to answer the question by 'applying to the job of manager the systematic analysis of Scientific Management'.[77] Drucker's method was 'to isolate that which a person does because he or she is a manager' and to 'divide the work into its constituent operations', which he identified as follows:

> A manager in the first place sets objectives. . . . He decides what has to be done to reach those objectives. . . .
>
> Second, a manager organises. He or she analyses the activities, decisions and relations needed. . . .
>
> Next a manager motivates and communicates. . . . He does it through his 'people decisions' on pay, placement and promotion. . . .
>
> The fourth basic element in the work of the manager is measurement. . . . He or she sees to it that each person has measurements available which are focused on the performance of the whole organisation and which, at the same time, focus on the work of the individual. The manager analyses, appraises and interprets performance.[78]

While he makes no mention of the overall subjection of these parts to the production of profit, the expansion of capital is clearly the overall aim, and the function of management is the function of capital. By so framing the function of management, Drucker was able to claim that most managers were inefficient because they persisted in carrying out non-managerial functions: indeed, he stated that most managers spent most of their time doing just that. Drucker gave as examples of the non-managerial roles carried out by managers the sales manager making a statistical analysis or dealing with an important customer and the foreman repairing a tool or filling out a production report. All these operations were necessary, but they were, according to Drucker, set apart from work that was common to all management.

It follows from Drucker's analysis that managerial work should be restructured. Managers, or at least top managers, should divest themselves of work that does not involve decision-making: they should concentrate on conception and leave execution to others. This, he maintained, would greatly increase managerial productivity. What he did not mention is that such a course would have detrimental consequences for those erstwhile managerial workers from whom conceptual roles and discretion have been taken. In so far as power and responsibility become concentrated at the top of the hierarchy, they disappear from the bottom, pushing sections of managerial workers further down the ranks of the new middle class.

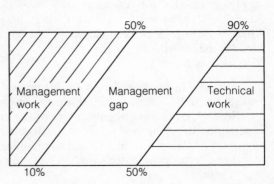

Figure *3.1* Management gap. After Allen, *Professional Management*, 1973

The same implications can be derived from the approach of the American writer, L.A. Allen. In establishing his 'principle of organisation levels', Allen put forward the following proposition:

'The lower his organisation level, the more technical work a manager tends to perform. At successively higher organisational levels a manager is primarily concerned with managing other managers.'[79] The organisation of managerial work, as conceived by Allen, means that at the top levels of management 'the chief executive ideally should devote at least 90 per cent of his time to management duties, and no more than 10 per cent to technical work', whereas 'foremen at the first level of supervision should devote no more than 50 per cent of their time to technical work, the other half to managing'.[80] Allen maintained, however, that there was a discrepancy between how much time particular levels of management should spend on managing and the actual amount spent. He estimated that most managers spend only half of their time managing, and foremen as little as 10 per cent. The gap between the desired percentage and the actual one Allen termed the 'management gap' and represented it as in Figure 3.1.[81] This 'management gap' can only be eliminated, according to Allen, 'when management at each level, starting at the top, concentrate on the management work they should be performing and build a strong organisation to which they delegate full responsibility and authority for technical work'.[82] Such an elimination would entail the restructuring of managerial work, however, and it remains the case that the assuming of more responsibility for management decisions by top management would result in a concomitant loss of responsibility further down the line, with the results that have already been indicated.

The interests of managers

The second major component part of managerial thought during the 1930s and 1940s identified by Child was the idea that managers were professionals. This idea was based upon the belief that managers performed a service on behalf of their client group, looking after the material and non-material rewards of their employees. This claim was reinforced by adherence to certain managerial principles, prominent amongst which were those of the human relations movement, which were regarded as scientific and verifiable. The third component Child delineated was closely associated with the idea of management as a profession; it was that industry should be run by those who, by ability and training, were best fitted to do so.[83]

There were serious limitations to the possible success of managerial claims to professionalism. Child noted that:

Management might, admittedly, aspire to satisfy some

professional criteria without a drastic restructuring of its traditional role – for instance, a controlling central organisation, or regulated recruitment based upon some fairly standard entrance requirements. Yet other criteria were clearly beyond its reach, given the prevailing conditions of private competitive industry and a system of industrial finance which normally ensured that the interests of capital were not disregarded with impunity over any length of time.[84]

In short, there was never any chance of managers achieving the independence associated with the 'classical' professions and they were always destined to remain, in Johnson's terminology, 'client controlled'.[85]

While managers were not to become true professionals, however, the reality of this situation was increasingly reflected in managerial ideology. Child detailed a movement away from a legitimatory emphasis, away from the 'concept of service, in which different interests would be impartially respected, to an assumption that managers should take the lead in defining these interests in relation to the goal of organisational effectiveness.' The attempt to secure the principle of managerial control was replaced by the 'justification of techniques designed to intensify the operation of managerial control'.[86] The decline in the legitimatory emphasis, Child claimed, was in large part explained by the absence of criticism of the management function as such. This, in turn, was partly because of the labour unrest of the post-First World War period, with its attendant demands for workers' control of industry, collapsed with the advent of mass unemployment. In addition, management's role was strengthened by the growth of vast and complex organisations: the performance of particular managers could be challenged, but the need for management appeared self-evident. Managers as a consequence became increasingly identified with the technical problems of management.

The development of management thought in this direction had consequences not foreseen by Child. As management became increasingly identified with the technical problems of management, the possibility of managers seeing themselves as technical workers, albeit with different interests from the shopfloor, emerged. Likewise, if it was not possible for management to become independent of capital, the reality of that fact became much more stark for sections of managers than had previously been the case. In contrast to earlier claims that managers were the detached and objective arbiters of the public interest or were looking after 'their' workers' interests, managers increasingly considered that the interests of everyone but themselves were being protected. After the Second World War it was generally felt by managers that the time had come to organise and assert their specific interests, to project themselves as a 'third force'. As a consequence, a range of such protective organisations now exist, the ideologies of which reflect the increasing differentiation of managers, from each other and especially from capital.

Conflict within management

The underlying changes in the class relations of sections of managers, and managers' reactions to them, have received little attention. Present levels of managerial unionism, although growing, would suggest that the joining of trade unions has been a far from widespread response of managers to the changed situation. But if collective resistance to the changes has not been prominent, neither should it be assumed that managers have necessarily greeted the changes with acquiescence and resignation. Conflict within the managerial function may not be overt and collective, but it exists nevertheless. The fact that it frequently takes the form of clashes between individuals is no less a consequence of capitalist organisation than the collective conflict between management and manual workers organised in trade unions. The conflict within the function of capital between line and staff functions, for instance, is structurally based. Melville Dalton, in *Men Who Manage*, 1959, was one of the earliest sociologists to draw attention to this. His study showed that staff posts, such as those involving inspection, planning, engineering and chemistry, carried less income, authority and prestige than line authority.[87] Understandably, therefore, staff were not satisfied to stay for long periods in advisory positions and looked for promotion into line authority. In order to achieve this move they needed allies among the senior line managers, and, in order to gain these, took two courses of action. Firstly, as method refiners and technique formulators, the staff were specialists in change and reorganisation, and as such they were seen as attacking lower line management on behalf of higher line authority. Seeing themselves as agents of senior management also led them to adopt a second, unofficial, role, as informers to top management about irregularities at the point of production. Dalton was able to document the power struggle between staff and lower line management that was the almost inevitable outcome of such organisation and the adoption of these two roles by staff. There are two limitations, however, to the usefulness of Dalton's work as a guide to the nature and extent of conflict

111

within management. There is no explicit discussion of class within the work and it was undertaken during the relatively favourable economic circumstances of the 1950s. The conflict discussed by Dalton was essentially about how to climb the managerial hierarchy and not about the problems of managers merely maintaining their positions.

The prospects of staff taking the traditional path to management *via* a technical specialism have diminished considerably, a development discussed in the work of Colin Fletcher. Fletcher believed he was witnessing the demise of traditional management roles specifically because of the impact of international monopoly capital on management structures, a phenomenon which he discussed in 'The End of Management', published in 1973.[88] This, he believed, was causing a 'crisis condition in the labour of superintendence',[89] as different groups of managers gained or lost under the impact. Fletcher distinguished a number of levels within management that corresponded to age groups. The 'old guard' were middle managers between fifty and sixty years of age, who had held their jobs for some time while their departments had doubled and trebled in size. Fletcher claimed that, having worked their way up a ladder, in which every rung was significant, this group formed 'a natural clique with memories of happier, less warlike days'.[90] There followed the 'ideas men' who had been 'brought into the company at considerable expense'. Members of this group were aged between forty and fifty years and had worked for at least three other firms. These managers were ranked above the 'old guard' and Fletcher described their work as follows: 'Their tasks are to stand outside the structure, pull together a future for the firm's products, and to engage in market research for new methods of production. They have no department and no immediate effect. For they counsel the Board.'[91] Next came a group that Fletcher termed the 'lumpen management'. Aged between thirty-five and fifty years, they were the ones on whom day-to-day operations depended. They were the 'backbone of the hierarchy' and did the bulk of the 'real work'.[92] Finally, Fletcher distinguished one further group, the 'rare hatchet men', aged between twenty-eight and thirty-five years:

> They joined the company as its earliest graduates and proved they would do anything they were told. They are the 'highest flyers' of all being heads of department, executives and close confidantes of the Board. They enjoy being totally dependent on the firm and welcome any change they are told to make. Their security comes in this dependence and movement. They

act as ideas men *within* their department; changing its structure; methods; personnel and title until it is dragged into the 1970s − less the greater proportion of its 'dead wood'.[93]

Fletcher claimed that this was the old world of management in transition. Only some types of managers had a future, others were tomorrow's 'dead wood', to be cut out and discarded. The 'old guard' and the 'lumpen managers' were the most likely victims and were offered either contracted responsibilities or early retirement. Those who had the greatest chance of survival, according to Fletcher, were the 'hatchet' and 'ideas' men, although both jobs were precarious, being subject to highly visible failure, as well as to attacks and sabotage from other staff who felt their own positions threatened. Fletcher detected a new type of manager, one he labelled the 'nouveau manager' and predicted that this type of manager would become increasingly predominant. He did not envisage these managers being fashioned in the mould of managers of the previous generation, with whom they shared few characteristics. Fletcher observed, however, that there was no immediate place in the structure of management for the 'nouveau manager' who acted as a personal assistant to other managers and that although such managers were trainees, no one was sure for what exactly they were being trained. He explained that the new type of manager had arisen because:

The Board wants fewer managers and more mobile, contract, technological operatives. The nouveau manager is to think like a director and act like a clerk. Rather than a management structure, fewer men are required to circulate in an amorphous quasi-management atmosphere. A few will be needed for the direct control of the workers as foremen. A few will be needed as specialist combatants with workers over changing conditions. But for the rest what is required is clever, near-creative clerks to collect data and collate it for the Board.[94]

Fletcher's observations were perceptive but exaggerated. In following the logic of his own rhetoric − the end of management − he looked at only one side of the process. The elimination and devaluation of certain managerial jobs involved the reconstitution of the authority invested in those jobs in the hands of others. Within Fletcher's typology the managers gaining authority would be the 'ideas' and 'hatchet' men or the Board directly. Likewise, the 'nouveau' managers, in their servicing role to the Board, would have scope to distinguish themselves. Even if it were possible for the Board to run the enterprise with 'nouveau'

113

managers acting as clerks, it would still not substantiate Fletcher's conclusion that 'though management may be validly "finished" managers need not be'.[95] Rather, he should have concluded that although particular layers of managers might be finished, management was not.

The decline of the foreman's authority

The rationalisation of management reinforces the importance of an examination of the lowest level of management, the foreman. Widespread attention has been paid to the position of the foreman, in both managerial and sociological studies. The information available, and foremen's much clearer propensity to organise collectively, highlight more clearly tendencies which are present throughout the management structure, and allow an evaluation of claims that the loss of authority by foremen illustrates the process of proletarianisation.[96]

That the foreman has lost power and authority within industry is beyond doubt. In the early decades of this century the foreman had the power to deal with planning and allocation of work, work methods, quality, safety and wages as well as to hire and fire.[97] No such power exists today. The growth in the size of companies and increasing professionalisation and specialisation in the structure of management has affected the foreman just as it has the majority of managers. Functional foremanship, the fragmentation of the foreman's duties into separate supervisory roles, was a foundation stone of Taylor's scientific management. The decline of the foreman's authority under scientific management organisation was highlighted when this in turn gave way to the human relations approach to leadership, popular in the 1930s.[98] This stressed the need for a new kind of supervision based not upon authoritarianism but upon the motivation of the work-group. Even if the foreman had been willing radically to change his mode of operation and become a leader, however – and there is no evidence that this was the case – the impact of this new approach would never have been anything but short-lived. The post-Second World War growth in trade union strength removed any real possibility of effective implementation. After 1945 the foreman was increasingly and effectively challenged in his now shrunken area of authority.

These developments – the loss of formal authority, the loss of technical roles, and the challenge of increased trade union strength – have continued, so much so that a recent extensive survey by the British Institute of Management came to the following conclusions about the position of the foreman:

(i)   'The front-line manager's authority has in recent years been eroded, in particular through increased union influence on the shopfloor and the growth of specialist departments. He may be uncertain as to his relationship with specialist departments and may feel they are not readily available to offer help and advice when he needs them. On disciplinary matters he frequently feels frustrated by union representatives and his ability to use labour flexibly is restricted by union practices. Sometimes he feels that higher management does not give him sufficient backing. The demands made on him, moreover, to achieve targets, do not take account of factors over which he has little control.'

(ii)   On the foreman's man-management role, it was noted that companies tended to place greater emphasis on his role in achieving management targets while neglecting to support him in his role as leader and motivator of the workforce to enable him to achieve these targets.

(iii)   his involvement in decision-making may be minimal.

(iv)   when it comes to communications, 'he is sometimes by-passed . . . and feels with some justification that union representatives may be better informed than he is on issues and policy decisions directly affecting the shopfloor and company plans . . . front-line managers appear to be particularly offended by the greater facilities union representatives have to consult with management, both informally and on formal consultative bodies.'[99]

A number of sociologists have attempted to conceptualise the position of the foreman taking into account these developments. A common approach has been to perceive the foreman as no longer part of management but as the 'man in the middle', that is, in a position between labour and capital. The elements of this approach are summarised by Stephen Hill:

> the foreman is caught in a position of role conflict, in which often incompatible pressures are received from both management and workers, who together form his role set; this results from an occupancy between two parties, seen as the foreman being an agent of management, but also in some sense a member of the shopfloor workforce; at the same time, according to this approach, the authority and status of the foreman's position has been eroded by structural changes in industry, so that the foreman has become powerless to control or influence his situation.[100]

Attractive as this approach is, a number of criticisms have been levelled at the formulation. Donald Wray, who examined the foreman's role in relationship to two crucial factors, 'the locus of

115

decision-making or the managerial function' and 'the focal points of union-management and employer-employee relations', concluded that the foreman was not so much in the middle of management-worker relationships, but peripheral to them.[101] Foremen were not included in the decision-making process, nor were they essential in the communication of decisions because a system of communications parallel to line authority tended to be used. He therefore characterised foremen as 'marginal men of industry'. This marginality, he argued, produced considerable strain which they might try to resolve in certain circumstances by 'defiantly adopting an alternative role . . . that of worker who may organise a union for bargaining with management'.[102]

The 'man in the middle' thesis has also been criticised by Colin Fletcher.[103] He tested the thesis in relation to three variables: the number of levels of supervision (stratification); the different organisation of tasks needed to manufacture different products (differentiation); and the social beliefs and backgrounds of foremen (identification). Fletcher found that the stratification variable affected the level of dissatisfaction felt. Senior foremen experienced a great deal more role-conflict than front-line foremen. He explained their greater level of dissatisfaction by their closer proximity to management and hence their clearer view of the nature of the decisions taken by management, decisions which they felt themselves capable of making. Differentiation was also found by Fletcher to influence the desire for more control. He noted that foremen in the machine shops wanted greater control, whereas those in the assembly area wanted clearer procedures that they could follow. This divergence was explained by Fletcher as responses to two dissimilar situations: the machine shop foremen were in charge of repetitious work and felt confident to demand more say and control over both supply and disciplinary problems, whereas the assembly shop foreman worked in a situation with a great deal of uncertainty, and wanted procedures to protect themselves from the consequences of that uncertainty.

The major emphasis of Fletcher's work, however, was on the empirical types of foremen that he found. He classified the foremen into three types – conservatives, radicals and revolutionaries. The conservatives were older, less educated, longer-serving, less careerist and more sociable with other foremen than were the radicals. The revolutionaries were more extreme than the radicals. They were also much younger, more educated, relatively isolated, selective about a small number of friends (many of whom were junior executives) and fundamentally critical of management. The failure of Fletcher to specify the relationships of the three variables to each other, and the emphasis placed upon the identification of the foreman, leads to the conclusion that Fletcher considered the determining factor in foremen's experience of conflict to be the ideas that they held. Neither historical changes in their class position nor employers' policies towards recruitment and promotion were examined. Yet only such examinations could have revealed the viability of the different orientations held by Fletcher's empirical types, for instance, his claim that revolutionaries considered themselves practising managers.[104] There was in Fletcher's work, therefore, a move away from an emphasis on the structural constraints on the role of the foreman present in earlier works. Whatever the weakness of these earlier approaches, they did consider the relations of the foreman to the two major social forces as centrally important in defining their position.

A more sophisticated account of the foreman's position, noting the historical decline of its authority, was advanced by John Child. He too identified different empirical types of foremen – the time-server, the super-craftsman, the frustrated achiever and the cadet.[105] The change in terminology, however, marks a significant change in perspective. The defining features of the types of foremen identified by Child rest not on the individual voluntarism of the foremen, but on management policies. He cites for example, the recruitment of university or college graduates (the cadets) as management trainees as highlighting a particular change in managerial recruitment policy. Child's perspective allows for an awareness of the importance of managerial strategies in defining the positions of foremen. In particular, it allowed him to note that different solutions to the problem of the role conflict of foremen were being discussed within management circles. While not explicitly concerned with the class position of foremen, Child's recognition of different possible managerial strategies has direct implications for the class position of foremen, and it is these strategies and their implications which are now examined.

Management and the foreman

Most managerial pronouncements on the role and position of foremen suggest that their position within management is clear and unequivocal and not the subject of any great controversy. These views are frequently accompanied by exaggerated and unrealistic claims as to the importance of the foreman in the efficient working of the company. As Sir John Hunter put it:

117

The importance of the supervisor's role in increasing our efficiency as an industrial nation cannot be stressed often enough. In a Britain geared to growth and progress the ever increasing pace of change accentuates the need for reliable links from top to bottom in every undertaking.[106]

It is arguable, however, that such statements, while designed to increase the morale of foremen, contribute to their further demoralisation, highlighting as they do the disparity between the projected view and the reality of the foremen's position.

This is not to say that serious attempts to appraise the position of the foreman have not been made by managerial writers. Two solutions in particular have been canvassed to resolve the recognised ineffectiveness and disaffection of foremen, and both, if implemented, would change the class position of the foreman. The first proposal is that the present foreman-level of supervision should be abolished. This abolition, consistent with the new human relations approach to management, would coincide with the establishment of 'autonomous' work-groups that would practise a degree of discretion previously the prerogative of the foreman. The first level of supervision would practise more administrative means of control. The adoption of this solution is more likely to take place in companies running process production factories, where much of the control and co-ordinating function can be integrated into machine design. There are, however, examples of companies modifying production lines to accommodate autonomous work groups, the Volvo and Saab plants being the best known.

Developments on these lines are not without difficulties. Trade unions may display an unwillingness to embrace new methods of organisation, especially if craft unions regard the flexibility involved in autonomous working groups as an attack upon their craft control of particular work. The other major difficulty is the reaction of the incumbents of the traditional foremen's position. The majority, according to a BIM profile, are relatively old and poorly educated[107] and are unlikely, therefore, to be regarded by management as matching up to the requirements of this new higher level of supervision. In consequence, they feel insecure and are likely to turn to union organisation to defend themselves, as indeed happened in the situation recorded by Nichols and Beynon at ChemCo.[108]

The other solution that management might adopt is to retain the foreman but to restructure his role to a more clearly managerial one. In this model of organisation the supervisor has managerial responsibility for the performance of his section and authority over personnel and disposal of resources. Such restructuring means that foremen would shed some of their collective worker function, which would be taken over by shopfloor workers. The BIM report illustrated this divestiture of part of the foreman's role, when stating that:

An examination of the content of the front-line manager's job shows there are tasks that are significantly time-consuming, yet not truly supervisory in themselves. How many hours, for example, may be spent by the front-line manager in activities that could equally well be done by a 'leading hand' with the right experience and ability and no formal supervisory authority? We acknowledge the value of developing 'leading hands' from among the shopfloor talent as a means of 'hiving-off' from the front-line manager those tasks which can only be done by him at the expense of his major function of managing people.[109]

For such a model to be implemented, a restructuring of authority within management would also be necessary and this would almost certainly involve the elimination of layers of middle management. Again, the BIM report noted that: 'In considering the organisational structure of the operating unit we believe it is desirable that there should be a minimum of intervening levels between top management and front-line management consistent with the span of control.'[110] This proposed elevation of the status of the foreman is also double-edged for the foremen themselves because it is accompanied by increasing scrutiny of their performance:

there should be a system by which the front-line manager can measure and monitor the areas for which he is to be held accountable. A first step should be a clarification of tasks, basic standards of performance, the scope of his responsibility and the extent of his authority.[111]

Far from welcoming this restructuring, present-day foremen have every reason to view the developments with some trepidation. There seems little reason to doubt that this redefinition of the role of the foreman would go hand in hand with a change in personnel. The present incumbents would not be considered able to perform this wider role and recruitment to such posts would be opened to outside competition, including graduates. The traditional foreman is therefore threatened by the adoption of either solution, be it the abolition of his present role or its restructuring.

There is evidence in both sociological and managerial writings

119

that the foreman's role within the function of capital has weakened. This is most graphically illustrated by their loss of authority on matters of hiring and firing and methods of work. This partial loss of function has been accompanied in some cases by increasing involvement in tasks concerned with unifying and co-ordinating the production process and which can be considered functions of the collective worker.[112] Seymour Melman, for example, reproduced an account of the work of a foreman in the car industry, in which it was clear that for much of the time the foreman's work was subordinated to particular work-groups.[113] The situation described was influenced by a collective piece-work payment system which induced a high motivation amongst the work-force and minimised the necessity for foremen to intervene over speed and methods of work. This particular system thereby ceded many areas of managerial control and removed the need for high levels of supervision.

The lack of managerial control of the work process has been the central reason for subsequent moves by managements to restructure relations and to abolish both collective and individual piece-work payment systems. In the late 1960s, in particular, there was a drive by employers to win shopfloor acceptance of 'productivity deals', an essential element of which was the replacement of piece-work rates by other payment systems and especially by measured-day-work.[114] These changes were designed to alter the relationship of foremen to the shopfloor: 'the discipline of the piece was to give way to the discipline of supervision'.[115] However, the extent to which this drive to change payment systems was successful and, where it was achieved, its consequences for styles of supervision are open to question. Certainly it is the contention of one recent writer, Richard Edwards, that the historical movement is away from what he termed simple control (direct supervision) to more structural forms (both technical and bureaucratic), both because of the increasing size of production units with their need for social planning, and because direct supervision gave rise to numerous disputes that could be avoided by alternative forms of supervision.[116] Moreover, continued management concern with the effectiveness of foremen as managerial representatives and discussions on the need to restructure foremen's roles to eliminate collective worker aspects testify to the fact that foremen have not been unambiguously subsumed back into management.

Managerial initiatives are, however, only one side of the picture; it is also necessary to examine the responses of foremen in particular situations because they are far from simply passive

spectators of managerial processes. In addition, the transformation of tasks from ones associated with the function of
capital to ones associated with collective work within the labour
process, based upon the distinction between control and
surveillance, on the one hand, and the work of unity and co-
ordination, on the other, is far from unproblematic – as critics of
Carchedi have pointed out. For both reasons empirical
investigations are needed to determine the extent to which
foremen can be considered to have been proletarianised.

On the basis of a case study, I have argued elsewhere that the
assumption made by Carchedi, namely that the decline of the
performance of the function of capital is paralleled by an increase
in the performance of work within the labour process, is not
necessarily correct.[117] The decline of the authority of the foremen
studied left them with only a minimal role in the production
process and at the same time failed to root them in a real labour
process. Their reactions to their effective demotions were also
important. Their continued accountability to management
without corresponding authority to deal with labour relations and
other matters led them to avoid conflicts with the shopfloor
workers. But, similarly, their lack of technical expertise and role
within the labour process made their identification with shopfloor
workers unlikely.

It is true, of course, that the work tasks of the foremen had not
totally atrophied. But such tasks – progress chasing, work
scheduling and job allocation – and their significance have to be
viewed in the context of the overall social relations within the
factory. Whether the tasks are or are not part of a labour process
depends neither upon their technical nature nor on taxonomy. In
different circumstances the same tasks can take on different
meanings. Where a substantial amount of control and confidence
resides in the work-force, foremen and management generally
have to accommodate themselves to it. The control aspect of
unity and co-ordination can thus be negated by the shopfloor.
Where that control is lost and the confidence broken, progress
chasing, work scheduling and job allocation are re-subsumed into
the capitalist function of control.

It is also likely that as the social character of their work
changes with changes in the balance of workplace power,
foremen will so follow the shifts in power, vacillating between
identification with higher management and shopfloor unionism,
depending upon which strategy appears most viable. Such an
approach stresses the role of class struggle in the determination
of class. While not denying the importance of structural analysis,
it confirms the sterility of attempts to classify middle-class

121

workers' relations in advance, in the manner of Poulantzas.

Conclusion

Modern management methods have arisen in the course of the twentieth century as a response to a series of problems that faced the owners and controllers of companies. Not least of these problems were those associated with the rise of monopoly capitalism, particularly the integration of a managerial hierarchy, which in turn promoted the growth of sub-divisions and specialisms within management. The result has been that not only are certain managerial employees at a very great distance from centres of decision-making, but also the fixed costs of management have grown extremely large.

The stagnation and recession experienced by capitalism on a world scale since the mid-1960s has heightened capital's awareness of the expense of management itself and both top management and managerial theorists have turned an increasingly critical eye on the effectiveness of the managerial structure. As a consequence, not only has there been an increase in the monitoring of managerial effectiveness, but also the continued reduction in the power of middle and lower management, and even the elimination of some layers.

This is not to argue that class relations within management can be identified simply or that managers' class positions are easily ascribed. As the work of Dalton and Johnson showed, it is not only the formal position within the hierarchy, or even the distinction between 'line' and 'staff', which is important when it comes to determining actual relations within the production process. Similarly, Pahl and Winkler, while utilising the distinction between allocative control and operational control, have stressed the difficulty of consistently identifying the respective types with occupational titles. Indeed, as they point out, any investigation must allow for the possibility that allocative decisions may be made at levels other than the top of the formal authority hierarchy.[118]

The need for further investigation notwithstanding, there is evidence of an increasing tendency for managers to perceive a clearer division emerging within companies between those with allocative control and those with operational control, or, to return to Bettelheim's terminology, between those with economic ownership and those with the powers of possession only. This conceptual distinction underpins the distinction between the effective controllers of the means of production and the new middle class. Moreover, the divisions are being reinforced by the recruitment and promotion policies of major companies. The organic unity of management and capital has been ruptured. This is not to argue that a layer of management has achieved proletarian status, but rather that management has polarised to the extent that it is possibly to identify a clearer coalescence of the new middle class. This polarisation means that even while carrying out the function of capital the new middle class has increasing need to defend itself against corporate capital. The form that this defence takes is frequently unionisation, a form examined in subsequent chapters.

4 The state and the new middle class

The development of capitalism in the twentieth century has seen not only the monopolisation of the private sector of the economy but also the expansion of state activities. Any attempt to analyse the changing nature of the class structure of these societies therefore has to include some consideration of the implications of this expansion. Social democratic theorists, whatever their other failings, have at least been clear on this. In the 1950s it was an integral part of social democratic theory that the changing balance of private and public ownership and vastly increased public expenditure and employment were crucial indicators that the class nature of British society had changed. Their contention, that the owners of private capital had lost power to the managers of companies, was paralleled by the claim that there had also been, in Crosland's words, a 'loss of power by the business class to the state'.[1]

This loss of power, according to Crosland, is apparent in three areas; increased economic regulation; nationalisation of basic industries; and the growth of social welfare. A corollary of analyses such as this, which view the state as neutral, is that state employees are seen as above class. As the number of state personnel has grown, the class basis of society is therefore seen to atrophy.

These conclusions have been contested by Marxist theory. Marxists have argued that the changes in state activities can be viewed simply as the latest stage in a continual process of establishing a framework designed to stabilise capitalist society by addressing problems that individual capitalist enterprises would find impossible to solve. This chapter takes up the Marxist perspective and views the state as operating on behalf of capital, albeit in a complex manner, but also attempts to demonstrate that structural changes in the state apparatus, brought about by the changing needs of capital, have had a corresponding effect on class relations within the state apparatus.

Marxism and the state

There has been, within the last decade, such a proliferation of Marxist works on the nature of the state that justice cannot be done here to all the complexities of the subject. Nevertheless, it is essential to put forward a relatively simplified model of the relationship of the state to society in order to provide a basis for further discussion. The starting point of Marxist analysis is the recognition that the state is the product of the social division of labour and, furthermore, that it is not neutral.[2] In other words, the functions performed by the state need not inevitably be separated from the vast majority of the members of society (law and order, for example), but are so under historically specific conditions because of antagonisms within civil society. In capitalist society the principal antagonism is between wage-labour and capital. The nature of this relationship varies, however, according to historical circumstances and this variation is also reflected in the role and nature of the state. This latter point notwithstanding, there have been attempts to periodise state activities in terms of general features of capitalist societies. Fine and Harris, for example, have distinguished the changing balance of state activities under three stages of capitalism: *laissez-faire*, monopoly and state monopoly. In the *laissez-faire* stage, the role of the state is rudimentary:

> It can be too readily assumed that the establishment of wage-labour heralds the rights associated with freedom of exchange, but these are rights that have to be won in class struggle. The restriction of these rights best serves the production of absolute surplus value and is best served by the lack of working class political representation. It has as its effect the localisation of capitalist relations, particularly in the competition for labour power, and the corresponding localisation of political power with the central state restricting rather than enforcing the granting of reforms to the working class.[3]

It was these repressive functions of the state on which classical Marxism focused. Under monopoly capitalism, however, the state's role was extended and changed. With the growth of machinofacture there occurred the real, as opposed to the formal, subordination of labour and the growing importance of the production of relative, rather than absolute, surplus-value.

125

This led to a contradiction between the interests of capital in general and the direction forced upon capital in particular by the forces of competition. To lengthen the working day continually, for example, threatened the physical destruction of the work-force, including women and children, and increased the cost of reproducing labour power by limiting the period of its productive potential. But as Fine and Harris note, the coercive forces of competition external to the capitalist made a limitation of the working day impossible without social intervention, i.e. by the state external to economic reproduction.[4]

The centralisation of capital also promoted the growing concentration of workers and thus provided the material base for trade unionism and for the placing of more effective political demands on the state. A combination of these demands and the political ascendancy of monopoly capital saw a transformation in the form of state power. This transformation, according to Fine and Harris, took the following sequence: 'Legislation on all reforms centred around a relationship between central government and local authority that was successively restrictive, permissive and compulsory as monopoly capital wrested political control from parochial capital.'[5] The growing organisation of labour under monopoly capitalism intensified the class struggle. At the same time, however, the struggle for political democracy as a means to social reform limited the fight, Fine and Harris claim, to one within a framework compatible with the continued existence of capitalist social relations of production: moreover, the demands placed upon the state encouraged its expansion and allowed it to mediate the antagonisms between labour and capital. As Fine and Harris argue:

> The partial 'resolution' of these contradictory tendencies that both promote and moderate class struggle under *monopoly capitalism* is to be found in the development of the economic role of the state. The state's predominance in economic reproduction is the distinguishing feature of *state monopoly capitalism* (SMC), the latest stage of the capitalist mode of production.[6]

State monopoly capitalism is therefore a product of the contradictions inherent in monopoly capitalism which draw the state directly into the circuit of capital. Fine and Harris posit three major characteristics of this state involvement in the process of circulation. Firstly, the state, through varied and complex mechanisms, replaces the private credit system as the dominant agent through which capital accumulation is regulated. Secondly, it greatly increases appropriation from the working class and capitalists *via* the highly socialised form of taxation, thereby increasing the state's ability to engage in contra-cyclical demand management and redistribution through subsidies. This mode of appropriation exists alongside previous forms based upon free exchange, but these are also increasingly affected by state activities: for example, exchange relations are modified by government wage controls. Finally, the state involves itself directly in the production process, *via* nationalisation, where individual capitals cannot carry out necessary restructuring and/or there is significant working-class pressure for state intervention.

The state's move into the centre-stage of economic reproduction is not without political dangers. It threatens, for example, to weaken the apparent separation of trade union economism and the political sphere, a separation important for the maintenance of capitalist control. Thus a struggle for wages or over redundancies 'would have a tendency under SMC to raise political issues immediately; the question of control of the state and its class nature'.[7] A political transformation of the state is therefore a necessity for the continued stability of capitalism. The central feature of the transformation is the incorporation of working-class political struggle, classically through social democracy. This allows the working class to process political demands while at the same time converting them into forms that are least harmful or, perhaps, positively beneficial, to capital as a whole. In addition, social democracy facilitates appeals by labour and other governments for economic sacrifices in order to maintain political power.

The characterisation of the latest stage of capitalism as one of state monopoly has been the subject of much criticism. Criticisms of the state monopoly capitalism theories of the Soviet bloc and many Western Communist Parties, for example, have concentrated on the alleged fusion of monopoly forces with the bourgeois state to form a single mechanism of economic exploitation and political domination.[8] (It is this fusion that in turn underpins the strategy of an anti-monopoly alliance between the working class and small capital.) Within the theory advanced by Fine and Harris discussed above, no such simple fusion between state and monopoly capital is implied. Indeed, a measure of autonomy is required by the state precisely in order to act against particular capitals in the interest of capital as a whole. As Fine and Harris emphasise:

> saying that the state is the focus for class relations at all levels (political, economic, ideological) muddies the water in other respects. For there is the problem of which class relations, and

127

also that of whether, if the state is a focus, the class relations are consequently pre-given and simply act through the state. As to which relations, the most fundamental factor is of course the antagonism of the bourgeoisie and the proletariat. But within these bounds the state's role is also determined by intermediate strata such as the 'petty bourgeoisie' and by class fractions such as the financial bourgeoisie as against the industrial bourgeoisie. As to whether class relations are pre-given the answer is clearly that they are not necessarily so.[9]

Nevertheless, Fine and Harris's formulation is open to criticism.[10] It is not clear, for example, at what stage monopoly capitalism becomes transformed into the state monopoly form, or whether social democracy is a necessary and irreversible factor of it. But it is not the intention here to enter into a debate as to which label, whether state monopoly, monopoly or late capitalism,[11] best characterises present-day metropolitan capitalist societies. The importance of any concept rests on its ability to help a comprehension of developments in the material world. The state's functions have increased in both scope and importance, and Fine and Harris's characterisation has the merit of focusing attention on these changes.

The British state

It can be argued that many features of state monopoly capitalism as characterised by Fine and Harris are present in Britain. They have been brought about as a result of restructuring state activity during and immediately after the Second World War and more recently by changes in government policies towards direct economic intervention particularly between the 1960s and the late 1970s. It is this latter period that is of most concern here, but, because changes in the immediate post-war world laid the basis for social democratic claims of a transformed British society, those changes are briefly examined within a framework of class analysis.

The need for increased war-time production enhanced the position and power of labour. The sacrifice made during the war gave rise to a widespread feeling for change which also made necessary major concessions to the working class immediately after it. The concessions took the form of the nationalisation of certain basic industries, the establishment of the welfare state and a commitment to high levels of public expenditure in order to guarantee full employment. Although administered by the 1945–51 Labour government, this basis of a post-war settlement between capital and labour was supported by successive Conservative administrations.

Nationalisation

Nationalisation was a forward step for labour. It was, however, conceded to stabilise capitalism not to transform it. The first wave of nationalisations carried out by the post-war Labour government consisted of sectors of industry which produced goods and services that were integral to the reproduction of the system as a whole and which could not be run profitably or efficiently by competing, private companies. Infrastructure industries, such as coal and the railways, needed massive capital investment beyond the scope of individual capitals. Partly for this reason, they failed to make a profit for long periods of their early history under nationalisation, but this in no way compromised their essentially capitalist nature.[12] Their economic performance was complicated by wider considerations of macro-economic management which caused havoc amongst long-term investment programmes (see below), but more particularly:

> Their prices were also kept down for anti-inflation purposes, causing large deficits. Since many of the nationalised industries were effective monopolists, the size of the nationalised surplus or deficit was largely determined by pricing policies. The early deficits were aggravated by the character of their capital structures (great dependence on loan capital with heavy burden of interest charges plus compensation payments to former shareholders).[13]

The resulting losses of some nationalised industries were therefore illusory. It was merely that the surplus-value was transferred to private industry *via* the concealed subsidy of low prices, high charges and interest payments.

Social welfare

Just as with the nationalisation of basic industries, the extension of social welfare in the period immediately after the war can be viewed as a gain by the working class, but one that not only failed to threaten capital in any fundamental way but was also ultimately beneficial to it. When the National Health Service was established in 1948, its aims of providing access to medical treatment on the basis of need rather than ability to pay was far from capitalist. However, it reflected the needs of employers for a healthy work-force (an ethos reflected in the low priority given

129

to expenditure on groups, such as mental and geriatric patients, not generally expected to re-enter the labour market) and, as in the case of the nationalised coal industry, aimed to improve inefficient and inadequate services through organisational rationalisation on the basis of central and regional planning.[14]

The extension of the welfare state was central to social democratic visions of improving society. Contrary to the claims of some of its theorists, however, social democracy in Britain never seriously challenged the capitalist nature of the society. Rather, it saw its attempts to deal with the problems, in a large part thrown up by capitalist social relations, as sufficient in themselves. While capitalism was expanding in the 1950s and welfare was expanding with it, this strategy had a strong appeal. But, as capital faced greater problems of profitability from the late 1960s onwards and generated more and more social problems, there was increasing hostility to the levels of state expenditure on welfare.

Economic regulation

The third plank of governments' post-war concessions to the working class was the maintenance of full employment. This was to be achieved by the Keynesian mechanism of contra-cyclical demand management designed to abolish or at least alleviate the worst effects of business cycles. As Bob Jessop has noted 'since demand management acts at the macro-level and does not involve direct controls on either capital or labour, there was little opposition to the principle of such interventions from financial and industrial capital or their political representatives in parliament and the administration'.[15]

If there was no opposition to such a policy in principle, there was opposition from certain quarters in practice. The dominant characterisation of this opposition is that it came from financial capital.[16] Based upon Britain's historic importance in the sphere of world trade and the role of sterling as a reserve currency, financial capital and its representatives in the Treasury and Bank of England tended to be dominant in any conflict with the interests of industrial capital. The requirement of the post-war political settlement that domestic expansion should continue was fulfilled, therefore, only so far as it did not threaten the position of financial capital and its interest that international confidence in sterling should be maintained. As domestic expansion sucked in imports and widened the balance of payments deficit, pressures mounted upon the government to deflate the economy. The result of these competing pressures for full employment and a strong pound was Britain's 'stop-go' cycle.

The consequence of this policy was the worst of worlds for both sections of British capitalism. The effects have been well summarised by Jessop:

> the policies intended to maintain the position of sterling discouraged and distorted industrial investment through high interest rates to attract foreign funds and prevent the flight of 'hot money', restrictions on investment outside the sterling area . . . and recurrent bouts of deflation to restrain home demand and 'free' resources for export production also inhibited industrial growth due to resulting high 'unproductive' state expenditure on the military sector − especially in comparison with Japan and Britain's competitors in Europe. At the same time the reflationary measures intended to *restore full employment* after each 'stop' phase tended to prevent the onset of economic crisis which could have precipitated the restructuring of industrial capital in the interests of more streamlined and profitable production.[17]

The full extent of the crisis of profitability in British manufacturing industry was masked by the unprecedented world boom that took place from the end of the war to the early 1960s. The low rate of growth, the falling percentage of Gross National Product going to profits, and the rising sum of capital needed for investment projects gradually undermined the satisfaction of industrial capital with existing state policies. The dissatisfaction led to pressure on the government to become more involved in strategic planning. Samuel Brittan accounted for the Conservative government's conversion to planning as follows:

> When Selwyn Lloyd (Conservative Chancellor of the Exchequer) entered the Treasury, he already thought that long-term planning of government expenditure was, like other things he believed in, 'common sense'. He was converted to the belief that planning has something to offer for the private sector as well by a conference of the Federation of British Industries, held in Brighton at the end of November 1960, to consider 'The Next Five Years'. . . . The Brighton Conference was attended by 121 leading businessmen and 31 guests, including the heads of government departments and of the nationalized industries, and a few economists. . . . During the course of 1960, some of the more active minds in the Treasury had, quite independently of the FBI, become interested in new ideas for adding some zip to British industry. . . . There were a very small number of officials who thought that it was worth putting together the forecasts and plans on which individual

industries were already working, to see if they fitted together.[18]

The first practical outcome of this conversion was the establishment in 1962 of the National Economic Development Council on a tripartite basis, comprising government, employees and trade union representatives. As important, however, was the much less public reorganisation of the Treasury, for this had important repercussions for all government departments. The changes involved an increase in administrative control of the Treasury. All spending of public funds was to be scrutinised within a framework of long-term trends of public need and availability of resources. Secondly, claims for expenditure were to be evaluated not on an *ad hoc* basis, as in the past, but against competing claims from other sectors, in an attempt to establish a coherent policy. To achieve these ends the Treasury was divided into three main sections. Of these sections, the Finance Group and the Public Sector Group carried out traditional Treasury functions. The National Economy Group, however, was a real innovation, amounting to an embryo planning group within the Treasury. It had as its brief the examination not only of general questions but also particular issues such as monopoly and restrictive practices, the supply of skilled manpower, and impediments to productivity.[19]

The short space of time between these two largely independent developments − the formation of the NEDC and Treasury reorganisation − and the 1964 General Election meant that there was little time for the achievement of practical results. Perhaps, therefore, the judgment of the impact of the developments should be that of Andrew Schonfield, who argued that 'it may be said that the intellectual and administrative preconditions for modern capitalist planning had been created or were in the course of being established'.[20] Certainly, these changes, together with the decline of British capitalism and the absence of an ideological attack on the move towards planning, gave a powerful impetus to the Labour Party's appeal at the 1964 election for the country to break from its old traditions. This appeal was embodied most concisely in a much-quoted speech of the Labour leader, Harold Wilson. Britain, with a Labour government, was set to become a modern, rational, technological society: a society not rent by class conflict but one of planned co-operation:

> Mr Chairman, let me conclude with what I think the message of all this is for Conference . . . we are redefining and we are restating our Socialism in terms of scientific revolution. But that revolution cannot become a reality unless we are prepared to make far-reaching changes in economic and social attitudes

which permeate our whole system of society. The Britain that is going to be forged in the white heat of this revolution will be no place for restrictive practices or for out-dated methods on either side of industry.[21]

The perspective was also enshrined in the Labour Party's election manifesto. The social and economic problems of Britain, it stated, could only be solved 'by a deliberate and massive effort to modernise the economy, to change its structure and to develop with all possible speed the advanced technology and the new science based industries with which our future lies. In short they will only be advanced by Socialist Planning'.[22]

From the mid-1960s a plethora of state institutions was established in Britain. Alongside the traditional state organisations concerned with social welfare (education, health, housing) new institutions were formed, often quasi-autonomous non-governmental organisations (quangos), which were concerned with intervention and restructuring relations (ACAS, IRC, Min Tech, NEB, etc). State expenditure was vastly increased both by this and the expansion of traditional services. It was increased, however, within a framework of promises of structural reforms to modernise the administration of Britain, and to promote the productivity and profitability of private capital. Within such a framework, major sections of capital could be carried along and, indeed, even play an active role in such developments.[23]

Once the possibilities of a regenerated British capitalism floundered on worsening international recession, the mood amongst influential ideologues of capital changed. This change was marked, for instance, by the reception given in 1976 to Bacon and Eltis's book, *Britain's Economic Problem: Too Few Producers*,[24] in which they argued that the public sector was an unproductive burden on the private sector, threatening private capital accumulation. It was also reflected in changed government fiscal policy: the centralisation of power towards the Treasury initiated by changes following the Plowden Committee was further developed by the Treasury which instituted a system of cash limits in 1976. The effect of this policy was to reduce total planned state expenditure in 1977–8 by £4.4 billion, or 8 per cent of total public expenditure.[25]

That which was forced upon the Labour government, by what it saw as force of circumstances, was whole-heartedly embraced by the Conservatives. The conversion of the Conservative Party to a monetarist philosophy was reflected by the victory of Margaret Thatcher over Edward Heath for leadership of the party in 1974. When the Conservatives were subsequently elected in 1979, the third element of the post-war settlement between capital and labour, the maintenance of full employment through demand management, already undermined by the previous Labour government, was now completely set aside. The adoption of monetarist policies meant and still means not only a reduction of public expenditure and employment but also an exacerbation of trends towards class polarisation within the remaining work-force, a development already maturing during the period of expansion. These developments can be observed within the nationalised industries.

It has already been argued that nationalised industries should be viewed as working within a capitalist framework. This is not to argue that from the outset they were paragons of capitalist efficiency. Successive governments, however, have attempted to rectify this state of affairs and the judgment of Raymond Williams, made in 1965, that 'they [the nationalised industries] have not only failed to alter the "profit before use" emphasis in the general economy but have also themselves been steadily reduced to this old criterion',[26] has been increasingly borne out. The movement towards this profit orientation, accepted by both Labour and Conservative Parties, is clearly displayed in the 1978 White Paper *Nationalised Industries*.[27] This laid down the importance of (a) financial targets based on a three-to-five-year period; (b) the objective of a 5 per cent real rate of return before tax on new investment; and (c) the publication of non-financial performance indicators so that the public could monitor the progress of the public corporations. Within such a framework the imposition of cash limits on borrowings has increased the pressure on them to generate cash from their own operations.

The move towards an increasingly explicit capitalist orientation coincided with a second wave of enterprises being taken into public ownership, both by nationalisation and majority share-holding by the NEB. Whatever the form taken, whether nationalisation, as in the case of ship-building and aerospace, or NEB control of British Leyland and Rolls Royce, the industries and companies were in need of massive restructuring. Once again, therefore, the idea of control of the commanding heights of industry for the common good was far from the reality of the case. The NEB in particular quickly veered away from its original conception of taking into ownership profitable parts of British industry. It became an emergency life-line for struggling private capital and worked with a ruthless profit orientation:

In its first two years, the only companies in which the NEB

acquired a controlling share – apart from the transferred companies – were companies which had gone bankrupt, but yet had profit potential. As the NEB guidelines put it, 'The NEB shall make acquisitions . . . only when they see the prospect of an adequate rate of return within a reasonable period'. . . . Eric Varley, the Secretary of State for Industry, directed that an adequate rate was to be 15-20% on capital employed for the whole of the board's activities by 1981. The only exceptions were to be British Leyland and Rolls Royce, for which an adequate return would be 10%. This overall target is very high when compared to the performance of most of British industry. . . . Against this background, a target of 15-20% in a period of deepening recession does not leave much room for the NEB to carry out what the guidelines call its 'wider responsibilities' such as 'creating employment in areas of unemployment' and 'promoting industrial democracy in undertakings which they [the NEB] control'.[28]

In practice the profit motive and the wider responsibilities were contradictory. The primacy of the former over the latter brought further unemployment to centres of already high unemployment and further weakened the main vehicle of industrial democracy in the enterprises it controlled, namely the trade unions. One such example was the closure in 1978 of British Leyland's Speke No. 2 plant, situated in Merseyside, one of the areas of highest unemployment in the country. As a report on the closure concluded: 'As things stand at the moment British Leyland (under the NEB and Edwardes) is putting the last stamp upon "nationalisation" for working class people. For them state ownership has meant redundancy – from start to finish.[29] Not only, therefore, has nationalisation failed to change the dynamic of the economy as a whole, it has also clearly failed to change relationships within the nationalised sector. Clearly these sectors, acting on an increasingly explicit capitalist basis, have 'reproduced, sometimes with appalling accuracy, the human patterns, in management and working relations, of industries based upon quite different social principles'.[30] In other words, it is possible to see in their workings the class relations distinguished in the private capitalist sector. More particularly, this means that in the state-owned company part of the revenue goes to the legal owners, the state (or is pumped into the private sector by under-pricing or the payment of premium prices for incoming goods), while the other part is accumulated by the real owners, the top management. It is possible therefore to concur with Carchedi's analysis that:

> As far as real ownership is concerned, it belongs to the managers both in the joint-stock company and in the state-owned enterprise. In both forms of enterprise, it is the manager who is the non-labourer/exploiter/non-producer/real owner. In both enterprises, the manager, as capitalist personified, is opposed to the labourer/non-owner/producer. In terms of production relations, then, there is no difference between these two types of enterprises. . . . Because both behave according to the laws of capitalist competition and accumulation, both produce commodities, in order to produce surplus value rather than of the customers' needs to be met, in short, *both advance money in order to increase it.*[31]

It is this very principle, however, that fails to operate in areas of public activity generally conceived of as social welfare which constitute the second foundation of social democratic claims that large areas of society no longer operate under capitalist principles. Here, therefore, class analysis cannot simply apply analyses deprived from the private sector. Moreover, there are mediating structures between government policy and the situation of social welfare workers which complicate any attempt to specify class relations. There has, therefore, to be an examination of these structures before welfare work itself can be viewed.

Class relations within the social welfare sector

Local government

The main agent for the administration of much of social welfare in Britain is local government. Education, housing and social services all fall within this sector, accounting for two-thirds of all local government expenditure and approximately 12 per cent of the Gross National Product.[32] The degree of autonomy of local government from the central state is, however, severely limited and is being even further curtailed. Not only are there statutory constraints, but there are also increasing financial constraints on local authority decision-making. Recent years have witnessed a growing dependency of local government on central government financing: for instance, 39 per cent of local government expenditure in 1965 came from central funds, rising to 55 per cent in 1975. Moreover, the enhanced authority that this has given to central government has been used to further reduce local autonomy. These developments, together with the structural reform of local government enacted by parliament in 1972, make it increasingly appropriate to view local government not as some benign remnant of local democracy, but as the local state.[33] The 1973 reforms created larger units of government in order, it was claimed, to achieve 'efficiency, economies of scale, functional effectiveness and an adequate capacity to plan and organise'.[34] In practice, however, these aims are far from neutral. A dual process of transition has occurred in local government: both its importance to capital has increased and its internal relations have become much more polarised by what has become termed as 'managerialism', but which is, in fact, a spread of, and dominance by, the capitalist labour process.

The need for more managerial control was noted by the National Board for Prices and Incomes (NBPI) in its report in 1967 on *The Pay and Conditions of Manual Workers in Local Authorities, The National Health Service, Gas and Water Supply*.[35] Complaining about the lack of a clear managerial hierarchy, the report commented that 'insufficient attention is given to equipping the officials concerned with the necessary managerial expertise and to encouraging cost consciousness'.[36] It was not within its remit to make detailed recommendations, but nevertheless it was made quite clear to the government that the Board regarded the matter as one of 'utmost importance'.

In fact, the first of a series of Government Committees had already turned its attention to the problem as defined by the NBPI. During the mid 1960s and early 1970s four official committees, under Maud, Mallaby, Redcliffe-Maud and Bains,[37] all reported on the managerial methods most appropriate to local government. One study of the effects of the reports concluded that although the four reports differed in detail the principles were shared. As in business, the message of the reports was 'integration, control from the top, more efficient use of money and labour, forward planning for a bigger impact on the job in hand'.[38]

The method appropriate to local government was the same as that appropriate to major capitalist enterprises: corporate planning. Following the reports, numerous councils employed private management consultants, all of whom shared common assumptions. The consultants' recommendations had, according to one prominent critic, John Benington, the following common features:

1 The creation of a Policy and Resources Committee (consisting of the Chairman of the major service committees or other senior elected members) to provide co-ordinated advice to the Council in the setting of its plans, objectives and

priorities.

2   The appointment of a Chief Executive to act as leader of the officers of the local authority and principal adviser to the Council on matters of general policy.

3   The setting up of a management system usually based directly or indirectly upon the American concept of PPBS (Planning, Programming and Budgeting Systems). The PPBS approach sets objectives, plans, programmes to try to meet those objectives, and develops a budget which attempts to measure outputs as well as inputs.[39]

The result of these proposals were two-fold. Firstly, changes were made in administrative procedures aimed at improving efficiency. These changes essentially concerned resource management *via* the techniques of O and M (organisation and management), OR (operations research), and CBA (cost benefit analysis). The second change was concerned not so much with the efficiency of the parts but the role of local government as a whole and saw the beginnings of the adoption of a more interventionist approach. The consequences of this change of emphasis have been wide-reaching. As Howard Elcock noted:

This view not only implies far more complex networks of communication between the local authority's own committees and departments, but also that the local authority should influence and coordinate the activities of other public and private sector bodies outside of its own control, such as Government departments, the nationalised industries, private industrial companies and providers of entertainment, sporting and cultural activities. The adoption of the 'governmental' approach further increases the need for a central organ in the local authority able to give a lead not only to the authority's own members and officers but also to others outside. A particularly good example is industrial development where local authorities, especially in areas with declining industries and high unemployment, have become involved in efforts to persuade domestic and foreign industrialists to undertake new investment in this area. Local authorities, often in collaboration with Regional Economic Planning Councils and other regional and national bodies, have attempted to 'sell' their areas to industrialists over whose decisions they have no control.[40]

The streamlining of local government and the centralisation of decision-making that has accompanied these developments, while enhancing the power of a minority of senior councillors, has tended to weaken the role of the majority. Councillors have become incorporated into a system of committees whose goals are to produce corporate plans. However sympathetic such committees are to the particular experiences of a councillor at ward level, they are charged with planning and providing authority-wide services and collect and collate information which sometimes appears to negate the experience of individuals. The corporate management approach has the effect of de-politicising issues and making more difficult any challenge to policy decisions. As Benington noted, 'The effect can be to generalise the issues to a point where conflicts of interest are no longer apparent and where they can be treated as neutral technical problems.'[41]

If one result of corporate management is to legitimise leadership and hierarchy, strengthening leading members of the council, it also has the much more significant effect of strengthening the powers of officers against councillors. Sometimes such an effect is quite consciously planned, as in Leeds where the Conservatives claimed that the creation of a corporate management structure would free committees and officers from the excessive political control imposed by their Labour predecessors.[42] More often, however, such effects are the result of reforms made in the search for efficiency, a goal shared by both Labour and Conservative councillors. One academic advocate of corporate management structures in local government, for example, has framed the argument thus:

> Optimal policy-making requires systematic thinking that is based on knowledge and orientated towards innovation on medium and long range policy issues. Not enough of such thinking can generally take place in action-orientated organisations because of both the pressure of acute problems and the way that a pragmatic organisational climate, based on experience and orientated towards executing policies, depressed innovation.[43]

The conclusion is therefore that the responsibility for the making of new policies and the reviewing of the effectiveness of old ones has to rest with small groups of experts.

Some councils have adopted this policy. The Lambeth local government structure assigned a key role to Policy Planning Groups (PPG). While committees were preoccupied with day-to-day agendas, the PPGs, assisted by the corporate planning staff of the Chief Executive, laid the basis for a more long-term plan. No elected members were directly involved in this process, with the consequence that, although amendments could be made at a later stage, the overall parameter had largely been laid down. While differing in particulars from other councils' reforms, those of Lambeth closely followed the general orientation as laid down by both the academic centre of reform, the Institute of Local Government Studies at Birmingham University, and the general literature on corporate management. The results of the Lambeth system have been described as follows:

> The vertical pyramid of control had grown taller and thinner. Directorate work was horizontally integrated in the Directors' Board. Whereas in the old days the majority group and the council itself had been a place where the affairs of many committees had been aired, in front of back benches and of the public, now, though group was still technically sovereign opinions were being formed and decisions hardened in Policy Committee. The Council meeting had long become, in the words of members, 'a set piece, a farce, a public relations show'. More important still, behind all the activity of group, committees and council stood the considerable organisation of officers. 'The real power in the town hall lies with the officers.'[44]

The parallels between the corporate structures of private companies and those of local authorities have already been noted. They can, however, be made more explicit. The structural reform of local government corresponds at one level to the restructuring of companies along multi-product, multi-divisional lines. A set of managers in both areas have been released from day-to-day executive tasks in order that the organisation achieves maximum productivity and efficiency.

This relationship between top management and those engaged in providing local services also calls into being two other contradictory developments. Firstly, it expands the new middle class in local government, a class which has no real control over policy and orientation but whose function it is to devise and supervise the demanded increases in productivity. Management Services grew to administer those various schemes. In Lambeth, for example, the growth has been from a couple of dozen to more than a hundred people in just a few years.[45] On the other hand, the same developments have led to a diminution of discretion and autonomy amongst other new middle-class workers. As Benington noted:

> Current management reforms more rarely, but occasionally, also include a measure of decentralisation and delegation down to the field level. However, in practice this seems to involve

increased administrative responsibility more often than any significant new powers in central policy making. The result is often that field staff are further burdened with day-to-day administration. So they become overwhelmed and even less likely to be able to raise the underlying policy questions which are often implicit in the individual problems which the public present to them, or which are apparent to them in their fieldwork. Current organisational developments thus may tend to harden the division between policy-making and implementation – between those who are incorporated into the 'management' part of the pyramid and those whose work brings them into contact with the outside world.[46]

In other words, there is, with the creation of an expanded layer of new middle-class employees, a simultaneous proletarianisation of other layers. This process can be clearly seen in one of the particular areas of local government responsibility: social services.

The restructuring of social work

The labour process in social work was reorganised as a result of the report of the Seebohm Committee, established in 1965 with the aim of reviewing 'the organisation and responsibilities of the local authority personal social services in England and Wales, and to consider what changes are desirable to secure an effective family service'.[47] Its brief showed state concern to underpin the family, but this aspect of its ideology is not of direct importance here. This concern, however, led the committee to argue the need for unified social services departments to be established in order to provide comprehensive services to families. The creation of these departments centralised decision-making within authorities, moving power from practitioners of social work up departmental hierarchies and from departments to policy advisory committees. The new, more efficient, organisation was envisaged as working as follows:

It is assumed that social workers work within technical administrative and legally-based policies conveyed to them through the Area Team Leader from the Director of Social Services. . . . These stipulations express prescriptions within which they must work, including the relationship they are expected to employ in performing their tasks and how to develop their roles.[48]

Once again it is possible to argue that the model adopted owed much more to organisational forms in private capitalist enterprises than to the specific problems of providing social services. This view is shared not only by a growing number of social workers and left-wing academics,[49] but also by more orthodox commentators. Bryan Glastonbury, for example, has noted that 'social services departments have originated less from our experiences with other types of service organisation, or out of local authorities, than from experience of industrial structures and management processes'.[50] Indeed, he goes as far as to maintain that an exactly parallel structure to that of industry has been established (see Figure 4.1).[51]

Industry	Function	Social services dept.
Board of Directors ———	Policy control ———	Central/local government
Managing Director ———	Operational control —	Director of Social Services
Section heads (sales, production, etc.) —	Specialist management —	Assistant Directors (field services, residential, etc.)
Line production managers —	Supervision of the production/ supervision process	Area team leaders
Skilled staff ———	Production/service tasks needing specific skills	Social workers
Labourers ———	Less skilled/ unskilled tasks	Welfare assistants, etc.

Figure *4.1*

This is not to suggest that all of the control mechanisms adopted by private sector companies are possible for social work. Nevertheless, where appropriate, they are advocated by writers such as Kogan and Terry, who urge those controlling social service departments 'to pay heed to efficiency, budgeting, economy, clarity of organisation and other management virtues'.[52] This means, in particular, more information on and control over the day-to-day practice of social workers: 'A department cannot be certain that it is functioning effectively unless there is a significant correspondence between filed activity on the one hand and overall departmental policy, as decided during priority setting, objectives setting, and budget making on the other.'[53] This bureaucratisation assumes, as a matter of fact, that the practitioners of social work are excluded from any of the control of priorities, objectives and budgets. As one group of critics of welfare work organisation has noted, 'the split is about knowledge of the whole process involved in the work. Some people have to carry organisation and others plan it: *the two groups are inevitably split* and do not have a cross membership. Thus above team leaders there are very few who ever *meet clients*; below team leaders there are very few people who are structurally allowed to plan or co-ordinate.'[54] It is still the case that the majority of social work management positions are occupied by qualified social workers and this has the advantage of lending credence to their management decisions. But with bureaucratic rationality increasingly dominant this situation may not last. It is argued by David Cooper, for example, that managers from social work backgrounds frequently find it difficult to abstain from involving themselves in substantive issues which should be delegated and have been ineffective in establishing managerial and procedural framework.[55]

If bureaucratisation is in the process of creating a clearer managerial stratum, it is also producing its opposite – a layer of employees who feel alienated from, and hostile to, the organisation in which they work. The changes in the organisation of work have, it has been argued, 'stripped away the veils of ideology around such things as "professional autonomy", and have increased welfare workers' perception of themselves as workers'.[56] Or, as Cooper and Glastonbury reluctantly conclude, 'many have lost faith in the organisation and turned instead to seek cohesion and strength through industrial action'.[57]

The National Health Service

The National Health Service was an outcome of a particular balance of social forces. It was a concession to working-class political pressure, but it was a concession which did not even threaten the power of the major sectional interest within the health care sector, the doctors, let alone the global interests of capital. As Noel and Jose Parry have argued, 'Rather than a service run on "socialist" lines, which the profession had feared, there was in fact a strengthening of controls exercised by doctors collectively over the institutions and organisations of medical care.'[58] Moreover, the very nationalisation of the service has resulted in a bureaucratisation and rationalisation that continued

143

private ownership could never have achieved. In this sense nationalisation has facilitated the progressive domination of the labour process by capitalist rationality. This is not to claim, like Bellaby and Oribabor, that the NHS is simply a capitalist production process with hospital workers producing surplus-value.[59] Money is not advanced to the NHS in order to expand it. But this in no way prevents the service being controlled by identical strategies and mechanisms to those organisations operated on a profit basis because pressure on the controllers of the NHS to reduce its unit costs is not lessened.

Once again it was the 1960s that first saw significant changes in the structure and management of the NHS and the labour process within it. The 1962 Hospital Plan[60] laid down guidelines for the establishment of large district general hospitals as the main units of production. This, in turn, enabled activities to be integrated, plant to be mechanised and services to be centralised. The aim was explicitly to achieve economies of scale. Any benefits to patients were incidental. Such developments were accompanied by, and further stimulated, changes in the organisation and methods of management. In particular it gave rise to modern management methods, including functional specialisation, throughout the NHS:

> In place of general administrators, specialist officers were created, particularly in the ancillary areas like catering, laundries, supplies and purchasing. Management services were streamlined and experienced both a rise in size and status, particularly work study, organisational methods (O & M), training and personnel. There were the beginnings of an inflow of managers with experience of private industry.[61]

One casualty of this increasing managerialism was the autonomy gained by nursing under nationalisation, which had accorded it parallel status to that of medicine and administration. Catering and domestic services became separate departments no longer subject to the control of the matron, who was relegated to a relatively low position in the emerging management hierarchy. With the implementation of the recommendations of the Salmon Report (1966),[62] the matron was seven steps down the hierarchy of control, responsible for co-ordinating and supervising a divisional unit of the hospital (see Table 4.1). The areas of decision-making were limited and the matron was subject to increased central control.[63]

These changes were advocated because it was considered by the Report that traditional nursing management was inferior to modern business administration methods. As a result, the lack of

TABLE 4.1 *The Salmon system of nursing management*

Grade	Title	Sphere of authority	Formerly for example
10	Chief Nursing Officer (CNO)	Group	—
9	Principal Nursing Officer (PNO)	Division	Large hospital
8	Senior Nursing Officer (SNO)	Area	Medium-sized hospital
7	Nursing Officer (NO)	Unit	Small hospital/ group of wards
6	Sister/Charge Nurse	Section	Ward
5	Staff Nurse	Section	Ward

managerial structure led to a misallocation of the matron's time: conception and execution were not systematically separated. In a passage that echoes Allen's managerial grid, the Report states:

> In nursing administration effective delegation is rarely seen
> . . . the matron of a sizeable hospital may head an array of
> deputy assistants and administrative sisters to whom she assigns
> duties, *but she does not find the relief that the top person of a*
> *business seems to find.* She often . . . retains work that she
> could well hand over to assistants.[64] (my emphasis)

Salmon implicitly called for a managerial structure based upon that used in the advanced sectors of monopoly capital, where bureaucratic hierarchies have taken over from individual owner-entrepreneurs.[65] This has meant tightening the managerial role of former matrons within their shrunken area of authority. The Report emphasised that the skills needed for nursing management were different from those needed for nursing: 'Nurses in top management need, most of all, well developed managerial skills. . . . Provided he or she has shown the proper managerial ability it does not matter the route taken to the top.'[66] With the acceptance of such thinking, the background of candidates for senior posts are of diminished importance:

> background discipline and nursing knowledge are becoming
> less important compared with 'abstract' managerial abilities
> that transcend local peculiarities and idiosyncracies. It is
> increasingly the case that nursing background is required less
> for its utility than to legitimise the position of managers over a

145

workforce, many of whom have frustrated professional aspirations. The future might see increasing resort to nursing degrees which, apparently, are proving extremely popular, and graduate entrants who will be able to pass through the ranks with indecent haste, ostensibly to gain experience, but in reality to obtain the minimum necessary legitimation for their future managerial roles.[67]

If Michael Carpenter is correct in arguing that the Salmon Report was in part anxious to create a career structure to entice back and hold middle-class recruits to nursing, it is also clear that promotion to its highest reaches will be less and less open to nurses starting at the bottom. The structure will produce a cleavage above the post of sister similar to that developing above the foreman in industry.[68]

The restructuring of the work process in nursing has left no layers untouched. Sisters also have been affected by an increasing specialisation:

First, operations such as taking routine tests (of urine, blood, etc.) and compiling case histories of patients have become the province of the Pathology Department and junior doctors or social workers respectively: they are no longer coordinated by the ward sister. Secondly, in three typical areas the ward sister has lost her power of decision to nurses superior in the hierarchy − determining the rota of work-allocation on the ward; disciplining junior nurses; and perhaps above all training.[69]

Furthermore, in spite of the fact that ancillaries have taken over many of the menial tasks traditionally performed by nurses, the increased division of labour has done little to enhance nursing: 'Typically, the nurse's task is broken down into constituent operations performed routinely by separate nurses on all patients (temperatures, blood pressure, injections and so on)' so that 'nurses seldom engage in the total process of care'.[70]

Nowhere is capitalist rationality clearer in hospitals than in management's treatment of ancillary workers. The two reports of the National Board for Prices and Incomes, 1967 and 1971, both highlighted the alleged low productivity of ancillary workers and blamed poor structures and standards of labour management.[71] Their recommendations were similar to those adopted in numerous private enterprises. The first report, NBPI 29, recommended reorganisation of the pay structure by job evaluation and earnings schemes related to performance. The later report, NBPI 166, proposed an Ancillary Work Efficiency scheme. Within these reports there were further calls for 'clearer allocations of management responsibilities, the wresting of ancillary work from nursing control, tighter job definitions, greater standardisation of methods and equipment, and more centralisation of production in fewer units'.[72]

As management became more concentrated, systematic and self-conscious throughout the 1960s and 1970s, it was not without major consequences on workers' organisation and consciousness. Union organisation and industrial action spread, particularly amongst ancillary workers but also amongst nurses. This trend is most clearly seen in the growth of the Confederation of Health Service Employees. Its membership of 77,000 in 1970 increased nearly threefold to 215,000 by 1979. The National Union of Public Employees' membership in the NHS also increased dramatically to 250,000 by 1979, while the National Association of Local Government Officers had over 84,000 members in the NHS at that time.[73]

Class relations in the public sector: a summary

As already stated, no widely accepted Marxist analysis of state employees has yet emerged. Indeed, it could be argued that no serious attempt to offer one has ever been made. Poulantzas, for instance, whose influence on class analysis has been widespread, has only a cursory treatment of state employees in his major work on class structure, *Classes in Contemporary Capitalism*, 1975. When he returns to the question in *State, Power, Socialism*, 1978, there is little more than a reiteration of the already stated position: all state employees outside certain nationalised industries and transport are either bourgeois or petty bourgeois. His analysis allows for a polarisation between mental and manual labour, but a polarisation that can never achieve for the petty bourgeois elements the full transition to proletarian status:

> This class place [of state employees] is distinct from the class origin of the state personnel (i.e. from the classes out of which it emerges): it refers to the position of the personnel in the social division of labour, such as it crystallizes in the state framework (in the form, amongst others, of the specific reproduction of the division between intellectual and manual labour at the very heart of intellectual labour concentrated in the State). It is a question of *bourgeois* class affiliation or place for the upper reaches of this personnel, and of *petty bourgeois* affiliation for intermediate and subaltern echelons of the state apparatuses.[74]

To maintain this argument Poulantzas needs to claim that:

> even sections of the state personnel which go over to the
> popular masses do not challenge the reproduction of the social
> division of labour within the state apparatus (i.e. the process of
> bureaucratic hierarchization); nor *a fortiori* do they normally
> challenge the political division between rulers and ruled that is
> embodied in the State. In other words they do not radically call
> into question their own place and role in relationship to the
> popular masses.[75]

Given the vague and a-historical nature of this formulation, it is
hard to attach much seriousness to it. If one interprets Poulantzas
as saying that the lower sections of state employees must be
excluded from the working class because they lack what amounts
to a revolutionary class consciousness, then the same criterion
would similarly exclude the majority of manual workers in
private industry, Poulantzas' archetypal working class.

Ranged against this categorisation is an extension of the
orthodox Marxist perspective to state employees which either
explicitly or implicitly divides them up into either bourgeoisie or
proletariat. Cynthia Cockburn, for example, in *The Local State*,
although claiming to base her analysis on Olin Wright's
framework, the central feature of which is the existence of
contradictory class locations, nevertheless sees only polarised
classes. She states:

> I adopt . . . [an] inclusive definition of the working class. For
> instance I include local state workers, except for senior officers
> associated with policy-making. I would argue that if their
> subjective inclination and their political practice identifies them
> as workers there is no objective constraint to their inclusion.
> . . . I reserve the term bourgeoisie for those who own
> substantial capital and who profit from the surplus value
> created by labour; plus those professionals, managers, etc. who
> identify with and further this process.[76]

Cockburn thus avoids the problem of an analysis of those
employees below senior officers who are not by subjective
inclination and political practice identified with the working class,
and yet cannot be classified as bourgeois.

In contrast to the partly voluntaristic basis of division implicit
in Cockburn's analysis, Fairbrother, in a recent pamphlet,
Working for the State, recognises the structural basis of divisions
between employees. Citing an example from teaching he states:

> while a school is *managed* by a local authority, in practice this

is a head teacher acting within guidelines set by the education department of the local authority. At the same time ancillary workers and teachers are supervised by head teachers but each may be answerable to different sections of management in the education department. Further, general education policy and practice is the responsibility of the Department of Education and Science, part of the central government structure. In this way the complicated structures of organisation and control, further divide one set of state workers from another.[77]

But having so defined the basis of the social division of labour within the state sector, Fairbrother proceeds to obscure it by a concentration on the difference between sectors. There are important ideological divisions, he states, but he is not concerned about the differing ideologies of managers and workers so much as the fact that the 'ideology of police work' is different from 'the ideology of social work'. Fairbrother thus obviates the necessity to differentiate state employees on a class basis by reducing divisions to differentiations within a homogeneous class category: 'While different managerial structures distinguish one set of workers from another they also provide a focus for employment and other grievances. In this respect, workers are able to unite around common concerns.'[78] It needs to be clearly stated, however, that there are many employees below senior management within the state sector whose interests in finding common cause with workers is far from unambiguous.

The desire to give an inclusive definition of the working class in the public sector has had more explicit theoretical underpinnings elsewhere. Ian Gough, for instance, treats state employees such as teachers, nurses and social workers as little different from productive workers.[79] He argues that such groups are wage-labourers, working under identical conditions to industrial workers. Furthermore, Gough maintains that such state employees are essentially productive, performing surplus labour which is later transformed into surplus-value. Contrary to this position, however, these state workers do not work under the direct control of capital; nor do they produce surplus-value. That they perform a useful social function is not at issue: that the dynamic of capitalist society is centred on the advancement of capital in order to expand it is. As Fine and Harris note,[80] only the classical Marxist distinction between productive and unproductive labour can explain why in times of crisis the capitalist state cuts expenditure on welfare services.

Such criticism of Gough would not necessarily exclude teachers, nurses and social workers from the working class, but

149

an inclusion cannot be based upon such thinking. It is necessary to examine the role of such groups in the public sector labour process. Viewed from this perspective, the above-mentioned case studies show that social workers and nurses are being increasingly proletarianised. The emergence of bureaucratic methods and hierarchical organisations has seen them adopt a trade union response to this development in increasing numbers. But above these groups, as far as the real controllers of the organisations, stretches a long line of new middle-class occupations, brought into being in part because of the actual or potential resistance of employees to the work methods and conditions imposed upon them.

There is, however, a limitation shared by both Gough and those who attempt to define class membership by an exclusive concentration on the tasks performed in the production process. Both ignore the relationship of the labour process itself to a more generalised class analysis. If, for example, the function of social work is in part to individualise and constrain working-class protest, does this not affect the class position of social workers, not only abstractly, but also in their practical, day-to-day relationships with 'clients'? There is a contradiction between their position of relative powerlessness within their organisations, which might be termed their proletarian condition,[81] and the tightening definitions of acceptable practice within social work, which makes the service they perform less responsive to working-class needs and which can be seen as part of a social control function.

In a study of the class membership of teachers, Kevin Harris noted a similar development.[82] The worsening conditions of teachers and their de-skilling were associated with an expansion of their control and surveillance function over their students. He was, however, unable to examine satisfactorily the implications of this development for his class analysis. He attempted to dissolve the contradiction using the distinction made by Poulantzas between objective place in the class structure and the alignment of agents at any one time. To utilise the distinction does little other than restate in different terms the orthodox Marxist distinction between objective and subjective positions. Leaving aside the fact that 'objective place' is an a-historical construct, Harris's formulation is open to other criticisms. In particular, there seems to be no relationship between class place and class action in the production process, on the one hand, and consciousness and class action outside the workplace on the other. However, if an alignment is a bourgeois one, it is to be expected that a teacher would not only, for example, reproduce history with a conservative slant but also reinforce the hidden curriculum of the school (assembly, uniforms, individual competition) that inculcates capitalist values. If, on the other hand, there was an alignment to socialist politics one would expect, within the structure of the school and its constraints, a teacher to provide both the 'knowledge' necessary for examination purposes *and* an idea that alternative perspectives are available. Similarly, while reproducing the hidden curriculum it would be expected that the teacher could by words, looks and deeds, distance him/herself from the rules and undermine them. There is, in other words, a dialectical relationship between people's objective position in the class structure and their consciousness and action.

The growing tension felt by teachers and other public service workers discussed in this chapter could be resolved in one of two ways. The consumers of the services they provide could increasingly be seen as the cause of the problems and the tension transformed into hostility to the client or patient. Alternatively, public service workers could form an alliance with working-class groups and consumers to challenge state policies towards benefit and service provisions, thereby transforming the relationship of providers and consumers from one of superior/subordinate to a more equal and co-operative one. Such a move would signify a change in the consciousness, practice and class position of such groups. The question as to which solution will be adopted, however, is purely a speculative one, which cannot be solved in theory. It depends not only upon the decisions of state employees alone, but also the confidence and organisation of the working-class as a whole, for only the latter provides the basis which makes alternative policies viable.

5 The theory of middle-class trade unionism

The change in the structure and composition of the work-force in Britain has inevitably brought about changes in the structure and composition of British trade unions. Trade unions have adapted to the changed world unevenly and sometimes reluctantly but with no great reflection on whether the recruitment of new middle-class labour presents them with special problems. This is understandable for institutions concerned with increasing or just maintaining their membership numbers. What is more surprising is that academic and socialist theorists have on the whole accepted the changing composition of unions as not meriting a major discussion on the nature and significance of new middle-class trade unionism. The recent discussions by Poulantzas, Carchedi and others has found little resonance within theories of trade unionism. This chapter argues that for both theoretical understanding and for more practical reasons this debate about the nature of the new middle class and its relationship to white-collar trade unionism is much overdue.

The growth of white-collar unionism in Britain

As white-collar employment has grown, so too has white-collar unionism. But the growth of this unionism has been far from uniform and has not simply reflected the growth in white-collar employment. Price and Bain showed that whereas between 1948 and 1964 the growth of white-collar unionism failed to keep pace with the overall growth of white-collar employment, between 1964 and 1970 the percentage grew at a much faster rate than the employment of white-collar workers.[1] Between these latter dates total white-collar union membership increased by 34 per cent, bringing the proportion organised from 29 per cent of the total in

1964 to 38 per cent in 1970. This growth continued throughout the 1970s. By 1974 36 per cent of all trade unionists in the TUC were white-collar workers, compared with 26 per cent a decade earlier (see Table 5.1)[2]

TABLE 5.1 *Membership of selected unions (thousands) 1964 and 1975*

	1964	1975	% change
AUEW (TASS)	65.9	125.6	+ 90.7
APECCS	79.2	132.0	+ 73.0
ASTMS*	(72.8)	325.1	+346.8
CPSA	146.3	214.4	+ 46.5
NUBE	56.2	100.2	+ 78.3
NALGO	338.3	541.9	+ 60.2
NUT	249.0	266.7	+ 7.1

* 1964 figures include membership of the Association of Scientific Workers, the Association of Supervisory Staffs, Executives and Technicians, and the Guild of Insurance Officials

Not surprisingly, as the number of white-collar trade unionists has rapidly increased so too has the attention paid to the causes of that growth. There now exists a vast number of books and articles, both academic and popular, devoted to unionisation and the specific characteristics of white-collar unionism. Despite the volume of work, within sociology there has been no great diversity of approaches to explaining white-collar unionism.[3] The debate between orthodox Marxism and neo-Weberian perspectives examined in Chapter 1 is reflected within the works on white-collar trade unionism, but the major divide is between a neo-Weberian paradigm seeking to establish a relationship between social class and unionisation and an 'industrial relations' perspective that implicitly, and sometimes explicitly, denies the significance of such a relationship.[4] These perspectives are reviewed in turn.

Sociological approaches to white-collar unionism

Although the dominant approach to white-collar unionism has stemmed from neo-Weberian stratification theory, it has been formed directly in opposition to an orthodox Marxism specifically concerned with white-collar trade unionism. Orthodox Marxism regards the position of the majority of white-collar workers as analogous to that of manual workers since they both share the

153

situation of propertylessness. Within such a perspective the unionisation of white-collar workers is the logical expression of either their proletarian position or their proletarianisation. Unionisation is thus regarded as part of a unilinear development towards class consciousness.[5] This teleological vision is well illustrated by the work of V.L. Allen. Allen subsumes all white-collar workers into the same economic category as manual workers, so emphasising their potential as trade unionists, stating that:

> The fact then that employees are in different market situations does not invalidate the claim that the prime determinant of the action of all employees are the conditions involved in having to sell their labour in order to subsist. The introduction of automatic methods of work, an increase in the competitive supply of labour, or, on the other hand, anything which reduces the value of the kind of labour power he offers, affects an executive in industry as much as the man who collects his garbage. In this sense all employees irrespective of their incomes, occupational status, authority position and social background fall into the same economic category.[6]

Allen recognised in practice that however much executive employees are subjected to the same prime determinant as manual workers, their actions are affected by other mediating factors. He stated that any collective action that this group undertakes is carried out 'within the context of their own social class values'.[7] He did not, however, specify the determinants of the 'social class' which he counterposed to his economic category. Middle-class values were further used by Allen to explain the refusal of groups of white-collar workers, the majority of whom had been insulated against trade unions by 'a false social image',[8] to adopt trade union organisation. Allen argued, however, that both the discrepancy between the objective economic position of white-collar workers and their failure to recognise it and become union members, and the discrepancy between their organisation into trade unions and their failure to engage in trade union type activity, would be resolved by a proletarianisation process. Through this proletarianisation process, both the conditions of white-collar workers and their responses would more and more approximate to those of manual workers. He stated that 'the social factors, which distinguish non-manual from manual workers and which stand in the way of a general and uniform response amongst employees to the problems which arise from selling labour power in a free market, are being eroded by mechanization and economic pressures'.[9] There would therefore be an 'inexorable spread of trade unionism in Britain' and, as that unionism grew, Allen foresaw that white-collar workers, initially cautious about links with the Labour Party and affiliation to the TUC, would increasingly realise the need for wider collective support. The inhibitions of white-collar workers would dissolve and the homogeneity of labour would be achieved.[10]

Views such as this, concerning the discrepancy between white-collar workers' objective position and their consciousness of that position, had earlier led Lockwood to make his influential study *The Blackcoated Worker* published in 1958. In so doing, Lockwood provided the most direct link between theories of class and the examination of white-collar unionism. He argued directly against those explanations that see the lack of progress of trade unions amongst clerical workers as caused by the workers' false consciousness of their real situation. Rather, he stated, it is necessary to discover:

> how far, in fact, the common fact of propertylessness has resulted in common economic consequences and identical social experiences for clerk and manual worker. In this way the ground is cleared for an examination of the variations in actual class positions which may account for variations in actual class consciousness.[11]

As noted earlier, Lockwood then utilised the distinctions between market, work and status situations to detail the superior class position of clerks *vis à vis* manual workers.[12]

When turning specifically to the trade unionism of clerks, Lockwood considered that this too reflects their superior class situation. Although the trade union movement is 'the main vehicle of working-class consciousness',[13] the unions of clerks exhibit different features from the main body of unions and the joining of white-collar unions does not therefore necessarily mean that clerks are fully class conscious.[14] To clarify this point Lockwood distinguished between group consciousness and class consciousness. He argued that the extent to which clerks' organisations have progressed from the former to the latter could only be measured in an indirect way, and indicated a number of indices. They were:

> by a change in the name and purposes of a clerical association, as when a friendly society is transformed into a genuine trade union; by the adoption and use of certain types of sanctions, such as strike action for the attainment of its goals; by the affiliation of the association to the wider trade-union movement; by its identification with the political wing of the

155

Labour Movement; by sympathetic behaviour in critical 'class' situations, such as the General Strike; as well as the general social and political outlook of the members and leaders of the association.[15]

Lockwood maintained that the work situation of clerical workers differs not only from manual workers but also from each other. The most important factor influencing the extent of unionisation in the work situation is, Lockwood maintained, the degree of bureaucratisation. Bureaucratic work conditions are favourable for group action, but this is not necessarily transformed into class conscious action because of the social distance between clerical workers and manual ones. The former work in close proximity to administrative authority and their association with it means that the relationship between the clerk and the manual worker lends itself to hostility and resentment on both sides.

But if the work situation of clerical workers was, for Lockwood, the prime determinant of the extent of unionisation, it was the market situation that primarily conditions the character of the union:

> Though no one set of factors suffices to explain the spirit that animates a particular corporate body, certain broad correlations may be established between the objective situations of the clerk and the character of his trade unionism. . . . Differences in economic position have been of prime importance. The internal economic stratification of the clerical labour force has produced differences in life chances quite as significant as those which demarcate clerks from manual workers in the same industry. If bank clerks and railway clerks differ so considerably in their attitudes towards the Labour Movement, this is primarily due to the fact that they have formed the 'aristocracy' and the 'proletariat' of the blackcoated world.[16]

Setting aside the very real disagreement, outlined in Chapter 1, as to the adequacy of Lockwood's conception of class, which was largely descriptive,[17] it must be acknowledged that his detailing of the effects of variations in market and work situations was a major contribution to the understanding of white-collar unionism. The criticisms that follow are therefore relatively minor ones which might easily have been incorporated within the framework that he established.

Firstly, and overmuch has been made of this by subsequent writers, Lockwood's analysis only dealt with those organisations that declared themselves to be trade unions and it thus ignored staff and professional associations which have been and still are important in the white-collar area and which carry out many of the functions of trade unions.[18] It would have been possible, however, had Lockwood so chosen, to relate the work and market situations of clerical workers to the character of such bodies. Secondly, trade union organisations were represented by Lockwood as simply crystallisations of membership attitudes. Such a representation thereby ignores the complicated internal relations of unions and the extent to which they can be regarded as unambiguous vehicles of class consciousness. These points are taken up again below, being common to all the writers discussed in this section.

A different aspect of white-collar unionism was the object of Kenneth Prandy's study, *Professional Employees*, 1965. Prandy looked at what he considered a fairly homogeneous group of employees, scientists and engineers, in order to compare the behaviour of such people in different situations and thus to suggest the relationship between situation and behaviour. Scientists and engineers, being both middle-class professional people *and* employees, are, according to Prandy, involved in two sets of competing ideas based on status and class ideologies, and institutionalised into professional associations and trade unions. These two sorts of institutions are, therefore, integrally connected to the stratification system because, Prandy maintained, professional associations embody status ideologies that sanction the existing order to the benefit of the powerful, whereas trade unions embody class ideology that involve a challenge to it. Prandy's particular interest in middle-class occupational groups centred upon the fact that 'since they are not situated at either extreme of the class-status continuum, they are most likely to hold views and exhibit behaviour which are a mixture of the class and status types. Being in the middle they are the most obviously subject to pressures from both directions.'[19]

Prandy claimed that the determining factor in whether class or status ideologies appear as more attractive to this group is the situation in which people find themselves working:

> Many scientists and engineers are employed in positions in which they either share directly in the exercise of authority, or in which their work gives them the feeling of being close to management. They therefore accept the employers' ideology of stratification, that they are part of a graded hierarchy. This has its concrete expression in the professional associations. Of those who do not share in the exercise of authority, some will

157

experience work conditions which emphasize the fact of this subordination. These individuals are likely to have attitudes which are more of a class type, and elements of this are found within the professional associations. The more these class conditions are present, the stronger will be the class attitudes, until eventually there comes a major change. For the individual this means a recognition of a conflict of interest with the employer, an acceptance of collective bargaining and membership of a trade union.[20]

On the most general level it is possible to agree with Prandy's thesis: people with a vested interest in the perpetuation of the present order will tend to subscribe to ideologies that legitimate it and, conversely, workers who do less well are more likely to subscribe to subversive ideologies. It has to be said, however, that the way Prandy formulated his thesis was vague and sometimes confused. The relationship that he posited between class and status, for instance, is contradictory. On the one hand, he claimed to be utilising a Marxist concept of class which acknowledges the objective antagonism between workers and employers due to their respective positions in the productive process. He further agreed that within such a perspective status ideology should be seen as the legitimising ideology of the employing class which obscures the class nature of society in their own interests. But having gone so far along this road, he went on to state that class and status ideologies have the same degree of validity, i.e. their respective world-views are just as accurate, a view not in accord with the derivative status that he had earlier placed on status ideology. He was able to do this by focusing on consciousness to the detriment of considering class as an objective relationship: on the one hand there is class consciousness and, on the other, status and, as they are both only ideas in people's heads, he concluded that they are both equally worthy of consideration.[21] Consciousness was recognised as being related to situations but there was no examination of how those situations were generated.

This latter criticism can also be made with regard to Prandy's use of 'authority' as a determinant of class. It remained essentially descriptive, in no way being related to the organisation of the productive process. Furthermore, it was not even a very accurate description because Prandy, in order to relate possession and non-possession of authority to status and class ideologies, did what Dahrendorf did before him, and dichotomised it: one has or has not authority. It is true that he qualified this usage but in practice maintained it, as when he stated of a group of scientists and engineers who were AScW members; 'They are part of the class to whom orders are given rather than that which gives them.'[22] This approach also led Prandy to consider only formal authority as indicated by occupational title rather than actual roles in production. He assumed that unless someone was officially designated as management they had no control functions, stating that:

Of the 24 new members (of the AScW) from the chemicals industry, 21 are in research and development work and 3 in process control. Of those from electrical engineering, nearly a half are employed in estimating for and preparing contracts, 10 are engaged in actual production, and 7 in testing. Thirteen are doing research and development, and 1 is in management. Apart from the one exceptional individual, all the members are, as the hypothesis requires, separated from the exercise of authority.[23]

Finally, Prandy's typology was one which placed class and status views on a continuum, with the views being institutionalised into either class or status organisations. Similarly, these organisations, while being predominantly one or the other, were recognised to be not simply class or status bodies, but contaminated to a greater or less degree with their opposite ideology. Whilst noting this qualification, however, Prandy ignored it in his analysis. The joining of a trade union was claimed to indicate a major break from normal, accepted middle-class standards'.[24] Trade unions, white-collar ones included, were seen by Prandy as expressions of class consciousness. While acknowledging Lockwood's claim that 'there is no inevitable connection between unionization and class consciousness', Prandy stated that this point should not be over-stressed.[25] Prandy, therefore, saw no necessity to examine the nature of the organisations that the engineers and scientists he studied were joining.

In contrast to Prandy, R.M. Blackburn placed the character of employees' organisations at the centre of his analysis. In his *Union Character and Social Class*, 1967, Blackburn set out to give a systematic treatment to the concept of union character.[26] All too often, he claimed, unions are assumed to be identical organisations. Even Lockwood who, as Blackburn acknowledged, saw the importance of union character, failed to consider the relationship between character and union size. Blackburn claimed that rather than merely considering character as being determined by market situation, it is also necessary to look at the influence of character on the number of people prepared to join

159

an organisation. Blackburn proposed therefore that any study of unionisation – 'the measure of the social significance of unionism'[27] – should include both dimensions, the size of union membership in a particular field, expressed as a percentage of potential members, which he labelled *completeness, and* the level of *unionateness*, which measured the degree of 'commitment of an organisation to the general principles and ideology of trade unionism'.[28] Following Lockwood, Blackburn outlined a number of indices that measure the degree of unionateness of a trade union. They are:

1   It regards collective bargaining and the protection of the interest of members, as employees, as its main function, rather than, say, professional activities or welfare schemes.
2   It is independent of employers for purposes of negotiation.
3   It is prepared to be militant, using all forms of industrial action which may be effective.
4   It declares itself to be a trade union.
5   It is registered as a trade union.
6   It is affiliated to the Trades Union Congress.
7   It is affiliated to the Labour Party.[29]

The relationship between unionisation and these two dimensions – completeness and unionateness – can be expressed, Blackburn claimed, by the formula unionisation = unionateness × completeness.[30] Or expressed differently, Blackburn claimed an inverse relationship between unionateness and completeness. In any white-collar situation a highly unionate organisation might achieve low completeness, or a less unionate organisation might achieve a higher completeness, but the level of unionisation in either case will be constant. Blackburn used this formula to examine the banking industry, in which the National Union of Bank Employees (NUBE) were seeking membership in competition with rival staff associations. The more unionate NUBE had a lower completeness than the staff associations, and Blackburn concluded that:

bank clerks, the aristocracy of clerks, are as ready to join
unions as almost any other occupational groups. Their
readiness to join is, however, dependent on union character.
An organisation must be sufficiently unionate to satisfy clerks,
but this does not require a particularly high level. Beyond this,
an organisation can be more unionate only at the expense of
completeness.[31]

There are two major criticisms that are specific to Blackburn's work. Firstly, although entitled *Union Character and Social Class* his study, in fact, had little to say about social class. Blackburn recognised that

> there is a conflict of interest between labour and capital . . .
> banks have been declaring record profits while staffs have been
> working longer hours, the real value of salaries are less than in
> 1939 and for most of the time since then differentials with
> many other manual and non manual jobs have been
> declining.[32]

He never distinguished, however, between those who carried out the respective functions of labour and capital, choosing instead to regard bank workers generally as a relatively homogeneous middle class. He made this clear in his statement: 'we are concerned with a single occupation, so that to a large extent the relevant class and status comparisons are between banking and other occupations'.[33] What differences there were within the profession were regarded as status ones rather than class ones:

> There are divisions corresponding to status within the
> occupation, one of which is, in fact, that between men and
> women. Apart from sex differences the only important relation
> between the staff organisations and the banks' status hierarchy
> is the tendency for the few who rise above the level of branch
> manager to regard membership of N.U.B.E. as inappropriate.
> There is some slight evidence that managers are more likely to
> prefer the staff associations, but beyond this there was no
> evidence of status within the bank being relevant.[34]

Furthermore, Blackburn's insistence that the class position of bank clerks is identical, is central to his analysis. This can be seen in his criticism of Lockwood's perspectives, when he wrote that 'if workers have the same class position . . . they cannot be represented by organisations with different characters'.[35] Hence the need for another variable − completeness.

Blackburn did not focus on the level of unionisation which he took as given. He was largely interested in the inverse relationship of the two component parts of unionisation − unionateness and completeness. Of the situation in banking, he stated that:

> the degree of unionisation is independent of whether there is
> one or two organisations. Thus a single organisation with the
> same completeness of unionisation would also have the same
> character of unionisation; or if a character of unionisation were
> more unionate with one organisation, such as NUBE, then
> completeness of unionisation would be lower.[36]

161

In so far as the level of unionisation does change either by organisations becoming more unionate, complete or both, the reasons for such a change, the attitudes of the employers, for instance, or the structure of industry, were external to the formula. Therefore the relationship between social class and unionisation was never considered by Blackburn.

Furthermore, Blackburn's arguments are in part tautological. Having posited the formula unionisation = completeness × unionateness, at any level of unionisation, which is taken as given, the two factors have to be inversely related. Nor can such a relationship be tested, because, although expressed as a mathematical formula, there is no way of placing values on unionateness. The seven components of this concept cannot be precisely applied to organisations because where differences emerge between organisations the significance of these differences depends upon the observer's evaluation and cannot be objectively weighted. Without such a weighting, it is not possible to say whether an organisation is more unionate than another.

This latter point gives rise to a further criticism, one which can also be made of Lockwood, regarding the relationship of union members to union policies. Unions are presented as having a fixed and uniform character that members or potential members take or leave. Blackburn stated that 'character is determined by factors pertaining to the total field in which a union recruits, so that in each sub-field the level of unionateness is largely determined by factors outside the situation'.[37] This fixed character then leads to different levels of completeness in different situations.

This perspective seriously underestimates the variations in the behaviour of union members both across the union and over time. The concept of union character, for both Lockwood and Blackburn, is essentially a generalisation from the formal policies of unions at national level. This both restricts the concept and, at the same time, suggests that policies formally adopted by trade unions are simply embodiments of members' wishes transposed to national level with no mediating factors. Both Lockwood and Blackburn thus ignore trade union activity at workplace level and the fact that decision-making within trade unions is a highly complex phenomenon.

In part the perspectives of Lockwood, Prandy and Blackburn are all predicated upon an unproblematic view of consciousness which is assumed to be coherent and uniform, whether it be status consciousness, group consciousness or class consciousness, or on a continuum between the three. Consciousness is acknowledged by these writers to reflect the situation of white-collar workers, but they do not explore the generation of these situations, nor the possible tensions and developments within them. In so far as situations are recognised to be changing through, for example, increasing bureaucratisation or government support for collective bargaining, these developments are not connected to a class analysis but remain part of some evolutionary, matter-of-fact world. The possibility of rapid shifts in consciousness, of consciousness reflecting new possibilities for action in concert or opposition with other groups on major issues, is never entertained.

Reflecting an unproblematic world, these accounts of white-collar unionism are conservative and none more so than that of Blackburn. The message that white-collar trade unionists might take from his work is that no matter what they do, the level of unionisation is fixed and beyond their control. To the extent that they push for more unionate organisations they will suffer a loss of actual or potential members.

The 'industrial relations' perspective

Despite variations in the works examined, all accept that class is an important influence on white-collar unionisation and union character. This view is not universally shared. Indeed, the 'industrial relations' perspective, closely associated with the work of George Bain, amounts to a sustained attack upon attempts to link class and white-collar unionism and it is therefore necessary to examine this perspective at some length.[38] In *The Growth of White Collar Unionism*, 1970, Bain brought together a mass of statistical data with which to assess various explanations of white-collar growth. In doing so he claimed:

No significant relationship was found between the growth of aggregate white collar unionism and any of the following factors: (a) such socio-demographic characteristics of white collar workers as sex, social origins, age, and status; (b) such aspects of their economic position as earnings, other terms and conditions of employment, and employment security; (c) such aspects of their work situation as the opportunities for promotion, the extent of mechanization and automation, and the degree of proximity to unionized manual workers; and (d) such aspects of trade unionism as their public image, recruitment policies, and structures.[39]

Instead, Bain claimed that there was a significant correlation

163

between aggregate growth and three stategic variables – employment concentration, union recognition, and government action. Arguing that white-collar workers join unions primarily 'to control more effectively their work situation',[40] he foresaw an increasing necessity for trade unions for white-collar workers. This necessity would arise, he claimed, because 'as their employment becomes more concentrated and bureaucratized, individual white collar workers find that they have less and less ability to influence the making and the administration of rules by which they are governed on the job'.[41]

There was a further implication in his conclusion that:

The model suggests that white collar unions will continue to grow in the future as a result of increasing employment concentration, but that their growth will not be very great unless their recognition by employers is extended. The model also suggests that the strength of these unions will generally not be sufficient in itself to persuade employers to concede recognition; this will require the help of government. In short, the future of white collar unionism in Britain is largely dependent upon government action to encourage union recognition.[42]

Bain's attack on the relationship between class and unionisation and union character is less than convincing for a number of reasons. There is no explicit discussion of the concept of class in the work. In so far as he utilised a class model, it is a dichotomous one in which the interests of white-collar workers were aligned with those of their employers. Discussing a range of occupational groups that included professional, scientific, technical, supervisory, administrative and clerical workers, Bain remarked that:

The members of the occupational groups listed above generally see themselves as belonging more with management than with manual workers, and are generally regarded by manual workers as one of 'them' rather than one of 'us' and by employer-managers as part of the 'staff' rather than part of the 'works'. The definition of 'white collar employee' used in this study is significant precisely because it is thought to be so by industry itself.[43]

There is, however, an implicit rejection of the link between class and unionisation through his dismissal of the significance of market and status situations, key components of Lockwood's analysis. But this dismissal was only a qualified one. Having stated the three key variables of his own model, Bain continued:

This in no way implies that other factors, including some of those discounted in this study, are not of importance in accounting for less aggregate patterns of union growth. For example, while the strategic variables may explain the existence of unionism *per se* among a given group of workers, which *particular* union is successful in organizing the group may be determined by union structures and recruitment policies.[44]

Aspects connected with social stratification therefore could have limited significance at workplace level. Or, put differently, whereas class factors might affect the growth of particular unions, aggregate union growth was dependent upon employment concentration, union recognition and government action and was independent of what was happening to class relationships. If, however, these three variables are examined it is possible to see within them a reflection of the changing class position of white-collar workers. Rather than these factors being a refutation of the relationship between class and unionisation, they serve to broaden the understanding of class relationships, which are not confined to a narrow employment relationship as perceived by Bain.

Employment concentration

As seen above, Bain did acknowledge the importance of growing employment concentration and the bureaucratisation of white-collar workplaces. Despite work situation, which includes these features, being a key component of Lockwood's conception of class, Bain made no connection between class analysis and these developments. The tendency for increasing employment concentration is integrally connected to the concentration of capital, a tendency identified by Marx as central to capitalism, and bureaucratisation can be explained as part of a strategy by employers to effectively control the workplace.[45] The increasing effect of these developments upon white-collar workers has implications therefore for the class position of white-collar groups and is not simply extraneous.

Union recognition

Similarly, if class is conceptualised as relations between social groups then the refusal of employers to recognise white-collar unions can be conceived as part of a class strategy. Within such a perspective Bain's work itself loses its detached academic appearance because it advocates the recognition of white-collar trade unions as being in the best interests of capital. This advocacy took place at two levels. Firstly, in both his research paper for the Royal Commission on Trade Unions and Employers' Associations (Donovon Commission), 1967, and his book *The Growth of White Collar Trade Unionism*, 1970, Bain articulated and then dismissed employers' fears of white-collar unionism. The employers' reasons for refusing recognition to white-collar unions were reduced by Bain to four basic arguments: employers considered that unions for staff workers were unnecessary; staff unionism would have 'dire consequences'; that a particular union might not be appropriate for the occupation, firm or industry concerned; and, finally, that a union was not representative of the employees concerned. Bain concluded that where employers' arguments had any legitimacy, their fears of the consequences of union recognition were exaggerated.

The second level at which Bain argued that it was in the interests of employers to recognise white-collar unions was more positive. Not only were employers' fears largely groundless, but there were also positive advantages attached to recognition of white-collar unions. This was because 'while it is not clear whether trade unions increase or decrease industrial conflict, it is certain that they at least make it possible for the conflict to be *contained, controlled and eventually* resolved'.[46] Furthermore, arguing the merits of independent trade union organisation as opposed to staff associations which many employers preferred, Bain pointed out that this strategy, was shortsighted.

it is doubtful if they [the staff associations] are even in the best interests of the employers. It is true that these organisations may not be as aggressive as trade unions in pushing up labour costs. But it is also true they do not have some of the advantages which trade unions can offer to employers. For inasmuch as these organisations are dominated by employers, they do not provide a very effective system of two-way communications or conflict resolution. In addition they do not possess the industrial relations expertise of unions. This can be a real disadvantage to employers when large-scale changes are required.[47]

If employers, instead of resisting white-collar unions, took early positive policy initiatives, Bain maintained that their chances of achieving an orderly collective bargaining structure would be greatly increased:

in the early stages of union growth, employers can very much influence which organisations their employers choose to join. By simply recognising one organisation as opposed to another and granting it facilities to participate in job regulation, they can increase its relative attractiveness to employees and thereby promote its growth. As the CIR noted in its First General Report, 'in areas where organisation is weak, there are good opportunities for policy initiatives which allow developments to be shaped on desirable lines'.[48]

The employer, he went on to point out, by granting negotiating rights to a union as soon as it appeared to be viable, could thus avoid multi-union situations arising.

Government action

The possibility that it is in the class interests of employers, if not individually at least collectively, to recognise white-collar unions is not necessarily sufficient to convince them to do so. Bain concluded that the shift towards recognition of white-collar unions could only be achieved by government intervention. He supported this contention by a historical analysis claiming that recognition of white-collar trade unions in both private and public sectors had only come about directly or indirectly as a result of government policies and the favourable climate they created for trade unionism.[49] His formulation, however, is far from clear. At one point, for example, he conceded that union strength was 'generally a factor in getting employer associations to concede recognition' although emphasising that it was 'rarely the most important'.[50] He also recognised that 'a certain density of membership is a necessary condition for any degree of recognition to be granted', which clearly implied that a benevolent government was not sufficient in itself to achieve recognition for white-collar workers.

Nevertheless, it is clear that Bain saw the most important factor as government intervention. It has been argued that in so doing Bain seriously underestimated the influence on recognition of trade union preparedness to take industrial action. Although the climate established by governments was important, Roy Adams maintained that:

the milieu alone was not sufficient to convince reluctant employers of the wisdom and desirability of collective bargaining. Instead, the critical element in the great majority of recognition cases was the direct threat posed by the unions

167

to the operations of the employers. Where the unions failed to mount such a threat, recognition was generally withheld despite the favourability of the milieu.[51]

Furthermore, in cases where white-collar unions did appeal to the government to intervene directly on their behalf, such an intervention was much more likely to be undertaken and, if so, carried more weight, if it was backed by union action.

Correct as Adams's criticisms are, however, they remain strictly within Bain's framework, with Adams concluding that 'although Bain correctly identified the key variables responsible for white-collar union recognition, he erred in his analysis of their interaction and relative strength'.[52] This still leaves unanswered questions. Why, for instance, should the level of white-collar unionism have remained low in private industry even where employment concentration has been high, employers have been willing to grant recognition and the government has supported collective bargaining? Why did ASSET, for example, which gained recognition from the Engineering Employers' Federation in 1944, have to wait until the 1960s before it expanded rapidly? To answer these questions a different framework is clearly needed. The following sections lay down the components of such a framework.

The sociology of new middle-class unionism

The theorisation of the new middle class outlined in Chapter 2 places new middle-class workers in a contradictory class location. As such, it allows for a tension between this social grouping and both capital and labour, a tension only partially acknowledged by theories such as Prandy's which describe white-collar organisations as embodiments of either status or class ideologies. The principal architects of the theories insisting upon the specific class determinations of such social groups, Poulantzas and Carchedi, have, however, made no extension of their analyses to encompass the nature of the organisations of these groups although two other writers basing themselves on similar analyses have made contributions that are pertinent, although not altogether satisfactory. Rosemary Crompton has raised the question of the significance of the division of middle-class workers between two different forms of organisation − trade unions and staff associations. Peter Fairbrother's work examined the already noted problem of the impossibility of a simple division of work tasks into either the function of the collective worker or the function of capital, and the consequences of this for middle-class trade unionism. Before drawing together the necessary features of an analysis of new middle-class unionism, the arguments developed by these two writers are briefly examined.

Crompton argued that it is perfectly compatible with their ambiguous class position that:

> some white collar workers should see their interests as being best fulfilled by co-operation with management (or the capitalist function) — for example, in staff associations — and others in the same occupation see their collective interests as being best served by identification with the labour function — in trade unions.[53]

The adherents to neither strategy, she argued, could be said to be falsely conscious of their class interests because their very situation did not allow their interests to be clearly defined.

Although Crompton recognised the ambiguous class situation of groups of white-collar workers, her model did not allow for organisations to reflect that ambiguity. Arguing explicitly against approaches that see staff associations and trade unions on a continuum of development towards 'unionateness', she insisted that the two modes of representation represent fundamental differences in approach. She implied, therefore, that it is possible to dichotomise staff associations and trade unions as representing the capitalist function, on the one hand, and the labour function, on the other. In so doing she returned to a position little different from that of Prandy. To maintain that there may be qualitative differences in both strategy and behaviour between middle-class collective organisations is quite feasible, but to insist that these will be institutionalised into trade unions and staff associations is not correct. The ease with which some staff associations either have been assimilated into trade unions or have evolved into organisations increasingly independent of capital has shown that there is no necessary dichotomy. Conversely, as a subsequent examination of particular TUC unions shows, co-operation with capital is not just the prerogative of staff associations.

This latter point is implicit in Fairbrother's analysis of white-collar workplace trade unionism. Having made the point that whatever the merits of the conceptual distinction between the function of capital and the function of the collective worker, in practice the two are often inextricably fused. He argued that the combination of these two functions in white-collar work should be emphasised to highlight the distinctiveness of the social basis of white-collar collectivities. Furthermore, the trade unionism of such workers reflected both of these social roles:

The examination of the ASTMS workplace union suggests that the structural position of white-collar factory workers (whether primarily supervisory or technical workers) is extremely complex. These work-tasks are associated with control, whether they are employed as controllers or co-ordinators. In addition, they participate in a routine and fragmented labour process. As a result workers are involved in contradictory relational demands, that is, ambiguous structural positions. Hence, such white-collar workers employed in manufacturing industry are able to emphasise different features of these relational demands. *They are able to distinguish themselves as a sector of the workforce with a set of distinctive collective interests.*[54] (my emphasis)

Fairbrother's work amounts to an insistence that the social organisation of labour is an important determinant of the nature of workplace trade unionism. He was not concerned with the character of particular unions as such. In making his points, however, he came close to inverting the mistaken relationship between membership and union character posited by Lockwood and Blackburn. Rather than viewing union character as an external given, imposed upon workplace groups, Fairbrother implied that union character is merely a reflection of the nature of workplace unionism, itself determined by the form of the social organisation of labour. The influence of national trade union structure and policies, and particularly the influence of permanent trade union bureaucracies are thus ignored by Fairbrother.

The inadequacies of both Crompton and Fairbrother's analyses do not stem inexorably from a perspective viewing groups of white-collar workers as a new middle class. On the contrary, it is possible to adopt such perspectives and construct a satisfactory account of the main features of white-collar trade unionism. To do so, however, the perspective must address a number of key problems that have been identified in the process of reviewing the variety of sociological approaches. These comprise: (i) some account of the growth of white-collar unionism at the aggregate levels; (ii) an evaluation of the role of state intervention in white-collar union growth and its relationship to the positions adopted by employers; (iii) the relationship between white-collar trade union workplace organisation and national union character.

Industrial militancy and the growth of white-collar unionism

There are a number of factors that affect the class position of white-collar workers. Both Lockwood and Bain noted the importance of employment concentration and bureaucratisation on the growth of white-collar trade unionism (although Bain did not consider these factors related to class). A factor not stressed by either, however, was the influence of generalised industrial conflict on the position and consciousness of white-collar workers. Following the analysis of the vacillation of white-collar workers in Germany, outlined in Chapter 1, and underpinned by the analysis of the structural ambiguity of middle-class workers in Chapter 2, it would be consistent of white-collar workers to join trade unions in periods of rising industrial militancy where both the need and the confidence to take action were present. In such periods, relations which are always present between labour and capital become much more exposed than in periods of social passivity.

This contention is borne out by historical analysis. White-collar unionism developed in the tide of worker militancy immediately prior to, during, and after the First World War. Between 1911 and 1923 the number of working days lost through strikes dropped below 10 million only during the war years; in 1912 the number of working days lost amounted to 38 million and in 1921 they reached 82 million.[55] It was during this period of heightened conflict that most white-collar unions were founded. The reverse side of this relationship between unionisation and industrial conflict was also borne out by the changed fortunes of these same unions during the 1920s and 1930s when some of them, especially those in the private sector, barely survived the demoralisation and the lower levels of overt conflict. After 1923, with the exception of 1926, the year of the General Strike, the total number of days lost in any year before the Second World War never again reached 10 million, averaging 3.2 million in 1927–38.[56] This low level continued in the immediate post-Second World War period, averaging only 1.9 million days in 1939–50. Even in the years 1951–65 the average number of days lost was 3.3 million, barely above the figure for the period of the Depression.[57]

The similarity of the figures of days lost between 1951 and 1965 and those during the Depression masks radically different patterns of industrial relations at workplace level during the two periods. In the 1950s and early 1960s, a period of labour shortage and buoyant order books, the number of strikes rose to a record level, but the severity of those strikes, measured in working days lost, fell. In this situation groups of workers could win concessions without recourse to official trade union machinery and this had wide repercussions. The actions of workers during this period cannot be described as individualistic, but neither did

171

their experiences suggest the need for industry-wide, let alone class-wide, solidarity. White-collar workers felt little need to organise themselves, relying instead on promotions and increased job mobility with its prospects of improvements in salary and working conditions, rather than trade union organisation and action.

The major period of sustained white-collar union growth, from the mid-1960s to the late 1970s, once again coincided with the disintegration of industrial stability. Not only did the number of strikes continue at a high level, and even increased, but disputes became markedly longer (Table 5.2).[58] The reasons for this high level of strikes and their longer duration can be found in greater employer resistance to workers' demands in the face of a changed economic situation. Unemployment rose steadily from 1.6 per cent in 1964 to 6.1 per cent in 1977;[59] the Retail Price Index, which had increased by 15.5 points between 1956 and 1962, increased by 90 points from 1962 to 1974, and a further 82 points in the years 1974 to 1977.[60]

TABLE 5.2 *Strikes 1964–78*

	Annual average			
	1964–8	*1969–74*	*1975–6*	*1977–8*
Number of stoppages	2,262	2,924	2,149	2,526
Workers involved per strike	465	540	338	414
Days lost per striker	2.9	5.4	6.4	9.3

White-collar workers were as affected by the changed situation as manual workers. Both were drawn into trade unions in order to protect themselves and were increasingly prepared to use the strike weapon. After 1969 all workers resorted to strike action much more frequently than they had done before, but the change was much more noticeable amongst white-collar workers than amongst manual ones.[61]

Trade unionism and the state

The 'industrial relations' perspective holds as a central tenet that the expansion of white-collar trade unionism is dependent upon the intervention of government and its promotion of trade unionism. This undoubtedly has been a feature of the stances adopted by successive governments, and especially those in power during the 1960s and 1970s, the period upon which this study focuses. The Labour government, for instance, following a recommendation of the Royal Commission on Trade Unions and Employers' Associations (Donovan Commission), established in 1969 a Commission on Industrial Relations (CIR), which was empowered to hear recognition disputes and to make recommendations for their settlement. Similar provisions have been a feature of subsequent industrial relations legislation, notably the *Employment Protection Act* (EPA), 1975, and even the Conservative government's *Industrial Relations Act*, 1971, which was widely held to be hostile to the trade union movement. What is more, these provisions have been widely used by white-collar unions and there is little doubt that such provisions have done much to expand white-collar unionism. It is argued here, however, in contradistinction to the 'industrial relations' perspective, that the adoption of such policies by governments is inextricably bound up with their responses to the growing industrial instability noted above. Those policies which provide a statutory right of recognition should therefore be regarded as integrally connected to class strategies and not outside them as held by those adhering to the 'industrial relations' perspective.

The central aim of government industrial relations policies has not been the abolition of industrial conflict, but its containment and resolution through the mechanism of collective bargaining. In such a perspective, trade unions have an important and legitimate role and their incorporation into a system of joint responsibility for an orderly system of industrial relations is therefore a priority. Given the confidence and potential disruptive power of trade unions in periods of full employment and an expanding economy, especially in those sections of industry where action by comparatively few workers could have a massive 'knock-on' effect, governments saw few alternatives. Rather than the recognition provisions of industrial relations legislation being regarded merely as a reward for trade union support for the Labour Party, or a 'sweetener' to encourage the acceptance of less palatable parts of Conservative industrial relations legislation, they should be regarded as part of a wider strategy of control.[62] As conditions change so will the strategies of control. The Conservative Government has revoked the recognition provisions of the *EPA* in the *Employment Act*, 1980, but this and wider changes in orientation are beyond the consideration of this study.

The strategy of containment of industrial conflict by the incorporation of trade unions can be seen in the evidence to and report of the Donovan Commission. The need for strong, responsible trade unionism was, for example, underlined by the evidence of the Ministry of Labour:

> It may also be felt that the role played in society today by trade unions is such that it is reasonable for the state to ensure that the trade union movement represents workers everywhere in the economy, i.e. can truly speak for all work-people. There is no doubt that trade unions have come to play an increasingly important part in the nation's affairs. This . . . is witnessed by recent developments in the field of incomes policy and by their membership of the NEDC.[63]

This perspective involved the promotion and extension of collective bargaining 'as the best way of conducting industrial relations' and this in turn required 'strong trade union organisation'.[64] Because neither of these could be achieved without recognition by employers of trade unions, and because there was some reluctance on their part to do so, especially when dealing with white-collar workers, the state, it was argued, also needed to take a more interventionist role in this area.

Intervention over recognition was nothing new. The Ministry of Labour, for example, had often been called in by trade unions during recognition disputes which had failed to make progress. When so doing, the Ministry considered that it was 'bound to appear to the employer as the agent for the trade union'.[65] What was new was the nature and scale of the intervention proposed by the Donovan Commission and subsequently enacted through the CIR and the Advisory Conciliation and Arbitration Service (ACAS), which ensured that conflict between state policy and individual capitalists increased.

Workplace trade union organisation and national trade union character

There are two levels of trade unionism that require study in their own right. Firstly, the prime area of trade union activity and organisation against capital is the workplace. Here the influence of members' positions in the social organisation of the work process on their trade union behaviour is highly significant. The degree of participation in union affairs, the source and nature of conflicts with senior management, and relations with other trade unionists provide the material for an analysis of workplace trade unionism. At the second level of analysis there is the study of the general features of trade unions, their character and behaviour. At this level, trade unions are recognised to have a dynamic which is distinct from the activities and wishes of its membership.

In other words, for the permanent officials running the union, the union appears to have its own organisational needs. These two levels of analysis come together when examining the existence and importance of the trade union bureaucracy. It is necessary briefly to outline the relationship of rank and file trade union activity to the official organisation because to talk of middle-class trade unionism makes an implicit contrast with working-class trade unionism. The general portrayal of white-collar unions as conservative suggests that manual worker unions are instinctively militant and ignores both the economic context in which all unions operate and the partially successful attempts by employers and the leadership of unions to institutionalise conflict.

The emergence of a trade union bureaucracy, comprising full-time, professional trade union officers, the 'Civil Service of the trade union world' the Webbs called them,[66] began after 1850. Their emergence reflected the shift in leadership 'from the casual enthusiast and irresponsible agitator to a class of permanent salaried officials chosen from out of the rank and file of Trade Unionists for their superior business capacity'.[67] The social existence of these leaders contrasted markedly with their members, and, according to the Webbs, this was reflected in their conception of their role. The Webbs quoted the assessment of a union member of the officials distinct outlook in *History of Trade Unionism*:

To the ordinary Trade Unionist the claim of the workman is that of Justice. He believes almost as a matter of principle, that in any dispute the capitalist is in the wrong and the workman in the right. But when, as District Delegate, it becomes his business to be perpetually investigating the exact circumstances of the men's quarrels, negotiating with employers, and arranging compromises, he begins more and more to recognise that there is something to be urged on the other side. There is also an unconscious bias at work. Whilst the points at issue no longer affect his own earnings or conditions of employment, any disputes between his members and their employers increase his work and add to his worry. The former vivid sense of the privations and subjection of the artisan's life gradually fades from his mind; and he begins more and more to regard all complaints perverse and unreasonable. With this intellectual change may come a more invidious transformation. . . . He goes to live in a little villa in a lower middle-class suburb. The move leads to him dropping his workmen friends; and his wife changes her acquaintances. With the habits of his new neighbours he insensibly adopts more and more of their ideas.

175

> . . . His manner to his members undergoes a change. . . . A great strike threatens to involve the Society in desperate war. Unconsciously biased by distaste for the hard and unthankful work which a strike entails, he finds himself in small sympathy with the men's demands, and eventually arranges a compromise, on terms distasteful to a large section of the members.[68]

That such developments were, if not desirable, inevitable was also the conclusion of the German sociologist, Robert Michels in his *Political Parties*, 1911. Despite their democratic and anti-authoritarian origins, trade unions were, according to Michels, as prone as other types of organisation to 'the iron law of oligarchy'.[69] The rule of the few succeeded because the leaders could claim specialised knowledge. Not only were they therefore difficult to remove, but they were also able to impose upon the organisation their own policies.

The emergence and consolidation of a conservative layer of officials took place during a period of relative social stability. Compared to Chartism, the horizons of the working class were extremely limited[70] and consequently the conflict between members and full-time officers was never sustained on a high level. Just as the fundamental divergence of the interests of workers and capitalists only becomes apparent in periods of crisis, so the conflict between members and trade union officials is best demonstrated in periods of major social conflict. This conflict frequently expresses itself in the formation of rank and file movements. As Brian Pearce has argued, 'The source of rank and file movements is the conflict between the struggle of the working class for better conditions and a new social order, and the increasing reconciliation between the leaders of the trade unions and the capitalist class, their growing integration into the upper reaches of bourgeois society.'[71] One such period was that between 1910 and 1914. The conflict was further reinforced by the agreement of trade union leaders virtually to suspend trade unionism for the duration of the First World War and led to a powerful shop stewards' movement in the engineering industry.[72] It found further expression in 1924 when under Communist Party leadership the National Minority Movement was formed.

It took the defeat of the 1926 General Strike to break the confidence and combativity of the rank and file in relationship both to capital and to their own leaders. The trade union leadership was instrumental in that defeat, showing in the process that what united left- and right-wing leaders was of far greater importance than that which divided them: left and right directed their energies towards compromises and not victory. The eventual surrender of the leadership took place in spite of a movement amongst their membership that was daily growing in strength, so much so that it is estimated that on the day after the strike was called off an extra 100,000 people joined the strike.[73]

The importance of trade union bureaucracies varies with the historical situation. Their importance in the 1930s stemmed from the demoralisation of their members in the General Strike and the fear caused by high levels of unemployment. Members unable to defend themselves looked to full-time officers. This tendency was reinforced in those industries where national collective bargaining was consolidated (building, engineering and railways). The role of bureaucracies in opposing rank and file action was of little consequence because of lack of activity at factory level.

This situation was transformed again after the Second World War. Full employment and the growth of the number of shop stewards, particularly in the engineering industry, led to a growth of disputes, the vast majority of them unofficial and of short duration. The attitude of official leaderships was of little importance when disputes were concluded often before officials even heard of them (Table 5.3).[74] As the growth of the economy slowed, however, and employer resistance stiffened, the official machinery of the union could no longer be ignored. The more severe the crisis, the longer and more defensive the struggles of workers, the more important is the role of the bureaucracy. Not only is finance for strikes a greater need but in order to win there has to be far greater mobilisation of support. The confidence and combativity of workers was initially reflected in official strikes but as unemployment undermined confidence the bureaucracy proved once again to be a conservative force. Even those whose ascent to leadership was based upon a movement for (limited) democratisation of union structures, notably Jack Jones, the

TABLE 5.3 *Patterns of strikes*

	No. of workers involved (000s)	No. of working days lost (000s)	Average no. of days per worker on strike
1914–18	3,159	26,460	8.4
1919–26	11,069	356,330	32.2
1927–38	3,669	38,590	10.6
1953–64	12,975	43,540	3.3

General Secretary of the Transport and General Workers Union, ended up as supporters of the Social Contract with its centralised restriction on wage rises.[75]

It is not the purpose here to echo the cry of 'sell-out' and to cast doubt on the good intentions of leaders. Such an emphasis implies that a more resolute leadership could withstand the pressures. Rather the analysis is intended to concentrate attention of the nature of trade unions and their internal relations, including the relationship of convenors and other lay officials with their members. The nature and importance of these relationships cannot be captured by a simple dichotomy between rank and file and bureaucracy. As Richard Hyman has argued:

> 'Bureaucracy' is in large measure a question of the differential distribution of expertise and activism: of the *dependence* of the mass of union membership on the initiative and strategic experience of a relatively small cadre of leadership − both 'official' and 'unofficial'. Such dependence *may* be deliberately fostered by an officialdom which strives to maintain a monopoly of information, experience and negotiating opportunities, and to minimise and control the collective contacts among the membership. But . . . the 'bad side of leadership' still constitutes a problem even in the case of a cadre of militant lay activists sensitive to the need to encourage the autonomy and initiative of the membership.[76]

It is not being claimed, therefore, that the great mass of workers are spontaneously militant and that they are constantly held back by a conservative caste of officials. It is the case, however, that the more habitual and institutional roles of officials, including those at factory level, may act as a brake on action when anger and militancy grip the shopfloor. Or as Hyman puts it, 'though often politically and socially more advanced or progressive than many of their members, [full-time officials] frequently perform a conservative role in periods of membership activism and struggle'.[77]

Middle-class workers, like their working-class counterparts, are members of trade unions for the purposes of collective bargaining. Conflict with their employers, however, is different in a number of respects and this in turn affects the relationship they have with their official union machinery. Firstly, conflict is less frequent than between manual workers and employers. It has been calculated that, for instance, if white-collar workers went on strike as frequently as manual workers then there would be two-thirds more strikes in the country as a whole.[78] This lower level of strike activity can be seen from Table 5.4.[79] Moreover, the conflict that does take place is less likely to be over issues of control of working methods because these are less often under attack. Conflict arises not so much over work tasks, which tend to be high trust ones, such as monitoring the work of others, but over the rate of pay for performing such tasks. This is illustrated in Table 5.5.[80] These figures may well underestimate the different preoccupations of middle class and working class trade union action because the figures relate to all staff workers, some of whom will not be middle class, having no supervisory duties or other functions of capital to perform. As a consequence of this the working-class groups within the staff worker category may account for a large proportion of the strikes by staff workers over working methods.

TABLE 5.4 *Number of strike days per 1000 employees in manual and non-manual groups (three-year moving averages 1966–73)*

Occupational group	1966–8	1967–9	1968–70	1969–71	1970–2	1971–3
Manual	194	249	380	386	452	419
Non-manual	16	21	46	55	69	49

TABLE 5.5 *Strikes in Federation engineering companies 1974 and 1975*

Causes of strikes	% Staff workers		% Manual workers	
	1975	1974	1975	1974
Pay-wage rates and earning levels	72.7	69.8	48.4	56.2
Working conditions and supervision	0.0	3.7	4.7	3.9
Manning and work allocation	2.3 } 3.9	3.0 } 11.0	13.2 } 24.1	12.2 } 19.8
Dismissals and other disciplinary measures	1.6	4.3	6.2	3.7

The different focus of the conflict that middle-class labour has with its employers involves much less of a change in its relationships with capital than does working class conflict. Not only does the conflict not centre upon working methods but its nature lends itself to negotiations by full-time officers rather than having to resort to guerrilla-type campaigns such as go-slows and work-to-rules that are more common practices on the shopfloor. This lack of challenge to the day to day commands of capital has two further consequences. There has been less need to institutionalise conflict *via* the growth of workplace-based union hierarchies. The exception to this is in the public sector where unions tend to recruit both new middle-class and working-class members. But even here the features are rather different. The activities of new middle class members in workplace union organisations tend not to be in the direction of mediating and controlling the actions of members of their own grades so much as those of working-class members. As has been noted elsewhere, the occupation of union positions by managerial workers in the public sector often proves to be an extension of managerial control into the union itself.[81] The second consequence of the type of activity in which middle-class members engage is that disputes when they do occur are more likely to be official.[82]

This comparative inactivity by the membership and high involvement by white-collar trade union officials frequently produces contrasting perspectives from the two groups. Full-time officials are only called into situations about which their members feel some sense of grievance. Such grievances arise infrequently in most workplaces but, because the full-time officials cover many workplaces, that which is episodic for the membership is the staple constituent of the work of full-time officials. The latter, therefore, although party to compromises with employers, work in a situation where conflict with employers is regular and, as a result, have a clear conception of dichotomy of interests. Such views are often reinforced by the officials' own previous membership of trade unions, particularly, as is often the case, of manual worker unions, and, in many cases, by a commitment to the trade union movement in general that played a part in the officials taking up the job in the first place.

Most of the time, therefore, groups of members do not have the same consciousness of conflict as their officials, tending rather to see management as a reserve bank of authority from which they can draw to reinforce their roles in the workplace. This is a feature about which many full-time officials feel uncomfortable, yet which is rarely discussed publicly by unions that organise middle-class labour. Where acknowledgment is made of this lack of trade union consciousness it tends to be made indirectly, emphasising their members' 'responsibility' and the importance to the members of rational demands as opposed to calls for action. Clive Jenkins, the General Secretary of ASTMS, and Barrie Sherman, its Research Director, pointed to this feature when remarking that 'the official has to argue a sophisticated case forcefully whilst, at the same time, stimulating and orchestrating possible industrial action amongst members for whom this is an alien tactic'.[83]

One further point needs reiterating. Any comparison between the character of middle-class and working-class trade unionism will be weighted towards similarity. Middle-class unions deal with only one aspect of their members relationship at work − that of conflict with their employer. Because of the structural position of middle-class labour this aspect of their work-life may be of only minor importance. Most of the day-to-day problems that emerge for middle-class labour are likely to be caused by the resistance of working-class trade unionists to the function of capital rather than action of the employer against the interests of middle-class labour. Collective action under trade union auspices is not appropriate in these circumstances. A trade union response would have to view the resistance of other workers as legitimate. Occasionally middle-class labour attempts to use trade union organisation to process grievances against shopfloor workers but most trade unions, and certainly those affiliated to the TUC, are sufficiently clear that to do so is outside their purpose and would threaten their institutional relations with other organisations. Where middle-class labourers have such problems, therefore, they are left to deal with them behind the back of the union.

6 The practice of middle-class unionism

The changes in the nature of the labour process and the structure of control within employing organisations have brought about changes in the work-forces of capitalist societies. In particular there has been a growth of middle-class labour staffing expanded managerial hierarchies. As earlier chapters have attempted to show, these hierarchies are not stable and free from conflict and one measure of the conflict inherent in these organisations is the increasing tendency of managers and supervisors to join associations which protect their interests. These associations reflect the widely varying positions of managerial employees within hierarchies of control, differing between those which are synonymous with the interests of capital, such as the British Institute of Management (BIM), and others, such as the Association of Scientific, Technical and Managerial Staffs (ASTMS), which have in membership not only managerial employees, but also draughtsmen/women, technicians, typists and clerks. Of the associations, those affiliated to the TUC tend to represent lower and middle management, and those with little trade union orientation higher layers of management. In contrast to the claims of certain sociologists, notably Prandy and Crompton, membership of organisations unambiguously declaring themselves trade unions does not simply reflect in managers a proletarian orientation. It also reflects an attempt to arrest the process of proletarianisation. In other words, the contradictory problems of middle-class labour, arising from its role in production, are also manifested in the policies adopted by its trade unions. This relationship is qualified to the extent that trade union policies are a product of a variety of processes and are not simply a result of the class composition of the membership. Nevertheless, the influence of the social relations of members on policies is apparent in the following case studies.

Organisations of managers

The British Institute of Management

The British Institute of Management (BIM) was established in 1948 with public funds. Its aims were to take the lead in promoting research into management problems, to co-operate in the development of training and educational schemes, and to undertake widespread propaganda concerning good management practice.[1] But in spite of the fact that it maintained a steady growth of members, increasing from 14,000 in 1968 to over 50,000 in 1976, there was increasing disquiet from within the Institute about the limited role that its aims and charitable status allowed it to play. It was felt that the BIM needed to establish itself as a major voice in the discussions on national and industrial matters which were dominated by the Confederation of British Industry (CBI and the TUC). Consequently, in 1976, the BIM shed its charitable status, hived-off its professional-style educational and research work into a new organisation, The BIM Foundation, and launched itself as a representational body. This change in direction, however, has been less than an unqualified success, for reasons that are directly related to the contradictions inherent in the position of many managers. They work for and help control the companies represented by the CBI and are thus closely identified with capital because of their function. Within these companies, however, they undoubtedly need to be organised into a coherent voice in order to make their opinions heard, a task which the BIM will not undertake. Hence the growing attraction of groups of them to trade unions, a number of which are keen to recruit them.

The BIM has rejected the representation of managers' interests to employers, restricting its orientation to lobbying the government of the day and issuing public pronouncements. There was a hint in 1978 that it might be considering a link-up with various non-TUC management associations.[2] Under such a scheme all negotiations and representations would have continued to be conducted by the individual associations, with the BIM making national representations to government on their behalf. The appeal of such a scheme was undoubtedly great, enabling as it would the BIM to make gains in both political authority and membership. The management associations would have gained from the strength of the BIM's established reputation. It was, however, not to be, because there were, and still are, considerable constraints on the BIM's freedom to move in this direction. Not least of these is its lack of financial independence from capital. Its rules allow not only for individual membership, but also for corporate membership, and the 12,000 or so employers in this category in 1978 ensured that the Institute was directly reliant on continued company support for a substantial part of its income.

The close links that the BIM has with capital are also apparent in its choice of leading personnel. Frequently its leadership has been interchangeable with that of organisations of capital. Lord Watkinson, its president in 1976, for example, moved on to become president of the CBI, and Sir Derek Ezra, who replaced him, was also on the council and president's committee of the CBI, as well as being a member of the Institute of Directors. The BIM has tended, therefore, to regard the centres of control with deference and respect, rather than work in opposition to them. It has chosen as speakers at its conventions leading industrialists like Sir John Partridge, a past president of the CBI, and Sir Jack Callard, former chairman of ICI, rather than people with whom middle and lower managers can directly identify. Given the nature of the leadership and its orientation, it is not surprising that much of the Institute's material reads 'like a precis of the CBI's own published views'.[3] Where it has made policy initiatives, such as setting up a joint working party, with the National Economic Development Organisation in 1978, within which it could express its views on the goals of industrial strategy, it has done so within a managerial framework, rather than in the interests of managers. As the then President, Sir Derek Ezra, put it: 'When the industrial strategy is formulated we are the people, those of us who are in industrial management, who will have to carry it out.'[4] This orientation was even clearer in the Institute's decision to launch its Strategy, Performance, and Utilisation of Resources (SPUR) campaign. The aim was to evaluate, through countrywide conferences and discussions, how managers could best contribute to the efficiency of the economy. In other words, the Institute's approach could be characterised as managers not asking what their company could do for them, but rather what they could do for their company. It is still, therefore, very much the British Institute of Management, rather than the British Institute of Managers.

Staff and managers' associations

The BIM's restriction of its activities to national lobbying and its refusal to organise managers at company level independently from and against their employers has not meant that managers have gone unrepresented. A plethora of competing organisations, from staff associations to white-collar sections of predominantly manual worker based and TUC-affiliated unions, has emerged and these now compete with each other in order to recruit Britain's managers. The nature of these organisations varies considerably, but evidence concerning the motives of managers who join is quite consistent: they want greater participation in the decisions that are taken by their companies. This demand for greater participation is not always accompanied by formal organisation into a representational body. An inquiry by Esso into their consultative arrangements, for example, revealed that their managers felt that they were not consulted as much as the manual workers.[5] The informal consultations that were supposed to take place with managers through line authority organisation simply did not happen. Nevertheless, managers shunned the idea of creating a formal representational agreement by joining a trade union. They preferred instead improved arrangements to allow them, at whatever level they worked, to discuss ideas and problems with their peers and superiors.

Whether such arrangements can work when not enforced by formal organisation is open to doubt. The significance of these moves by managers is that they are part of a process of detachment from identification with capital. In a survey of executive grade employees in West Germany conducted in 1971–2, Heinz Hartmann found that over half the managers interviewed believed that they could not be subsumed into interest groups that coincided with either employers or workers.[6] On the contrary, they believed that they constituted a separate interest group, a 'third force'. Consistent with this view, over one-half of the managers requested more formal participation in decision-making. Hartmann saw in such views definite signs of group formation, with 'a fairly clear conception of common and specific interests' and a 'surprisingly strong propensity to organise'.[7] Furthermore, he mentioned that there was a willingness to bring the weight of such organisations to bear on top management, even if there was also a tendency to shy away from open conflict and to display a preference for 'discursive confrontation'.[8]

This tendency of managers to develop a group identity in contradistinction to both capital and labour is encapsulated in the formation of staff associations. Greg Bamber noted no reluctance on the part of managers to form their own collective organisations.[9] There is, however, a great deal of variation in the nature of the staff associations so formed. Some have been formed on the initiative of employers, or at least with their active assistance, as a response to the possibility of managers joining a TUC-affiliated union. The advocacy of this approach is not restricted to employers. In a survey of over 1,000 managers working for a major British company, David Weir found that 76 per cent of male managers and 67 per cent of female managers considered that they were insufficiently consulted on matters that directly affected them, and an overall 64 per cent wanted a more formal consultative system. He pointed out, however, that:

> even though there are some slightly negative features of management attitudes to the company, it is not to be taken for granted that there will necessarily issue an overt support for potential unionism . . . the greatest single area of agreement in terms of new procedures for consultation and new mechanisms for participation lie in the area of company based staff associations, rather than in extending into the company the white collar unions which are organising in the industry at large.[10]

Noting a widespread belief within the company that something had to be done to ensure a move towards greater participation, such as more formal procedures of consultation, and more opportunities for employees to become involved in policy formation, Weir concluded that if 'the company can meet these demands without moving the whole way towards full-blooded unionism, it may just move to a situation which would satisfy the majority of the staff in these grades'.[11]

There is increasing evidence that organisations formed on the initiatives of employers often do not remain dependent on employers and not infrequently end up merging with TUC affiliates. If they are to satisfy managers' aspirations they have to be seen to be independent and effective. The National Unilever Managers' Association commented that:

> It has been suggested that some companies have pre-empted the genuine unionisation of managers by establishing controlled managers' associations which masquerade as independent unions. No doubt there are examples of such marriages of convenience but they must be regarded as a temporary expedient which cannot survive in the long term.[12]

Indeed, it is much more common nowadays for independence from employers to be a feature present at the formation of employee organisations. This is because the criteria for registering as an independent union under the *Trade Union and Labour Relations Act*, 1974 debar employer support, and such registration is necessary to gain access to the provisions of the *Employment Protection Act*, 1975. This is not to say that given the choice between a company-based staff association and a much broader based TUC-affiliated union the employer will not look more favourably upon the former, but it does mean that it is not always easy to draw a hard and fast line between a staff association and a trade union.

Despite the growing independence of staff associations, they still tend to be unstable and short-lived organisations. This situation is integrally connected to what may be considered the main distinguishing feature of staff associations, i.e. their belief in the sufficiency of purely internal company organisation. This in turn is partly a reflection of the lack of inclination on the part of managers seriously to challenge the power of their employers. When no significant gains are made by a staff association, interest is hard to sustain. Even if managers organised in staff associations do possess the inclination to press their claims upon employers, internal organisation normally severely restricts the resources available to do so. One of two developments therefore tends to take place after the initial organisation of staff associations. Aware that it is not possible to run the organisation effectively without proper back-up facilities, and that the wider influence of such organisations on their own is negligible, certain staff associations either attempt to liaise with similar bodies or merge with TUC affiliates.

A number of managers' associations, some more widely based than others, have made these moves. Perhaps the most prominent and important example of an organisation taking the first course is that of the Association of Managerial and Professional Staffs (AMPS). The Association has 10,000 members, of whom 70 per cent are managers, largely located in the chemical industry, and particularly in ICI. The Association, which claims to have agreement with over fifty companies, views itself as a 'third force' in industry, as is shown by the statement made by its president when criticising the Bullock Report:

Both the representatives of employers and of the TUC on the Bullock Committee appear to have made the assumption that managers and professional staffs will automatically always align themselves with the employer, and do not, therefore, need separate representation on the proposed new Boards of directors.

The fact is that managers are neither employers' men nor followers of the policies of unions representing other grades. They are their own men, with their own distinctive and

> informed views on the way their firms should be run. They
> certainly identify with the interests of their companies. . . . But
> they also have expert knowledge and readiness to criticise the
> way in which their companies are being run and, if necessary,
> to identify themselves also with organisations which will enable
> them to make that criticism more effective.[13]

This approach recognises the need to protect managers' interests against capital but also displays a belief that the ultimate aims of its members are in accord with those of their employers. Not surprisingly, therefore, the Association stresses its moderation through its faith in arbitration, legal remedies and rational arguments, as opposed to industrial action. Such a view of unionism calls for little commitment from its members. As a recruiting leaflet puts it:

> Think of union membership like belonging to a motoring
> organisation − some day you're almost sure to be stranded by
> the roadside.
> Relationships can get over-heated too − like motorcars.
> Why spoil your future with a rash remark when, for example, a
> union can negotiate the best conditions for your ambition to
> thrive in independently, avoiding personal conflict.[14]

By projecting itself as a moderate organisation, the Association attempts to distance itself from the image of manual trade unions. It reinforces this attempt by barely disguised hostility to such unions: 'AMPS is recognised by professional institutes. Professional managers, engineers and scientists need the understanding of professional representatives. What would a broom-pusher know about professional ethics?'[15] The Association sees managers' problems as arising not only from their employers but also from shopfloor unions, as is shown in the following report in its journal:

> A member has proposed that AMPS should undertake a survey
> of occupational health risks to managers facing day-to-day
> implications of industrial relations legislation.
> The object of the survey would be to discover whether
> managers suffered more from 'stress' diseases such as heart
> attacks, cancer, suicide and mental disturbances.
> 'We claim that the workload and stress of managers has been
> increased and possibly the health hazards for managers
> handling militant trade unions are as great as those of workers
> handling toxic chemicals', comments Dr Maurice Green,
> president.[16]

188

The Association was not satisfied with its ability to influence wider events and therefore, in 1978, took the initiative in forming the Federation of Industrial Management and Professional Associations (FIMPA), representing 33,000 managers and professionally qualified employees, in order to press its own views and those of similar organisations on the government. The possibility of creating a unified association out of the nine participatory organisations must also have been apparent to AMPS, which provided the chairman to FIMPA (who was also president of AMPS), although as yet no such developments have taken place. On an even wider front, AMPS also participates, as does FIMPA, in the Managerial Professional and Staff Liaison group (MPLSG). Founded in 1978, after the British Medical Association (BMA) had been informed, when making representations to the government, that it was not speaking on behalf of a sufficiently large number of people, MPLSG claims to represent a combined membership of 500,000. Once again AMPS provided the chairman of the new organisation, in the form of the executive secretary of AMPS.

Despite the growth of non-TUC management associations, however, the majority of managers who are in collective organisations are in TUC unions, either having been recruited directly into them or having joined associations that subsequently merged with TUC affiliates. Managers in the steel industry, for example, formed the Steel Industry Management Association (SIMA) in 1968. The experience of this Association suggests that the prognosis for those associations adhering to a 'third force' strategy is not hopeful. Having 12,000 members, mainly in the nationalised sector of the steel industry, the Association was a well organised and cohesive force. It also advocated the 'third force' concept most explicitly, as an article on the Association and its General Secretary detailed:

> Bob Muir, SIMA's General Secretary has a vision. He wants to see the managers of this country develop into a third force. . . . It would be a force positioned between capital and labour. It is essential, he says, that all the managers of an organisation should belong to the same union. That stage being reached, he foresees ultimately a separate, coherent voice for the management profession. For want of a better label he would call it a Congress of Managers which would also bridge the gap between TUC-affiliated unions and non-affiliated unions. It would speak for managers of all industries.[17]

Elsewhere, the General Secretary made a similar point when he

189

commented that the Bullock Report 'has also failed to accept that managers are the separate "third force" in industry and should have their right of participation'.[18]

The Association believed that managers were in a unique position and deserved special treatment by the employer. In accordance with these beliefs the Association adopted 'as a principle, the concept of the "Managerial Obligation", a concept which can be embraced by every true manager'. This policy stated:

1   Managers do not sell their services to their enterprise either by time (e.g. by the hour, by the shift, etc.) or on a piece-rate; Managers provide a quality of service in fulfilling a responsibility to make events happen in a way which will achieve the objectives laid down by the policy-making Directorate.

2   This quality of service by Managers as the outstretched arm of the policy-making Board involves Managers in a very close and interdependent relationship with the Directors who trust the Managers to put loyalty to the common enterprise above most other considerations.

3   In fulfilling their responsibilities to make events happen in order to achieve the objectives of the enterprise, Managers have to exercise substantial powers of individual judgement and discretion.

4   In turn, Managers allow between themselves that there must be some degree of the right of the individual to exercise conscience in any situation where the individual's loyalty to the enterprise might be in conflict with his obligation of loyalty within any voluntary association of a trade union nature.

5   Thus, whilst a managerial trade union may formally require through its Rules that Members shall, inter alia, comply with the objectives and obligations of their Association, there is an unwritten understanding that a particular case of non-conformity on grounds of conscience would, given acceptable justification, be excused from penalty.

6   At the same time, if managerial motivation and effectiveness are not to be vitiated, it is expected of employers that they shall respond to these standards by demonstrating a genuine willingness to negotiate with integrity, thereby avoiding any provocation of managerial trade unions to resort to forms of sanctions traditionally adopted by craft and shopfloor trade unions.[19]

The policy, while obviously weighted against industrial action, does not rule it out and, while stressing managers' links with the

Directorate, the union was nevertheless serious about its independence, as its General Secretary made clear:

I would separate the operational manager from the company board. As soon as an operational manager is in a separate group his capability to apply sanctions becomes credible, and operational managers must be prepared in the last analysis to apply sanctions, either to offset the industrial muscle of the shop floor unions, or to prevail in the interests of the managers on the decisions of the employers.[20]

Despite a viable organisation and a willingness ultimately to take industrial action, such as a successful work to contract and job description in 1974, SIMA was, nevertheless, unable to make much headway on issues that it considered important. In particular it failed to gain a seat on the British Steel Corporation Board, alongside the TUC unions. It, therefore, subsequently changed its orientation. Instead of attempting to steer a course between capital and labour it applied in 1978 for membership of the TUC. Its application was rejected and the TUC recommended that it sought affiliation with an appropriate TUC union. It seems unlikely that the TUC had in mind the Electrical, Electronic, Telecommunication and Plumbing Union (EETPU), but in 1980 the two executives agreed merger terms.[21] In so doing, SIMA followed a route already taken by the Association of Managerial Electrical Executives and the UK Association of Professional Engineers which had joined the EETPU. Such a change in orientation, while indicating SIMA's changed evaluation of the possibilities of building a 'third force', does not necessarily indicate a new-found solidarity with fellow workers. This latter point was illustrated by SIMA's actions during the 1980 steelworkers' strike, which was widely considered to have been engineered by the British Steel Corporation (BSC) and the government. SIMA issued a secret internal memo advising their members what to do in the event of a strike. It read as follows:

MEMBERS OF SIMA should
1 CARRY OUT their normal duties and give assistance as is necessary in all strikes (whether official or unofficial) involving members of other trade unions.
2 CO-OPERATE with the Corporation by undertaking extraordinary duties in order to maintain production operations.
3 GIVE ASSISTANCE on such additional duties as are necessary . . . this automatically includes security protection of plant (this normally being the province of ISTC members).

191

4   IF members of ISTC opt to return to work then it is part of managerial obligations for SIMA members to carry through whatever production etc. operations that may be feasible.[22]

A TUC union that is itself based upon a managerial membership, the Electrical Power Engineers Association (EPEA), has also been particularly active in trying to attract non-TUC managerial associations. Indeed, the lengths to which it has gone in order to do so have made it far from popular among its fellow affiliates. Based exclusively in the electrical supply industry, there was little chance for the EPEA to increase its membership much beyond its 1976 membership of 35,000. In that year, however, it started to recruit managers and professional engineers outside this industry. It had an immediate, if not major, success when the 8,500-member Association of Supervisory and Executive Engineers decided to merge. This in turn enabled the union to launch the Engineers and Managers Association (EMA) as a federal body in the following year. Towards the end of 1977 the Shipbuilding and Allied Industries Management Association (SAIMA), with 1,600 members, became a constituent part of the EMA. In 1979, the Association was able to extend its influence into the aerospace industry when the British Aerospace Staffs Association, with 5,000 members, voted to merge, followed by the 450 members of the BAC Professional Staffs Association at British Aerospace's Preston plant. Not surprisingly, this expansion outside the EPEA's traditional recruiting field has not been welcomed by those TUC unions with aspirations to recruit shipbuilding and aerospace management staffs. A bitter public battle has been conducted, particularly between the EMA and TASS, with frequent recourse being made to the Bridlington disputes procedure of the TUC and, occasionally, the High Court.

The traditional base of the EMA and its policies make it an ideal pole of attraction for organisations which, although they decide that TUC affiliation is a necessity, wish to retain as much of their conservative character as possible. The Association's rules provide it should not be affiliated to any political party, it believes in a sound system of differentials, and it also believes that unionisation can strengthen the managerial function. In this latter regard it has stated:

In a recent well published case involving serious unofficial action in the Supply Industry, the Association unequivocally supported the industry's management, and therefore its own members running the power stations, in the assertion that it was their responsibility to run the industry. The Association refused point blank to yield this responsibility to an unofficial shop stewards' committee. As a union, essentially of managers at different levels, we are from time to time likely to find ourselves in the situation of supporting top management's resolve to carry out the policies to which they have committed their managers in their line role; and it is in this country's interest that we should.[23]

The Association of Scientific, Technical and Managerial Staffs

The Association of Scientific, Technical and Managerial Staffs (ASTMS) is the largest of the private sector unions recruiting predominantly new middle-class labour. The membership comes from a wide variety of industries including engineering, chemicals, insurance and banking and stood at over 400,000 in 1982. The heterogeneity of the membership derives not only from the wide span of recruitment but also from the widely differing positions of authority which its members occupy. ASTMS claims senior managers, as well as engineers, scientists, supervisors and clerical staff. In any study of the relationship between social class and trade union character, therefore, the Association is of particular importance.

Not the least important feature of the union is that, despite the social class composition of its membership, and contrary to traditional models which associate white-collar unions with conservatism, the Association has a reputation for militancy and for being politically inclined to the Left. As such it appears to offer support for those theorists arguing that the joining of trade unions by sectors of middle-class labour reflects a proletarian response to their problems. A closer examination of the policies and structure of the union does not, however, bear out this view.

The appeal of ASTMS

ASTMS has been extremely successful in attracting members, growing by 1,055 per cent between 1948 and 1974.[24] This growth suggests that major aspects of the ideology of the Association accord with those of large sectors of middle-class labour. There is some evidence that for a brief period in the mid-1960s the Association's predecessor, the Association of Supervisory Staffs, Executives and Technicians (ASSET), believed that its growth resulted from the proletarianisation of middle-class labour which was then about to form the vanguard of the trade union movement.[25] Such a view was firmly superseded by one based upon organising white-collar workers as a middle class. This latter orientation involved making allowances for three features of the consciousness of middle-class labour: that it was more reluctant to take collective industrial action than the working class; that it felt superior to manual workers; and its resentment over what it considered to be the relatively higher pay and improved conditions won by manual trade unions.

The association has recognised the reluctance of potential members to take industrial action by presenting a model of trade unionism that requires the minimum of commitment from them. Trade union membership is presented as a form of insurance policy to be referred to only when there is an annual salary claim or threat of redundancy: 'The insurance industry recently advertised by using the slogan "get the strength of the insurance companies around you". In this modern capitalist world it would be remiss of the white collar workers not to take that advice in industrial terms and join a trade union.'[26] Within such a view of trade unionism there is little emphasis on the self-activity and organisation of the membership. Indeed, trade unionism is presented as an alternative to collective action. This view was clearly displayed by Clive Jenkins, the General Secretary of ASTMS, and Barrie Sherman, the Research Director, in their *Collective Bargaining* published in 1977:

> If you feel unwell you visit a doctor; if you have toothache you visit a dentist; if you are involved in litigation you visit a solicitor; if collective bargaining needs to be done, workers approach a trade union. We live in the age of the professional and in the case of trade unions this applies not only to the negotiations, but also to their research, legal and educational staffs.[27]

By emphasising the professional nature of the organisation, ASTMS is able to portray itself as different and superior to the organisations of manual workers, which are characterised as being conservative and representing a shrinking and increasingly impotent membership. The need to so present itself stems from the Association's assessment that its members and potential members feel themselves to be superior and more worthy than manual workers because of their positions within the social relations of production. ASTMS consciously panders to these feelings, one example being displayed in an issue of *Finance News*, its paper for insurance, shipping, banking and commercial membership. Sandwiched between two photographs, the top one of terraced housing and the one below of semi-detached housing, was the caption, 'Few insurance workers would want to start married life in the type of house shown above. To live in a street like the one below is a natural aspiration for white collar staff.'[28]

Feelings of superiority, however, are not necessarily the ones that motivate people to join unions. The element of resentment is more important and amongst the people that ASTMS recruits this feeling is as likely to be directed against shopfloor gains as it is against management. This is reflected in the propaganda of ASTMS, which has walked a narrow path between support for shopfloor demands and hostility towards them because they undermine the status and differentials of its members:

> The skills and expertise that scientists and engineers have acquired painfully over many years are not being rewarded by remuneration, security of employment or promotional prospects. The professional, whether a man or a woman, whether a scientist, engineer or computer specialist, has seen other less skilled, less qualified groups of workers catch up with and indeed surpass his or her salary, whilst at the same time enjoying more secure employment. This is not to say that others do not deserve their wages and salaries; what it does say is the time is approaching when skill, qualifications and responsibility will also have to be adequately rewarded.[29]

Despite protestations to the contrary, the overwhelming impression given is that the less skilled and qualified do not deserve their improved pay and conditions and it is hardly surprising therefore that ASTMS members recruited on the basis of this outlook have not readily identified with shopfloor struggles. The fact that the Association denies this interpretation is important because it indicates the parameters within which ASTMS works. Hostility towards other sections of labour has to be contained and channelled otherwise it would threaten the relationships of ASTMS with the wider trade union movement. Furthermore, hostility towards other sections of labour is useful when recruiting only if it can be turned against the employer.

The structure of the union

What distinguishes the structure of ASTMS from many other unions is the importance attached to workplace groups. There were approximately 10,000 such groups in 1979, each of which elected officers to conduct negotiations and maintain communications with the branch to which they were attached. Whereas there are obvious virtues in encouraging the undertaking of responsibilities at workplace level, it is also the case that within the context of the wider policies of ASTMS and the nature of the membership, such an orientation tends to reflect

195

and reinforce the very narrow and instrumental commitment of members of the new middle class to trade unionism. The issues discussed at work-group level are overwhelmingly parochial and it is often felt that contact with other groups of ASTMS members is unnecessary. Instead of the group being a smaller unit of the branch, it becomes a substitute for it. The group structure not only isolates members from those in other factories or workplaces but also insulates them from fellow members within the same workplace. Moreover, the necessity for this type of organisation stems directly from varying and contradictory positions adopted by the membership.

The structure tries to accommodate, with as little friction as possible, not just the differing ideas but also different levels of trade union activity and commitment amongst its membership, levels which are themselves conditioned by different roles in the production process. Within the same firm, therefore, militant test engineers can be engaged in industrial action while production engineers, foremen and managers can go about their work undisturbed by any need to show support. That there is no compulsion to support other groups in dispute has been made clear by a number of disciplinary cases brought within the union. In one such case it was concluded that 'it was against union policy to insist that managerial staff should be bound by decisions to participate in disputes called by members not in their bargaining unit; or that they should be bound by decisions taken by committees of members in subordinate grades'.[30] ASTMS's policy and structure seek to remove higher grades from the scenes of disputes by placing them in separate work-groups. Where an ASTMS member is directly implicated in a dispute by, for instance, being the manager directly in charge of the work-group concerned, the Association makes no demands on that person and the managerial function is respected.

Differentials, incomes policies and collective bargaining

The Association's willingness to portray itself as an organisation that respects and is prepared to fight for the superior position of the new middle class *vis à vis* manual workers has been one of the major reasons for its success. In this role as champion of middle-class labour, the emphasis of the union on the necessity and justice of pay differentials for skill and responsibility is central. Such a policy fully incorporates the aspirations and ideology of large parts of the membership and middle-class labour generally. There is in the demand for such differentials an implicit assumption that were shopfloor wages to be held at the same level or reduced, the Association's members would be satisfied to continue to work at their present salary levels. This tends to make the demands reactionary and hostile to shopfloor improvements. Certainly there is little in the union's position on this issue to enhance its left-wing reputation. Indeed, a correspondent to the Association's newspaper, the *Journal*, pointed out approvingly that 'the union fight for skill and responsibility differentials is more akin to Conservative than to Socialist philosophy'.[31]

The Association's defence of its position rests upon the contention that the better paid its members, the more this helps to 'lift the whole concept of adequate pay at all levels, and is therefore an aid to all trade unionism'.[32] But in order for this to be the case, the salaries of ASTMS members would have to be the object of parity claims or claims for narrower differentials by shopfloor workers and there is little evidence that this is the case. More common by far is the situation where ASTMS has welcomed a stable relationship between salary and wage levels that involves a fixed formula for settling salary claims after shopfloor claims have been negotiated.[33]

Although there is employer resistance to the size of differentials paid to ASTMS members, many employers accept differentials in principle. Where such agreements are made, and many of them are informal ones, there seems some justification for the feelings of shopfloor workers that they go into collective bargaining carrying ASTMS members on their backs, because the eventual outcome of the negotiations will automatically benefit members of ASTMS without them engaging in any struggle. Where such agreements have been reached they have been threatened not so much by employer hostility as by a succession of government imposed incomes policies. Not surprisingly, therefore, ASTMS has been among the unions most opposed to such policies.

Political orientation

The Association's strident opposition to incomes policy has been regarded as a sign of its left-wing leanings, although, as has been argued, the motivation behind the opposition stems from a very conservative philosophy. The major reason for the Association's left-wing image is, however, its relationship with the Labour Party and indeed its close involvement with the Tribune Group of Labour MPs, for long regarded as the most extreme left-wingers in the organisation. This involvement presents a paradoxical picture of a union with a largely conservative and passive membership strongly supporting the Labour Party.

This paradox is explained by examining the relationship of the members to the stance adopted by the Association towards the Labour Party. In 1975 ASTMS affiliated 185,000 members, i.e. 57 per cent of its total membership, to the Labour Party. The annual accounts, however, reveal that in 1975 fewer than 50,000, i.e. approximately 16 per cent of the membership, paid the levy.[34] By 1978 only 13 per cent of members paid the levy, but the Association continued to affiliate a much larger number to the Labour Party.[35] This it did by charging a much higher political levy than the amount needed to affiliate an individual to the party and using the difference to pay for extra affiliations. Yet even with this decline in membership support for the Labour Party, there is a wealth of evidence that the Association is committed to increasing the union's political involvement.

The Association's political orientation is a result of a combination of pragmatic responses to problems facing the union and the political philosophy of important elements of the Association's leadership. The former aspect is well illustrated by Irving Richter's study of the political activities of the General Secretary, Clive Jenkins:

> Close observation . . . of Mr Jenkins' work . . . indicated that a major and perhaps preponderant share of his time and energy on and off his job was devoted to political operations designed to enhance ASSET's bargaining position as well as Mr Jenkins' prestige and authority. In a variety of political activities Jenkins had a reputation of being a left-winger; in his ASSET Parliamentary Committee role, however, he was distinctly eclectic and opportunistic. He limited himself to strategies that would yield organisational and bargaining improvements.[36]

The political orientation of ASTMS reflects and reinforces a lack of self-activity amongst large sections of the membership. Just as the union places emphasis on the ability of its professional negotiators to solve collective bargaining problems so it presents its MPs as a higher level of representatives who are willing to take up and solve wider issues at the very highest levels. Sections of the membership with major problems are not encouraged to take industrial action but to send delegations to parliament and lobby the relevant minister. The Parliamentary Committee normally facilitates and supports such action. On one occasion, however, members complained to the NEC when only one of the Association's MPs turned up to support a delegation to a minister. In reply, the President of ASTMS pointed out that there had only been one other time when the representation of MPs had been inadequate and that generally union deputations to Ministers included a high percentage of MPs.[37]

In order to be successful this policy of using political connections and pressure-group activity requires either considerable outside pressure to be brought to bear by ASTMS, or groups of ASTMS members, on ministers, or the Association needs the ear of influential MPs. The former has not been the case, hence the concentration on the latter. The logical development of such a perspective is seen in the union's activities around the 1964 general election. Richter noted that 'the focal activity of the entire full-time staff in the General Election was on behalf of "Brother Wilson", the Labour Party Leader and potential Prime Minister'.[38] In addition, Wilson's Constituency Labour Party received the largest cash contribution made to any CLP by the Association as well as the use of some office equipment even though it was far from being a marginal constituency. At the same time the Association gave only token contributions to the general election fund of the Labour Party because, in the words of one executive member, 'we've got to put it where it counts for us'.[39] It was clearly felt that any assistance given to a future Labour Prime Minister would reap great dividends.

Over and above the Association's involvement in politics for pragmatic reasons, there is a more coherent political philosophy at work. Whereas the Association has a membership of over thirty MPs whose views cover the spectrum of Labour opinion, those mostly closely associated with ASTMS have been Tribunite MPs. Ian Mikardo's long-standing association with the union has made him the most prominent of these, but other important figures have included Brian Sedgemore, Arthur Lewis, Jeff Rooker, Martin Flannery, Judith Hart, Jo Richardson, Ron Thomas and Stuart Holland. Together these MPs have formed an important component of the Bennite left, the most distinctive feature of which has been its support for what has become known as the 'Alternative Economic Strategy' the demands of which include import controls, an end to the role of sterling as a reserve currency, price controls and incomes policy, increased powers to the National Enterprise Board, industrial democracy, public ownership of the financial institutions, and maintenance of Labour's social programmes. The National Executive Committee of ASTMS has been identified with all these positions with the exception of an incomes policy and, because of a restive insurance and banking membership, public ownership of the financial institutions.

It is highly unlikely, given their expressed lack of support for the Labour Party, that the majority of the membership identify with the policies of *Tribune* or their own NEC. Despite this, however, the union has not been torn apart by political divisions. The explanation for the membership's tolerance of such positions is two-fold. Firstly, many have remained untouched and unaffected by what they regard, often quite correctly, as rhetorical declarations which carry little practical import. Secondly, where Association members work in ailing parts of the economy, such as footwear, electronics and motor vehicles, the Association's demands for government intervention have been welcomed as the only alternative to capitulation to closures on the one hand, or direct action on the other. The consistent advocacy of a more active NEC role has found some sympathy amongst the membership, not because of any reservoirs of strong anti-capitalist ideology, but rather because it has been seen as the best way of saving their jobs.

This is not to suggest that the policies of the Association have no positive base of support within the membership. Policies, although influenced by the leadership of the Association, are not simply imposed upon the membership, but arise out of the decision-making processes of the union. There are sections of the membership which identify whole-heartedly with the political orientation of the Association: the union activists are much more likely to be Labour Party members and agree to the support of the Labour Party. There is some evidence to indicate that these members tend to be drawn from those whose occupational roles have less to do with the function of capital and are more concerned with tasks within the labour process. These sections have attitudes towards trade unionism which are much more akin to those in much more working-class based unions,[40] but faced with conservative and passive fellow members, these sections view the substitutionalism of the leadership, which is paraded as professionalism, as progressive. They tend, therefore, to support the 'broad left' perspectives of the leadership.

Conclusion

The common-sense view of white-collar unions, reinforced by sociological writings, is that they are generally more conservative and less likely to be identified with the Labour Party. Although this view holds with some of the organisations examined, it is clearly not the case with ASTMS. The weakness of such attempts to relate social class and trade union character is that they ignore the processes of policy-making within unions and members' relations to those policies. By shaping the Association on the lines of traditional manual unions (i.e. by being unionate), ASTMS, according to Blackburn's analysis, should have attracted only a small minority of potential members.[41] While the specific density of the membership of the Association is difficult to calculate because of its almost unlimited ambitions to become a general white-collar union, it is clearly not the case that the union's character has deterred large numbers of potential members. ASTMS has done considerably better than competing organisations with much more moderate images. The left-wing stances adopted by the leadership of the Association have attracted attention, as have the personality and outspoken comments of Clive Jenkins, the General Secretary. But neither of these features of the Association have impinged upon the day-to-day activities of members or potential members. Jenkins conveys the impression that the Association will make great strides on behalf of a membership not required to act, while its political orientation calls upon the government to intervene to improve the position of its membership. Both aspects can peacefully co-exist with a conservative membership in a period in which their conditions are not subject to any rapid decline. Neither is it the case, therefore, that the alternative model of the relationship between class and unionisation, presented by Prandy and to a lesser extent Crompton,[42] is any closer an approximation to reality. Although ASTMS is a trade union, as opposed to a staff or professional association, it does not simply project a class ideology but also incorporates many features that reflect the class position of middle-class labour.

More generally, there appears to have been a clear trend in the 1970s towards what is, historically, a quite rapid unionisation of managers and supervisors and for that unionisation to be reflected in affiliation to the TUC. It should be noted, however, that such a movement does not necessarily represent an abandonment of a 'third force' strategy in principle but rather a disillusioned response to its ineffectiveness. The converse is also true. Affiliation to the TUC does not represent a positive break with previous thought nor does it indicate a new identification with the labour movement. It is merely a more effective way of pressing managers' interests which are still seen as being quite distinct from and in opposition to, those of manual workers. In short, staff associations do not represent a simple identification with capital, nor do trade unions represent a simple identification with labour. The movement from one sort of organisation to the other merely reflected the fact that not only do the majority of managers not have economic ownership of the means of production, but they also have diminishing powers over day-to-day decisions and their own conditions of work. These changing circumstances necessitated the putting aside of ideological objections to TUC-affiliated unions in order for managers to press their interests more effectively.

With the weakening of trade union power and confidence, and the prospect of a Conservative Government increasingly hostile to trade union organisation, a simple evolutionary path towards greater managerial unionisation seems unlikely. Moreover, as the balance of power swings further towards management, it is likely that sectors of the new middle class will abandon an orientation towards the labour movement and seek an accommodation with capital.

7 Conclusion: the politics of the new middle class

One of the criticisms of structuralist attempts to delineate a new middle class by its functions in the production process is that such a methodology is unable to say anything about the relationship between class so defined and the forms of collective action in which it might typically engage. While undoubtedly theorists of the new middle class have largely failed to articulate the relationship between class location and political action this does not have to be the case. Indeed, the examination of new middle-class unionism in this study is an attempt to illustrate the relationship − trade unionism being one typical form of collective action by the new middle class with features distinguishing it from working-class unionism. Nevertheless, bearing this in mind, and with the proviso that there is no one to one correspondence between class location and the representation of class interests at the political level, the more general problem of the interests of the new middle class and their political orientation remains.

Central to the argument of this book is that what determines the political orientation of the new middle class is the interaction between the structural position its members occupy between labour and capital and the balance of class forces both at the local and societal levels. Within such a perspective any radicalisation of new middle-class employees faces definite constraints. The higher the authority possessed by members of the new middle class and the less they perform work within a real labour process, the less likely their support for a socialism built upon workers' control and self-emancipation. In so far as radicalisation takes place because of a societal crisis it is likely that it adopts the ideological form of state socialism, which amounts in reality to no more than state capitalism.[1]

Poulantzas is one of the few theorists to attempt to generalise

203

the specific interests of the new middle class into a coherent ideology and one that has many features compatible with the above perspective. The main thrust of this ideology is, according to Poulantzas, 'anti-capitalist' modified by 'reformist illusions'.[2] Thus while the class experiences exploitation and demands larger incomes and a more rational system of pay determination, it nevertheless avoids the question of the ownership and control of the means of production. The fear of proletarianisation is manifested in its adherence to wage differentials and this attempt to distance itself from the proletariat is also reflected in its demands on capital for participation rather than workers' control. It seeks not to replace the hierarchical organisation of work but rather to reorganise it in order to enhance its own position, leaving the position of subordination of the working class unchanged. The attachment to hierarchy likewise manifests itself in its aspirations for promotion and a career.

The relative isolation and powerlessness of the class also conditions its attitude towards the state, which it sees as inherently neutral. Just as it views itself as an intermediate class, the mediator between the bourgeoisie and the proletariat, the new middle class similarly believes that the state should arbitrate between social classes. Having specified the features of this anti-capitalist ideology, reformist or not, however, Poulantzas qualifies it by claiming that these attitudes towards the state can express themselves as support for a 'strong state' in the form of social Caesarism, and notes the close relationship between sections of the new middle class and various kinds of Bona-partism and fascism.

Poulantzas makes no claim that all middle-class labour will adhere to the main features of this ideology and also recognises that different sections of the class will be more attracted to some aspects than others. Nevertheless, elaborating on the perspectives of Poulantzas it is possible to claim that fundamental features of the ideology appeal to a wide section of the new middle class in spite of the fact that there are tensions between the features because they represent attractions to different poles of the class structure. Support for trade union organisation stems from the subordinate position of the class within managerial hierarchies. At the political level this reflects itself in support for social democracy and increased state planning and aid to industry, which are perceived as a source of opportunity and advantage to large sections of middle-class labour. These sections include not only those directly employed by the state, who have an obvious vested interest in the expansion of state activities, but also those threatened by insecurity and redundancies through the operation of the capitalist market. The attitudes and activities of ASTMS members to the state in such periods of employment crisis has already been noted. These attitudes have traditionally been represented in Britain through the Labour Party. The turn of the Labour Party away from adherence to an explicitly working-class ideology after 1959 and towards a portrayal of the need for a vibrant, technologically advanced, planned economy, with high levels of investment, was designed quite consciously to appeal to the interests of professional, managerial and administrative groups. Their position was to be advanced by the dramatic expansion of those areas calling upon their expertise.

In contrast to this orientation, other aspects of the ideology of middle-class labour rest more comfortably within free enterprise policies. The emphasis of the class on the need for wages differentials to be maintained or increased, and the problems it encounters in confrontations with workers on a day-to-day basis provide fertile ground for appeals to it from the Conservative Party. The concentration of the Conservative Party on the need to reward skills and responsibility, to attack 'irresponsible' trade unionism, to reduce taxes and increase social inequality, echo the desire of many of the new middle class to maintain its power and petty privileges over other sections of labour.

It is not the case, therefore, that, as Goldthorpe has argued, there is a lack of correspondence between the class position of managers, administrators and professionals and its manifestation in identifiable collective action.[3] It is simply that the British electoral system promotes the dominance of two parties, or at least has done so thus far, and thereby encourages the new middle class to find representation of its interests within either of the parties, rather than in a separate, predominantly new middle-class party. The result has been that because of the contradictory position it occupies between the two main classes and because of the wide span of its ideology, the representation of the new middle class has been split between the two main parties.

The recent attempt by the Social Democratic Party (SDP) to 'break the mould' of British politics by the establishment of a new centre party has presented the new middle class with an opportunity of more direct and less diluted political representation, an opportunity which many of the class have embraced enthusiastically. Raphael Samuel, an acute observer of the rise of the SDP, argues that it 'seems to appeal especially to frustrated professionals, who would like to exercise their energies on a wider front . . . it also seems to have recruited vigorously among middle managers and industry's young cadets'.[4] But, although distinctly professional middle-class in make-up, the expression of the interests of the class in concrete policies is rather harder to discern. In appearing to be all things to all men, and, quite consciously with the SDP, to all women, what is said becomes less important than its style of presentation. Hence the importance attached by the party to the qualities of calm, reasoned argument.

Style is, however, also a reflection of the particular social milieu of its membership. Central to Samuel's argument is that the style of SDP politics − its reasonableness and narcissism − reflects the new cultural compactness of the middle class. The new middle class is now more confident, outward-going and consumerist than its pre-war predecessor which was 'less a class than a society of orders'.[5] It is this cultural compactness which has established the preconditions for the successful political representation of the class by the SDP.

In making this analysis, however, Samuel mistakenly conflates the middle class outside the capitalist production process with those who staff the professional and managerial hierarchies within it. While the participation in the SDP of individuals from the former backgrounds, such as shopkeepers, garage owners and self-employed professionals is not in dispute, there is ample evidence that much of this sector of society is less than at home with the 'distinctive moral temper' of the party.[6] That the characteristics of the party come from its new middle-class members, rather than the traditional middle class, is also implied by the weight of Samuel's own evidence. This is further borne out by the study of the party by Hugh Stephenson, which concludes that the party aims to take ideology out of politics and to replace it with professional and managerial values.[7]

Whatever the initial success of the SDP, it faces, as does any party basing itself on the new middle class, enormous problems of survival. Such a class does not have the numerical weight to form the basis of a mass political party. The emergence of the SDP does not, therefore, lessen the probability that the new middle class will have to look to either capital or labour as its principal ally or the importance of examining the likely nature of any allegiance.

The relationship between the class position and political orientation of managers, administrators and professionals has recently been examined by John Goldthorpe. Following the Austro-Marxist, Karl Renner, Goldthorpe classified these groups as the constituents of a service class. The essential feature of this class is that its relationship with its employer, unlike the relationship between wage labour and capital, contains 'an important measure of trust'[8] arising from the degree of autonomy and discretion necessarily afforded to it while carrying out tasks delegated by the employer. Given the absence within his definition of a likely basis of conflict between the service class and capital, it is not surprising that Goldthorpe views this class as 'an essentially *conservative* element within modern societies'.[9] This view is further reinforced by pointing to the unattractiveness to the class of radical egalitarian programmes. Goldthorpe claims, moreover, that attempts by the class to pursue their material interests through trade union type action should not be taken as indicative of proletarianisation, but rather as an attempt to prevent it.

A number of criticisms can be levelled at Goldthorpe's conception of a service class. By claiming that the structural basis of the class is the relationship of trust between it and its employer, Goldthorpe overestimates the degree to which that trust operates and underestimates the heterogeneity of the groups which comprise the class, as an examination of the methods of corporate control of managerial hierarchies would have shown. A further consequence of defining away the sources of antagonism between the service class and capital is that Goldthorpe does not establish those divergent interests which are fundamental for class formation. The problem of class boundary is also reproduced below the service class. Goldthorpe imagines there to be a clear line between managers, administrators and professionals, on the one hand, and routine clerical and sales workers, technicians, foremen and other supervisory personnel, on the other. The latter groups, he argues, although sharing staff status, lack 'the prospective rewards implicit in the service relationship in the form of security of status and recognised career lines'[10] and therefore should be regarded as intermediate groups within the class structure. Contrary to the impression given by Goldthorpe, however, the rewards are not absolutes and the differences in security of status and career lines operate within the service class as well as between it and intermediate groups. The absence of an examination of the internal relations of the service class allows Goldthorpe to project the idea that were its interests to be threatened it would affect the class in a uniform way, strengthening its support for capitalism. In particular, he states, support should increase for varieties of 'liberal' or 'bargained' corporatism, the advance of which would further buttress the principles of meritocracy and technocracy to the benefit of the class. Given the restricted membership of the service class, the conservative nature of its political allegiance is not really in doubt. Goldthorpe, however, does raise another possibility. In the event of a severe crisis, it is possible to foresee a radical reaction of the service class, with support being given to authoritarian movements. To those who seek fundamental change in society, therefore, warning is given: certainly as far as the service class is concerned, radical change is more likely to be in the direction of fascism than socialism.

Goldthorpe's warning, is, however, only a specific version of a theme prominent in sociology, namely that white-collar workers provided an important base of support for fascism in Germany and other countries before the Second World War and that this establishes their inclination to participate in authoritarian movements. This thesis has taken on a trans-historical form, ignoring social and cultural differences between societies. More pertinently, here, it ignores the influence of the balance of class forces on the orientation of the new middle class, a point taken up below.

Standing diametrically opposed to those theorists who see the new middle class as the embodiment of conservatism are the theorists of the new working class. Serge Mallet, in particular, viewed technicians in advanced industries not as conservatives but rather as the vanguard of the struggle for socialism.[11] At the centre of his analysis was the contention that, although indispensable and therefore relatively well-treated by capital, the new working class was not socially integrated. The significance of this lack of integration was that not only did it not identify with management goals, but it would also increasingly demand greater control of the production process, a development which would threaten the basis of the social relations of production. It hardly needs saying that developments have not gone in this direction. The submission that quantitative demands would be transformed into qualitative ones about control of the enterprise proved false and, with memories of the radical actions and demands of technical workers during the 1968 May Events in France fading, the impact of the theory has declined.

This is not to say that Marxists have abandoned technicians or white-collar workers generally to the middle class. As has been indicated, orthodox Marxists have continued to claim that by the criteria of income level and work situation, white-collar workers have been objectively proletarianised. To this perspective has been added a recent upsurge of interest in the existence of groups of employees not easily assimilated into either the capitalist class or the proletariat, but which are, nevertheless, considered to be subject to a process of proletarianisation.

Braverman, for example, examining the occupations of 'draughtsmen, technicians, engineers, accountants, nurses, teachers, supervisors, foremen and petty managers', notes two stages in their proletarianisation. First, these occupations become part of a mass labour market that assumes the characteristics of all labour markets, including the necessary existence of a reserve army of unemployed exercising a downward pressure on pay levels. Secondly, as soon as the employment of such occupations becomes sufficiently large to warrant it, capital subjects them to the 'forms of "rationalization" characteristic of the capitalist mode of production'.[12] While later qualifying the extent to which these occupations have been proletarianised, Braverman nevertheless states that 'in such occupations, the proletarian form begins to assert itself and to impress itself upon the consciousness of these employees'.[13] The reactions of employees to these processes are seen to be unproblematic.

The assumption is also made that the relative depression of their pay and the fragmentation and monitoring of their work are sufficient criteria for the inclusion of these employees in the proletariat. The social function of this fragmented labour is ignored, together with the consequences of the function for their practical day-to-day relations. As Crompton has stated 'a capitalist function is not transformed into a labour process by the manner of carrying it out'.[14]

Even a recognition of the necessity for a qualitative change in work role, namely the elimination of the function of capital, is no guarantee, however, that analysis will not overestimate the extent of proletarianisation. Crompton, whose use of the term proletarianisation includes the necessity for the loss of capital functions, has examined the process and its relationship to unionisation in the insurance industry.[15] She argues strongly that from the 1960s there has been a concerted and successful attempt to de-skill the jobs of insurance clerks and to remove their decision-making powers. It is not clear, however, the extent to which the developments she notes are simply attacks on the control of skilled labour or whether they involve a loss by clerks of the function of capital or merely its attenuation. If the function of capital has been weakened, rather than removed, unionisation of middle-class clerks may have been a reaction designed to arrest the process rather than simply a proletarian response. As Crompton herself notes, union membership 'does not seem to have been heavily biased towards proletarianised females'.[16] Crompton does not raise the possibility that trade union members continue to be middle-class because she continues to carry over from her earlier work the implicit assumption that trade unions are a proletarian form *per se*.[17]

The acceptance that proletarianisation of the new middle class is proceeding apace threatens to be a new orthodoxy amongst sections of Marxist sociologists. Moreover, and more importantly, the political developments which correspond to this process are left unexamined, leaving the impression that the forces available and willing to change society are being strengthened. There is an almost total absence of wider political and social considerations, including the effects of the confidence and organisation of capital and labour on the consciousness and political orientation of the new middle class. The interaction of these factors is complex and historical and comparative studies would be needed to reveal the relative weight of each. Duncan Gallie's study of a French and a British oil refinery illustrates how the contrasting patterns of relations between capital and labour in the two countries influenced the managerial style and ideology of refinery managers.[18] Though not mentioned by Gallie, this has obvious implications for the new middle classes of France and Britain.

In the French refinery managerial power remained formally absolute and management conceded no right of control over any aspect of refinery conditions to the trade unions. The situation in the British refinery was very different. The shopfloor representatives had achieved considerable gains towards control of a wide range of issues, including work conditions, grading, manning levels, deployment of personnel and the use of contractors. It is clear that these gains did not simply stem from a more militant British trade union movement – indeed by nearly all criteria the French unions were more militant – but were conceded as part of a managerial strategy – designed to incorporate the unions into running the plant. Gallie maintains that such an option was not open to French management, faced as it was with a trade union movement which had a clear class ideology and which saw its role as mobilising the work-force for far-reaching structural transformation of society. In contrast to the French unions, the British ones placed little emphasis on raising the consciousness of their members, restricting their role to representing the work-force. In consequence, the French management were much more autocratic and defensive than the British. The difference in the two styles and the effect of the differences on managerial ideology was neatly summed up by a British manager comparing himself with his French counterpart:

> I coax things along. I don't believe in insisting all the time on managerial prerogative. I don't think one should allow oneself to get het up by problems. I think, R [the French Director] allows himself to get anxious about things too quickly. He lives by emergencies. He thinks he is defending capitalism and all

that . . . But I try to put myself in the position of a spectator watching management and the unions, and not to feel completely identified with the Company.[19]

In a more ideologically polarised society, such as France, management tends to be more authoritarian and more coherent. There is less room for dissension within the hierarchy of management and consequently a less stable base for managerial trade unionism. To unionise in such a society means a much greater ideological leap and the probability is that unionisation would only take place at a point of major social conflict in which unions generated the belief that they were going to win.

By ignoring these wider social and political influences, the movement of the new middle class towards the proletariat can be reduced to a very mechanical process and frequently takes the form of representing the rising level of trade union membership as an indicator of the process of proletarianisation. But, as this study has been at pains to point out, not all trade union membership signifies a whole-hearted embrace of working-class perspectives. Moreover, even amongst unions with an over-whelmingly working-class membership there is abundant evidence of a high degree of disenchantment with their performance, a factor which if it develops far enough will certainly deter the spread of unionism to further sectors of the new middle class.

The disenchantment with trade unions is, in part, a result of the structural weakness inherent in trade unionism.[20] Based upon occupational differences and predicated upon the existence of someone with whom to bargain, their very *raison d'être* is tied up with the continuation of capitalism. A consequence of the acceptance of capitalist society is a reformist politics that, during periods of relative trade union strength, frequently finds union leaderships embroiled in the workings of the state, framing and overseeing social legislation designed to erode the need for industrial action by their members. This reliance on state patronage and legislation can quickly prove a critical weakness during economic crises. In this respect the position in Britain today has strong parallels with that of Germany before the Second World War. Anderson described it as follows:

The decline of Trade Union strength and influence did not become really visible before the great depression and mass unemployment began. But it is important to remember that mass unemployment was not the only cause that eventually reduced the German Unions to a shadow of their former selves. The Unions' growing dependence on the State, their

211

submissiveness and self-emasculation, were, to say the least, very important contributory causes.[21]

This is not to suggest that Britain is on the verge of witnessing the rapid growth of a fascist movement composed of the new middle class. It has to be recognised, however, that unions have proved far from successful in converting defensive battles within capitalism into offensives for socialism. Without such a strategy, and with the likelihood of the economic problems of capitalism remaining, not only will sections of the new middle class not feel confident to identify with the socialist movement, they might also look actively for other solutions. A recent study of Fiat's plants in Italy by Marco Revelli illustrate the crucial importance of the balance of class forces on the consciousness and activity of the new middle class.[22]

In October 1980 there was a five-week strike of production workers against mass redundancies at the Turin plant of Fiat. The strike appeared to be solid, with up to 15,000 men and women involved daily in picketing the plant. However, following a mass demonstration by 20,000 foreman, middle management and white-collar workers (and a small minority of production workers) under the slogan 'work is defended by working' the strike collapsed. Revelli distinguishes two underlying reasons for this unprecedented mobilisation of the new middle class in support of capital. The first reason can be traced back to 1973 when Fiat began an investment programme aimed at restructuring the production process in order to reduce the power of its work-force. It chose do to so by adopting a more flexible production cycle which isolated and nullified the effects of industrial action taken by groups of workers. Because the system was no longer based upon the traditional assembly line, action by specific groups could no longer paralyse the production process upstream and downstream. Having avoided confrontation during the implementation of the system, Fiat were ready by 1980 to attempt to justify this investment by lowering staffing and raising productivity. Revelli contends that having allowed the changes to take place the production workers had placed themselves in a structurally weak position to resist the logical outcome. Despite their willingness to fight, Revelli maintains that the workers recognised this and that 'defeat was in the air right from the start'.[23] More importantly for this analysis, the same conclusion was almost certainly conveyed to the new middle class.

The second reason for the mobilisation of the new middle class against Fiat workers is rooted in the anxiety about its role in the production process that followed the reorganisation of the

212

factory. The adoption of new forms of technology within the plant had allowed some of the functions of command and control to be transferred to machines, rendering the foremen, in particular, exposed to fears of obsolescence. Computers now registered the completion of work, diagnosed technical stoppages, determined when tools needed replacing and co-ordinated material supplies. As a result, a problem of legit-imation and an identity crisis spread through the lower levels of the command structure. In the white-collar area as well there were widespread fears that mechanisation and automation were going to have an even more dramatic effect than among manual workers. Revelli concludes that:

> Unlike the working class (which, faced with the erosion of their own identity due to technological innovation, have thus far responded via forms of conflict), this extended 'techno-structure' has reacted by proposing to management a sort of *pactum subjectionus* whereby they would offer *loyalty* in exchange for *security*. This is the deeper meaning of the demonstration of October 14th, a frightened mass sees its own role being eliminated, sees its jobs being threatened; it offers management an alliance, a political support in the confrontation with the workers, and hopes to achieve, in exchange for this total loyalty, a respect for its own status; it hopes that management will decide not to carry to its logical extremes the process of rationalisation.[24]

Revelli's account of the role of the middle-class labour at Fiat is sufficiently alarming to conjure up images of pre-war fascism. Certainly, Italy is a sharply polarised society, in which the new middle class is unlikely to have the luxury of abstentionism in major social struggles. Whether the crisis mirrored in Fiat is widespread enough to call for the mobilisation of the class on a national scale is not a question that can be answered here.

As far as Britain is concerned, such developments do not appear to be immediately likely. The general retreat of trade unionism at both the organisational and ideological levels does not require capital to mobilise directly the new middle class as a physical force against the working class. The absence of this need, however, will not prevent a move towards the closer integration into companies of managerial employees by a tightening of the ideology of, and discipline within, management. This was certainly the case at British Leyland where the determination to ensure that managers managed, following the appointment of Michael Edwardes as chairman, saw hundreds of managers displaced and a recognition in every one of those left that with their jobs under threat there were to be no compromises with shopfloor control.[25] Certainly given this change in the balance of class forces, the renewed authoritarianism of top management will no longer acquiesce to fresh middle management unionisation and will probably actively seek the reduction of the present level.

More generally, at the level of party politics, the rise of the SDP could be characterised as a reaction by the new middle class to the fear of an imminent polarisation of British politics. In the view of the SDP the growing extremism of the Left and the dogmatism of the Right threaten to force upon it a choice between either alignment with one or the other extreme or political ineffectiveness. Shunning this uncomfortable vision, the professional occupiers of the middle ground look back to the politics of consensus and offer the electorate 'a better yesterday'.[26] Whatever the electoral appeal of such an orientation the economic circumstances for its implementation should the SDP come to power are not favourable. In the immediate future the majority of the new middle class will choose or be forced to ally with either the interests of capital or those of labour: which way they choose will depend not only on their roles in production but also on which class appears to be the dominant class of tomorrow.

Notes

Introduction

1 The leading exponent of the thesis was F. Zweig in *The Worker in an Affluent Society*, London, 1961.

2 Harold Wilson, quoted in Paul Foot, 'Parliamentary Socialism', in Nigel Harris and John Palmer eds., *World Crisis*, London, 1971 p. 86.

3 See, for example, Harold Wilson's speech to 1963 Labour Party Conference, *Labour Party Annual Conference Report 1963*, pp. 134– 40.

4 See, for example, P. Wilmott and M. Young, *Family and Kinship in East London*, London, 1957, and *Family and Class in a London Suburb*, London, 1960; Brian Jackson, *Working Class Community*, London, 1968. For a critique of these approaches to class analysis see Eve Brook and Dan Finn, 'Working Class Images of Society and Community Studies', in *On Ideology: Working Papers in Cultural Studies*, 10, 1977, pp. 77–105.

5 For the most influential study, see David Lockwood, *The Blackcoated Worker*, London, 1969.

6 Jeremy Seabrook, *Unemployment*, London, 1982; André Gorz, *Farewell to the Working Class*, London, 1982.

7 Robert Price and George Sayers Bain, 'Union Growth Revisited: 1948–1974 in Perspective', *British Journal of Industrial Relations*, vol. XIV, no. 3, 1976, p. 346.

8 Ibid., p.348.

9 Daniel Bell, *The Coming of the Post-Industrial Society: A Venture in Social Forecasting*, London, 1976, p. 17.

10 Richard Hyman recorded that in France *professions libre, cadres et employees* increased from 24 per cent of the labour force in 1962 to 30 per cent in 1968. In Italy, *digirenti e impegiati* rose from 9 per cent in 1954 to 14 per cent in 1963 and 20 per cent in 1973. In Germany, *Beamter und Angestellter* rose from 30 per cent in 1962 to 40 per cent in 1972. Richard Hyman, 'Occupational Structure,

Collective Organisation and Industrial Militancy', in Colin Crouch and Alessandro Pizzorno (eds), *The Resurgence of Class Conflict in Western Europe Since 1968*, vol. 2, 1978, p. 57.

11 R.M. Blackburn, *Union Character and Social Class*, London, 1967, pp. 71–9.

12 Enid Mumford and Olive Banks, *The Computer and the Clerk*, London, 1967, p.21.

13 Nicos Poulantzas, *Classes in Contemporary Capitalism*, London, 1975, Guglielmo Carchedi, *On the Economic Identification of Social Classes*, London, 1977, Erik Olin Wright, *Class, Crisis and the State*, London, 1978.

14 Harry Braverman, *Labor and Monopoly Capital: the Degradation of Work in the Twentieth Century*, New York, 1974.

1 Sociology, Marxism and the class structure of capitalist societies

1 For such a thesis see I.M. Zeitlin, *Ideology and the Development of Sociological Theory*, New Jersey, 1968.

2 The best testimony to the impact of Marx's thought is, as T.B. Bottomore pointed out, both the unrelenting criticism and the tenacious defence to which it has been subjected. See T.B. Bottomore, *Classes in Modern Society*, London, 1965, p. 21.

3 A good example is the work of the American Marxist C. Loren, *Classes in the United States: Workers against Capitalism*, California, 1977.

4 Alan Hunt, 'Class Structure in Britain Today', *Marxism Today*, June 1970, p. 167. It should be noted that Hunt is an academic sociologist.

5 Karl Marx and Friedrich Engels, *Manifesto of the Communist Party*, in Karl Marx and Friedrich Engels, *The Communist Manifesto*, with an introduction by A.J.P. Taylor, Harmondsworth, Pelican, 1967, p. 86.

6 Ibid., p. 88.

7 A.J.P. Taylor, introduction to *The Communist Manifesto*, op. cit., p. 41.

8 G.D.H. Cole, *Studies in Class Structure*, London, 1968, p. 89.

9 Anthony Giddens, *The Class Structure of Advanced Societies*, London, 1973.

10 Ibid., p. 101.

11 Karl Marx, *Theories of Surplus Value*, London, Lawrence & Wishart, 1969, vol. 2, p. 573.

12 Georg Lukács, *History and Class Consciousness*, London, 1971, p. 59.

13 Robert Schaeffer and James Weinstein, 'Between the Lines', in Pat Walker (ed.), *Between Labour and Capital*, Hassocks, Sussex, 1979, p. 148.

14 Ibid., p. 149.

15 Ibid., p. 166.

16 G. Ross, 'Marxism and the New Middle Classes', *Theory and*

Society, vol. 5, 1978, p. 167.
17 Ibid.
18 Hunt, op. cit., p. 170.
19 Ibid.
20 Ibid., p. 171.
21 Ibid.
22 Using just this criterion it has been concluded that 90 per cent of the American population is working class. See C. Loren, op. cit.
23 Hunt, op. cit., p. 172.
24 H. Frankel, *Capitalist Society and Modern Sociology*, London, 1970, p. 208.
25 Frank Parkin, *Marxism and Class Theory*, London, 1979, p. 4.
26 J.H. Clapham, *The Economic Development of France and Germany, 1815–1914*, Cambridge, 1923, pp. 283 and 303–9.
27 Quoted in H. Lebovics, *Social Conservatism and the Middle Classes in Germany*, Princeton, 1969, p. 3.
28 Clapham, op. cit., p. 301.
29 Walter Kendall, *The Labour Movement in Europe*, London, 1975, p. 340.
30 The party was, in fact, constitutionalist and reformist. As George Lichtheim commented: 'The "Erfurt Programme" adopted in 1891 was mainly the work of Kautsky, and it embodied as much of Marx's analysis of capitalism as the mental comprehension of its readers seemed likely to permit. . . . [But] the bulk was unimpeachably democratic and "reformist" ' George Lichtheim, *Marxism*, London, 1964, p. 260.
31 These figures are taken from Hans Speier, 'The Salaried Employee in Modern Society', *Social Research*, vol. 1, no. 1, 1934, p. 112.
32 Hans Speier, *The Salaried Employee in German Society*, WPA Project no. 465–97–0391, New York, 1939, p. 86. Speier noted that 'In 1929, the most comprehensive statistical inquiry into the social origin of salaried employees, it was discovered that, including those employees who have inherited their occupation, 71.7 per cent originate in the middle class and only 3.3 per cent in a higher stratum; labour contributed 25 per cent.'
33 Ibid., p. 9.
34 See, for instance, V.I. Lenin, 'The Proletarian Revolution and the Renegade Kautsky' in *Collected Works*, vol. 28, Moscow, 1964, pp. 231–50.
35 Karl Kautsky, *Bernstein und das sozialdemokratische Programm*, Stuttgart, 1899, quoted in Peter Gay, *The Dilemma of Democratic Socialism*, New York, 1970, p. 211.
36 Gay, op. cit., p. 212. − 204
37 Eduard Bernstein, *Evolutionary Socialism*, New York, 1909. Originally published as *Die Voraussetzungen des Sozialismus und die Aufgaben der Sozialdemokratie*, Stuttgart, 1899.
38 Gay, op. cit., p. 206.
39 Ibid., p. 173. − 165
40 This view is echoed by Martin Nicolaus in 'Proletariat and Middle

217

Class in Marx: Hegelian Choreography and the Capitalist Dialectic',
Studies on the Left, 7, 1967, pp. 22–49.

41 Gay, op. cit., p. 209. –201

42 Ibid., p. 210.

43 Ibid., p. 211.

44 For an account of all three, see Lebovics, op. cit., pp. 49–138.

45 For an account of their work see ibid., Ch. 6, and Walter Struve, *Elites against Democracy*, Princeton, 1973, Ch. 2, esp. pp. 361–5.

46 This concept, with its dismissal of the 'old order' on the one hand and communism on the other, bore a marked resemblance to the position taken up in later years by the Nazi Party. When Hitler seized power in 1933 it was not with the active support of the 'Tat' circle. Zehrer, an editor, was close to the Strasserites, the left-wing of the Party, and had a Jewish wife. He, not surprisingly, quickly retired from political journalism. The other editor, Fried, abandoned his criticism of capitalism and was accommodated within the Third Reich. For further details, see Lebovics, op. cit., pp. 203–4.

47 The D.H.V. was founded in 1893 by anti-semitic political leaders rather than by salaried workers. It represented anti-semitic, anti-parliamentary, anti-liberal and anti-Marxist principles. The D.H.V. eventually went into the Nazi 'German Labour Front' as the principal organisation in the 'salaried employees column', the leader of which was a National Socialist functionary of the D.H.V. See Speier, op. cit., 1934, p. 125.

48 Emil Lederer, *The Problem of the Modern Salaried Employee: Its Theoretical and Statistical Basis*, W.P.A. Project no. 165–6999–6027, New York, 1937. In 1937 the New York State Department of Social Welfare and the Department of Sociology at Columbia University jointly sponsored a W.P.A. project of translating foreign social science monographs. In all about twenty-five were translated and deposited in the Columbia University Library as well as distributed on a limited basis. One major topic was that of the 'white-collar worker' in Germany and about ten studies on the topic were translated including works by Emil Lederer, Lederer and Marschak, Fritz Croner, Hans Speier, Carl Dreyfus, Erich Engelhard and Hans Tobis.

49 Ibid., p. 2.

50 Ibid., pp. 3–4.

51 Ibid., p. 7.

52 George Sayers Bain and Robert Price, 'Who is a White Collar Employee?', *British Journal of Industrial Relations*, vol. X, 1972, p. 326. They contrast what they claim was Lederer's 'brain/brawn' approach to his later works. This, as is shown, however, did not contain a significantly different approach, and there is no justification therefore in holding Lederer responsible for founding the approach that defines white-collar work by its physical content.

53 Lederer, op. cit., p. 8.

54 Ibid., p. 8.

55 Emil Lederer and Jacob Marschak, 'Der Neue Mittelstand', in *Grundiss der Sozialokönomik*, ix Abteilung, I Teil, Tübingen, 1926; translated as *The New Middle Class*, W.P.A. project no. 165–97–6999–6027, New York, 1937.
56 Lederer and Marschak, op. cit., p. 16.
57 Ibid., pp. 16–17.
58 Ibid., p. 22.
59 Ibid.
60 Ibid., p. 24.
61 Ibid., p. 25.
62 Ibid., pp. 44–5.
63 Ibid., p. 45.
64 Ibid., pp. 41–2.
65 Ibid., p. 43.
66 Emil Lederer, *State of the Masses*, New York, 1940.
67 Hans Speier, op. cit., 1934, pp. 111–33, 1939.
68 Speier, 1939, pp. 14–15.
69 Speier, 1934, p. 116.
70 Ibid., pp. 131–2.
71 Speier's analysis was one of the first to emphasise sex as an important differentiating factor in employment and promotion opportunities.
72 Speier, 1939, p. 77.
73 Speier, 1934, pp. 127–8.
74 Ibid., p. 128.
75 Ibid., p. 132.
76 Ibid.
77 Ibid., p. 133.
78 These pamphlets and articles are published collectively in Leon Trotsky, *The Struggle Against Fascism in Germany*, London, 1975.
79 Speier, 1939, p. 6.
80 Ernest Mandel, introduction to Trotsky, op. cit., p. xxii.
81 Leon Trotsky, 'The Turn in the Communist International and the Situation in Germany', in Trotsky, op. cit., p. 17.
82 Ibid., p. 18.
83 Daniel Guérin, *Fascism and Big Business*, New York, 1973, p. 50.
84 Daniel Bell, *The Coming of the Post Industrial Society: A Venture in Social Forecasting*, London, 1976, p. 77.
85 For an account of Austro-Marxism and selected readings from key texts produced by members of this tendency see T.B. Bottomore and P. Goode, *Austro-Marxism*, Oxford, 1978.
86 Part of this was translated as 'The Service Class' in Bottomore and Goode, op. cit., pp. 249–52.
87 Quoted in Ralf Dahrendorf, *Class and Class Conflict in an Industrial Society*, London, 1972, p. 94.
88 Bottomore and Goode, op. cit., p. 251.
89 Ibid.
90 Fritz Croner, *Die Angestellten in der modernen Gesellschaft*, Frankfurt, 1954. There is no English translation. A summary of

219

Croner's theory is contained in his 'Salaried Employees in Modern Society', *International Labour Review*, LXIX, February 1954, pp. 97–110.

91 Quoted in Dahrendorf, op. cit., p. 91.

92 George Sayers Bain and Robert Price, op. cit., p. 334. They do not, however, cite any historical examples.

93 Ivy Pinchbeck, *Women Workers and the Industrial Revolution 1750–1850*, London, 1969, p. 282.

94 Helena Hayward and Pat Kirkham, *William and John Linnell. Eighteenth Century London Furniture Makers*, London, 1980, see particularly Ch. 1, 'The Linnell Family', and Ch. 3, 'Management, Marketing and Finance'.

95 C. Wright Mills, *White Collar. The American Middle Classes*, New York, 1972, p. 297.

96 Ibid., p. 353.

97 Ibid.

98 Ralf Dahrendorf, op. cit., p. 253.

99 Ibid., p. 54.

100 Ibid., p. 55.

101 Ibid., pp. 56–7. This conclusion is the starting point of a later work. See Ralf Dahrendorf, *Conflict After Class: New Perspectives on the Theory of Social and Political Conflict*, London, 1967.

102 Ibid., p. 165.

103 F.D. Klingender, *The Condition of Clerical Labour in Great Britain*, London, 1935.

104 Speier, 1934, p. 112.

105 Geoffrey Crossick, 'The Emergence of the Lower Middle Class in Britain', in Geoffrey Crossick (ed.), *The Lower Middle Class in Britain 1870–1914*, London, 1978, p. 41.

106 Ibid.

107 This argument has been advanced by Perry Anderson, 'Components of the National Culture', in Alexander Cockburn and Robin Blackburn (eds), *Student Power*, 1969, pp. 214–84.

108 John Westergaard and Henrietta Resler, *Class in a Capitalist Society*, London, 1975, p. 29.

109 Anthony Giddens, op. cit., p. 41.

110 Quoted in H.H. Gerth and C. Wright Mills (eds), *From Max Weber*, London, 1967, p. 69.

111 Theo Nichols, 'Social Class: Official, Sociological and Marxist', in J. Irvine, I. Moles, J. Evans (eds), *Demystifying Social Statistics*, London, 1979, p. 159.

112 Gerth and Mills, op. cit., p. 181.

113 Ibid., p. 182.

114 Ibid.

115 Ibid., pp. 186–7.

116 Ibid., p. 187.

117 Giddens, op. cit., p. 78.

118 Rosemary Crompton and Jon Gubbay, *Economy and Class Structure*, London, 1977, p. 17.

119 David Lockwood, *The Blackcoated Worker*, London, 1969, pp. 15–16.
120 Giddens, op. cit., pp. 177–97.
121 See, for example, John H. Goldthorpe and David Lockwood, 'Affluence and the British Class Structure', *Sociological Review*, vol. 11, no. 2, July, 1963, pp. 133–63.
122 C.A.R. Crosland, *The Future of Socialism*, London, 1956.
123 Goldthorpe and Lockwood, op. cit., p. 134.
124 See particularly John H. Goldthorpe, David Lockwood, Frank Bechofer, Jennifer Platt, *The Affluent Worker in the Class Structure*, Cambridge, 1969.
125 David Lockwood, 'Sources of Variations in Working Class Images of Society', *Sociological Review*, vol. 14, no. 4, November 1966, pp. 249–67.
126 Frank Parkin, *Class, Inequality and Political Order*, London, 1972, p. 31.
127 Ibid., p. 24.
128 In Frank Parkin (ed.), *The Social Analysis of Class Structure*, London, 1974.
129 The terminology of this latter mode of closure changes from solidarism in the earlier work to usurpation in the latter. The argument, however, is essentially the same.
130 Frank Parkin, op. cit., 1979, p. 46.
131 Parkin (ed.), op. cit., 1974, p. 5.
132 Ibid., p. 13.
133 Parkin, 1979, p. 94.
134 Ibid., p. 113.
135 Hunt, op. cit., p. 167.
136 H. Frankel, op. cit., p. 207.
137 Watergaard and Resler, op. cit., p. 27.
138 Ibid., pp. 95–6.
139 Ibid., p. 96.

2 Marx, Marxism and the new middle class

1 Hal Draper remarked of such attempts: 'It offers a splendid opportunity for pointless quotation-mongering through which a new "theory of class" can be discovered in Marx every week' Hal Draper, *Karl Marx's Theory of Revolution*, New York, 1977, vol. 1, p. 17.
2 See ibid., p. 17 and Bertell Ollman, *Social and Sexual Revolution*, London, 1979, pp. 33–47.
3 Karl Marx and Friedrich Engels, *Manifesto of the Communist Party*, in Karl Marx and Friedrich Engels, *The Communist Manifesto*, with an introduction by A.J.P. Taylor, Harmondsworth, Pelican, 1967, p. 79.
4 Karl Marx, *The Poverty of Philosophy*, in Karl Marx and Friedrich Engels, *Collected Works*, vol. 6, 1976, p. 197.
5 E.P. Thompson, *The Making of the English Working Class*,

Harmondsworth, Penguin, 1968, p. 10.

6 Karl Marx, *Capital*, vol. 3, London, Lawrence & Wishart, 1974, p. 791.

7 Draper, op. cit., p. 507.

8 An analysis of the weaknesses of the *Manifesto* and how Marx's later works compensated for them is given by Stuart Hall, 'The "Political" and the "Economic" in Marx's Theory of Classes', in Alan Hunt (ed.), *Class and Class Structure*, London, 1977, pp. 15–60.

9 See pp. 7–14.

10 Particularly important in this respect is Abram L. Harris's, 'Pure Capitalism and the Disappearance of the Middle Class', *Journal of Political Economy*, 1939, pp. 328–56.

11 Marx, *Capital*, vol. 3, 1974, p. 175.

12 Karl Marx, *The Eighteenth Brumaire of Louis Bonaparte*, in Karl Marx, *Surveys from Exile*, Harmondsworth, Pelican, 1973, p. 147.

13 Marx, *Capital*, vol. 3, 1974, p. 885.

14 Marx, *Capital*, vol. 2, 1978, p. 422.

15 Karl Marx, 'Results of the Immediate Process of Production', in *Capital*, vol. 1, 1976, p. 1042.

16 Ibid., pp. 1044–5.

17 The particular importance of this point will be discussed later when examining the work of Nicos Poulantzas, pp. 71–8.

18 Marx, *Capital*, vol. 2, 1978, p. 448.

19 Ibid., pp. 190–1.

20 Harris, op. cit., pp. 343–4.

21 Marx, *Capital*, vol. 3, 1974, pp. 289–90.

22 Ibid., p. 300.

23 Marx, 'Results . . .', *Capital*, vol. 1, 1976, p. 981.

24 Ibid., p. 981.

25 Ibid., p. 988.

26 Ibid., p. 990.

27 Ibid.

28 He stated, for instance, that 'The capitalist functions only as *personified* capital, capital as a person, just as the worker is no more than *labour* personified'. 'Results . . .', *Capital*, vol. 1, p. 989.

29 Marx, *Capital*, vol. 3, 1974, p. 886.

30 Marx, 'Results . . .', *Capital*, vol. 1, 1976, p. 1021.

31 Ibid.

32 Marx, *Capital*, vol. 1, 1976, pp. 643–4.

33 Marx, 'Results . . .', *Capital*, vol. 1, 1976, p. 1040.

34 This is the point missed by Ralph Miliband in *Marxism and Politics*. Having noted Marx's extension of the concept of productive labour Miliband is at a loss to find criteria with which to exclude the 'executive labourer' from the working class. Because he does not examine the function of capital, he is reduced to placing an erroneous interpretation on Marx's statement that 'in order to labour productively, it is no longer necessary for you to do manual work yourself; enough if you are an organ of the collective labourer,

and perform one of its *subordinate* functions'. Miliband concludes that 'the "working class" is therefore that part of the "collective labourer" which produces surplus value, from a position of subordination, at the lower end of the income scale, and also at the lower ends of what might be called the "scale of regard" '. The significance of the extension of the collective worker is thus negated by essentially Weberian criteria of class (income level and status). Ralph Miliband, *Marxism and Politics*, Oxford, 1977, pp. 23–5.

35 Marx, 'Results . . .', *Capital* vol. 1, 1976, p. 989.
36 Ibid., pp. 985–6.
37 Marx, *Capital*, vol. 3, 1974, p. 380.
38 Ibid., p. 383. This has been little noted. The passage in full reads:

> The conception of profit of enterprise as the wages of supervising labour, arising from the antithesis of profit of enterprise to interest, is further strengthened by the fact that a portion of profit may, indeed, be separated, in reality, as wages, or rather the reverse, that a portion of wages appears under capitalist production as [an] integral part of profit. This portion, as Adam Smith correctly deduced, presents itself in pure form, independently and wholly separated from profit (as the sum of interest and profit of enterprise), on the one hand, and on the other, from that portion of profit that remains, after interest is deducted, as profit of enterprise in the salary of management of those branches of business whose size, etc., permits of a sufficient division of labour to justify a special salary for a manager.

39 Ibid., p. 383.
40 Ibid., pp. 383–4.
41 Ibid., p. 386.
42 Ibid., p. 389.
43 Ibid., p. 386.
44 Marx, 'Results . . .', *Capital*, vol. 1, 1976, p. 1048.
45 Ibid., p. 1048.
46 Ibid., p. 450.
47 Marx, *Capital*, vol. 3, 1974, p. 388.
48 Charles Bettelheim, *Economic Calculation and Forms of Property*, London, 1976, pp. 68–75.
49 Guglielmo Carchedi, *On the Economic Identification of Social Classes*, London, 1977, pp. 89–90.
50 See pp. 48–50.
51 The phrase literally means 'false costs', but it was used by Marx to refer to incidental costs. See Marx, *Capital*, vol. 1, 1976, footnote to pp. 446–7.
52 See pp. 66–7.
53 Carchedi, op. cit., p. 45.
54 Ibid., p. 49.
55 Terry Johnson, 'What is to be Known?', *Economy and Society*, vol. 6, 1977, p. 200.

56 Ibid.
57 Ibid.
58 Peter Fairbrother, 'The Bases of Collectivity: a Study of White-Collar Workplace Trade Unionism', unpublished paper presented to the Conference of Socialist Economists, Conference 1979 and John Urry, 'New Theories of the New Middle Class', unpublished paper, University of Lancaster, May, 1975.
59 Johnson, op. cit., p. 206.
60 Ibid., p. 218.
61 Carchedi, op. cit., p. 90.
62 Marx, *Capital*, vol. 3, 1974, p. 389.
63 Nicos Poulantzas, *Classes in Contemporary Capitalism*, London, 1978, p. 21.
64 Ibid., p. 14.
65 Ibid., p. 210.
66 Ibid., p. 216.
67 Ibid., p. 214.
68 Ibid., pp. 224–30.
69 Ibid., pp. 230–70.
70 Ibid., p. 257.
71 Marx, *Capital*, vol. 3, 1974, p. 300.
72 Ibid., pp. 289–301.
73 For instance, Poulantzas quotes from 'Results . . .', 'In so far as it produces commodities, labour remains productive; it is materialized in commodities which are simultaneously use-values and exchange-values. . . . *Thus only labour that is externalized in commodities is productive*' (Poulantzas, op. cit., p. 219, my emphasis).
The Pelican translation of 'Results . . .', however, reads: 'Labour is productive, therefore, is it is converted into commodities' (*Capital*, vol. 1, 1976, p. 1039). Poulantzas also fails to note that Marx went on to repeat his definition of productive labour as that which directly produces surplus-value, with no qualifications as to the necessity for labour to be externalised into commodities.
74 Marx, 'Results . . .', *Capital*, vol. 1, 1976, p. 1044.
75 Ibid.
76 Ibid., p. 1045. Marx went on to criticise 'the desire to define productive and unproductive labour in terms of their material content' (ibid., p. 1046).
77 Poulantzas, op. cit., p. 212.
78 Marx, 'Results . . .', *Capital*, vol. 1, 1976, p. 990.
79 Poulantzas, op. cit., p. 238.
80 Ibid., p. 256.
81 Ibid., p. 272.
82 Marx, 'Results . . .', *Capital*, vol. 1, 1976, pp. 1054–5.
83 Poulantzas, op. cit., pp. 302–3.
84 Ibid., p. 326.
85 Ibid., p. 257.
86 Erik Olin Wright, *Class, Crisis and the State*, London, 1978, p. 62.
87 Ibid., p. 63.

88 Ibid., pp. 64–74.
89 Ibid., p. 73.
90 Ibid., pp. 77–8.
91 Ibid., pp. 80–1.
92 Barbara and John Ehrenreich, 'The Professional-Managerial Class', in Pat Walker (ed.), *Between Labour and Capital*, Hassocks, Sussex, 1979, p. 12.
93 Ibid.
94 Ibid., p. 9.
95 Ibid., p. 21.
96 Ibid., p. 24.
97 Harry Braverman, *Labor and Monopoly Capital*, New York, 1974, p. 409.

3 Monopoly capitalism and the rise of the new middle class

1 Maurice Dobb, *Studies in the Development of Capitalism*, London, 1978, p. 123.
2 Ibid., p. 138.
3 Ibid., p. 260.
4 Quoted in Sidney Pollard, *The Genesis of Modern Management: a Study of the Industrial Revolution in Great Britain*, London, 1965, p. 11.
5 A. Ure, *The Philosophy of Manufacturers*, London, 1835, pp. 15–16.
6 E.J. Hobsbawm, *Labouring Men: Studies in the History of Labour*, London, 1968, p. 297.
7 Craig Littler, 'Deskilling and the Changing Structures of Control', in Stephen Wood (ed.), *The Degradation of Work? Skill, Deskilling and the Labour Process*, London, 1982, p. 125.
8 See Dobb, op. cit., p. 267.
9 Ibid., p. 266.
10 Hobsbawm, op. cit., p. 298.
11 Pollard, op. cit., p. 38.
12 Hobsbawm, op. cit., p. 298.
13 Dan Clawson, *Bureaucracy and the Labour Process: The Transformation of US Industry, 1860–1920*, New York, 1980.
14 Ibid., p. 83.
15 Daniel Nelson, *Managers and Workers: Origins of the New Factory System in the United States 1880–1920*, Madison, 1975, p. 4.
16 Quoted in Clawson, op. cit., p. 114.
17 Ibid., p. 117.
18 The same is true for Great Britain. Littler comments that 'the traditional foreman's power started to be modified almost as soon as it emerged from the decay of the internal contract' (op. cit., p. 134).
19 F.W. Taylor, *The Principles of Scientific Management*, New York, 1911, p. 48.
20 For a detailed assessment of the philosophy of scientific management see Harry Braverman, *Labor and Monopoly Capital*,

New York, 1974.

21 Ralph C. Nelson, *Merger Movements in American Industry 1895–1956*, Princeton, 1959, p. 37.

22 Alfred D. Chandler, Jnr., *The Visible Hand: The Managerial Revolution in American Business*, Cambridge, Mass., 1977, p. 411.

23 Alfred D. Chandler Jnr., *Strategy and Structure: Chapters in the History of the Industrial Enterprise*, Cambridge, Mass., 1972, p. 32.

24 Ibid., pp. 42–64.

25 Chandler, op. cit., 1977, p. 463.

26 Leslie Hannah, 'Visible and Invisible Hands in Great Britain. The Advent of the Modern Corporation in Britain', in Alfred D. Chandler and Herman Daems (eds), *Managerial Hierarchies: Comparative Perspectives on the Rise of the Modern Industrial Enterprise*, Cambridge, Mass., 1980, p. 53.

27 Derek Channon, *The Structure of British Enterprise*, London, 1973, pp. 50–85.

28 John Child, *British Management Thought*, London, 1969.

29 C.A.R. Crosland, *The Conservative Enemy*, London, 1962, p. 92.

30 Ralf Dahrendorf, *Class and Class Conflict in an Industrial Society*, London, 1972, pp. 35–71.

31 Writers in this vein include Sam Aaronovitch, *The Ruling Class*, London, 1961; Michael Barratt Brown, 'The Controllers', *Universities and Left Review*, no. 5, 1959; Gabriel Kolko, *Wealth and Power in America*, London, 1962 and C. Wright Mills, *The Power Elite*, London, 1959. There are exceptions, however, prominent amongst which are Theo Nichols, *Ownership, Control and Ideology*, London, 1969, and Robin Blackburn, 'The New Capitalism', in Perry Anderson, (ed.), *Towards Socialism*, London, 1965, pp. 114–45.

32 Karl Marx, *Capital*, vol. 1, Harmondsworth, Pelican, 1976, p. 739.

33 Marx, 'Results . . .', *Capital*, vol. 1, 1976, p. 990.

34 Marx, *Capital*, vol. 1, 1976, p. 450.

35 Stuart Holland, *The Socialist Challenge*, London, 1975, p. 70.

36 See R.E. Pahl and J.T. Winkler, 'The Economic Elite: Theory and Practice', in Philip Stanworth and Anthony Giddens (eds), *Elites and Power in British Society*, London, 1974, p. 118.

37 James Burnham, *The Managerial Revolution*, London, 1962.

38 I.C. McGivering, D.C.J. Matthews and W.H. Scott, *Management in Britain*, London, 1960, p. 72.

39 The exception to this was John Kenneth Galbraith, *The New Industrial State*, London, 1969. He argued (p. 74) that the complexity of organisation in large corporations meant that power had passed to a 'technostructure' which he defined as 'the association of men of diverse technical knowledge, experience or other talent which modern industrial technology and planning require. It extends from the leadership of the modern industrial enterprise down to just short of the labour force and embraces a large number of people and a large variety of talent'.

40 Sidney Pollard, op. cit., p. 157.

41 Rosemary Stewart, *The Reality of Management*, London, 1967, p. 15.
42 Alfred D. Chandler Jnr., in Chandler and Daems, op. cit., p. 1.
43 See, for instance, Dorothy Wedderburn, *White Collar Redundancy: a Case Study*, Cambridge, 1964.
44 Richard Berthoud, *Unemployed Professionals and Executives*, *Policy Studies Institute*, vol. XLV, no. 582, May 1979.
45 Marx, *Capital*, vol. 1, 1976, p. 929.
46 Gerald Newbould, *Management and Merger*, London, 1970, p. 176.
47 Gerald Newbould and Andrew Jackson, *The Receding Ideal*, Liverpool, 1972, pp. 130–48.
48 A.P. Sloan Jnr, *My Years with General Motors*, New York, 1965, p. 50.
49 See John Child, 'Organisation Structure and Strategies of Control', *Administrative Science Quarterly*, vol. 17, no. 2, 1972, pp. 163–76.
50 Philip Stanworth and Anthony Giddens, 'An Economic Elite: a Demographic Profile of Company Chairmen', in Stanworth and Giddens, op. cit., p. 86.
51 D.T. Bailey, 'The Business of Accountancy: East and West', *Journal of Management Studies*, vol. 12, 1975, p. 37.
52 Ibid.
53 Terry Johnson, 'The Professions in the Class Structure', in Richard Scase (ed.), *Industrial Society: Class, Cleavage and Control*, London, 1977, p. 107.
54 Theo Nichols and Huw Beynon, *Living with Capitalism: Class Relations and the Modern Factory*, London, 1977, p. 38.
55 Peter F. Drucker, *Management*, London, 1979, p. 348.
56 Lord Robens cited in Huw Beynon and Hilary Wainwright, *The Workers' Report on Vickers*, London, 1979, p. 38.
57 H. Leavitt and L. Whisler, 'Management in the 1980s', *Harvard Business Review*, vol. 36, no. 6, Nov./Dec. 1958, pp. 41–2.
58 Stewart, op. cit., p. 180.
59 M. Weir, 'Are Computer Systems and Humanised Work Compatible?', in R.N. Ottaway (ed.), *Humanising Work*, London, 1977, p. 48.
60 Quoted in M.J.E. Cooley, 'Taylor in the Office', in Ottaway, op. cit., p. 73.
61 Peter Fairbrother, 'Consciousness and Collective Action: a Study of the Social Organisation of Unionised White Collar Factory Workers', unpublished PhD thesis, Oxford, 1978, pp. 342–3.
62 William Kornhauser, *Scientists in Industry: Conflict and Accommodation*, Berkeley, 1962, p. 136.
63 C. Sofer, *Men in Mid-Career: a Study of British Managers and Technical Specialists*, Cambridge, 1970, p. 277.
64 Ibid., p. 278.
65 Nichols and Beynon, op. cit., p. 40.
66 W. Robins, unpublished paper on executive redundancy, cited in R.D. Anthony, *The Ideology of Work*, London, 1977, p. 296.
67 Rosemary Butler, 'Employment of the Highly Qualified

1971–1986', *Unit of Manpower Studies Research Paper, no. 2*, Department of Employment, 1978, p. 29.

68 See Frederick Herzberg, *Work and the Nature of Man*, London, 1968; A.H. Maslow, *Motivation and Personality*, London, 1970; Douglas McGregor, *The Human Side of Enterprise*, New York, 1960, and C. Argyris, *Understanding Organizational Behaviour*, London, 1960.

69 See Michel Bosquet, 'The Prison Factory', *New Left Review*, no. 73, May 1972, pp. 23–4.

70 Argyris, op. cit., pp. 7–24.

71 For an account of the introduction of a job-enrichment scheme in such a situation, see Theo Nichols, 'The "Socialism" of Management: Some comments on the New "Human Relations" ', *Sociological Review*, vol. 23, no. 2, May 1975, pp. 245–65. For a trade union view on such schemes, see K. Graham, 'Union Attitudes to Job Satisfaction', in Mary Weir (ed.), *Job Satisfaction*, London, 1976, pp. 265–72.

72 Keith Robertson, 'Managing People and Jobs', in Mary Weir (ed.), op. cit., p. 34.

73 Braverman, op. cit., p. 87.

74 Taylor's most important works have been collected together in F.W. Taylor, *Scientific Management*, New York, 1947.

75 See, in particular, Braverman, op. cit.; Michael Rose, *Industrial Behaviour: Theoretical Developments Since Taylor*, London, 1975.

76 Craig R. Littler, 'Understanding Taylorism', *British Journal of Sociology*, vol. 29, no. 2, June 1978, p. 190.

77 Drucker, op. cit., pp. 19–20.

78 Ibid., p. 20.

79 L.A. Allen, *Professional Management*, New York, 1973.

80 Ibid., p. 58.

81 Ibid.

82 Ibid., p. 59.

83 Child, op. cit., p. 219.

84 Ibid., p. 222.

85 Terry Johnson, 'The Professions', in Geoffrey Hurd (ed.), *Human Societies*, London, 1978, p. 122.

86 Child, op. cit., p. 232.

87 Melville Dalton, *Men Who Manage*, New York, 1959.

88 Colin Fletcher, 'The End of Management', in John Child (ed.), *Man and Organisation*, London, 1973, pp. 135–57.

89 Ibid., p. 156.

90 Ibid., p. 147.

91 Ibid.

92 Ibid.

93 Ibid., p. 148.

94 Ibid., pp. 149–56.

95 Ibid., p. 157.

96 See Erik Olin Wright, *Class, Crisis and the State*, London, 1978; Richard Edwards, *Contested Terrain: the Transformation of the*

Workplace in the Twentieth Century, New York, 1979, pp. 191–3.

97 See John Child, 'The Industrial Supervisor', in Geoff Esland, Graeme Salaman and Mary-Anne Speakman (eds), *People and Work*, Edinburgh, pp. 70–87.

98 Ibid., pp. 73–4.

99 *The Front-Line Manager*, British Institute of Management, 1976, pp. 31–2.

100 Stephen Hill, 'Supervisory Roles and the Man in the Middle: Dock Foremen', *British Journal of Sociology*, vol. XXIV, no. 2, June 1973, p. 205.

101 Donald E. Wray, 'Marginal Men of Industry: the Foreman', *American Journal of Sociology*, vol. 54, 1949, pp. 298–301.

102 Ibid., p. 301.

103 Colin Fletcher, 'Men in the Middle: a Reformulation of the Thesis', *Sociological Review*, vol. 17, no. 3, 1969, pp. 341–54.

104 Ibid., p. 350.

105 Child, op. cit., 1975, pp. 82–3.

106 *Supervisory Training: A New Approach for Management*, HMSO, 1966, p. v.

107 *The Front-Line Manager*, p. 27.

108 Nichols and Beynon, op. cit., pp. 44–67.

109 *The Front-Line Manager*, p. 27.

110 Ibid.

111 Ibid.

112 The question as to the extent to which the work of unity and co-ordination can be regarded in practice as separate from control and surveillance is discussed below. See pp. 121–2.

113 Seymour Melman, *Decision-Making and Productivity*, Oxford, 1958, pp. 99–102.

114 See Tony Cliff, *The Employers' Offensive: Productivity Deals and How to Fight Them*, London, 1970.

115 Martyn Nightingale, 'UK Productivity Dealing in the 1960s', in Theo Nichols (ed.), *Capital and Labour: A Marxist Primer*, London, 1980, p. 317.

116 Edwards, op. cit.

117 R. Carter, 'Managerial and Supervisory Workers: Class Unionisation and Union Character', unpublished PhD thesis, University of Bristol, 1980, pp. 230–72.

118 Pahl and Winkler, op. cit., p. 121.

4 The State and the new middle class

1 C.A.R. Crosland, *The Future of Socialism*, London, 1956, p. 26.

2 For an extensive treatment of Marx's views on the state, see Hal Draper, *Karl Marx's Theory of Revolution*, vol. 1, New York, 1977.

3 Ben Fine and Laurence Harris, *Rereading Capital*, London, 1979, pp. 113–14.

4 Ibid., pp. 114–15.

5 Ibid., p. 118.

6 Ibid., p. 121.

7 Ibid., p. 125.

8 See, for example, Bob Jessop, *The Capitalist State*, 1982, pp. 57–77.

9 Fine and Harris, op. cit., p. 96.

10 For a critical review, see Simon Clarke, 'The Value of Value: Rereading *Capital*', *Capital and Class*, 10, Spring 1980, pp. 1–17.

11 For an influential work on monopoly capitalism, see P. Baran and P. Sweezy, *Monopoly Capital*, London, 1966; for the concept of late capitalism, see Ernest Mandel, *Late Capitalism*, London, 1975.

12 For a development of this argument, see John Hughes, *The Nationalized Industries*, London, 1955.

13 Sam Aaronovitch, 'The State and Production', in Sam Aaronovitch and Ron Smith, *The Political Economy of British Capitalism*, London, 1981, pp. 127–8.

14 See Harry Eckstein, *The English Health Service*, Cambridge, Mass., 1958.

15 Bob Jessop, 'The Transformation of the State in Post-War Britain', in Richard Scase (ed.), *The State in Western Europe*, London, 1980, p. 29.

16 See Frank Longstreth, 'The City, Industry and the State', in Colin Crouch (ed.), *State and Economy in Contemporary Capitalism*, London, 1979, pp. 157–90.

17 Jessop, op. cit., 1980, p. 32.

18 Cited in Mandel, op. cit., p. 495.

19 Andrew Schonfield, *Modern Capitalism: the Changing Balance of Public and Private Power*, London, 1978, pp. 103–5.

20 Ibid., p. 109.

21 *Report on 1963 Labour Party Conference*, 1963.

22 Cited in David Coates, *Labour Party and the Struggle for Socialism*, London, 1975, pp. 99–100.

23 Not only was capital well represented on government committees but there was also an increasing flow of personnel from private to public institutions. See Cynthia Cockburn, *The Local State: Management of Cities and People*, London, 1977, John Benington, *Local Government Becomes Big Business*, London, 1976, and Steve Bolger, Paul Corrigan, Jan Docking and Nick Frost, *Towards Socialist Welfare Work*, London, 1981.

24 R. Bacon and W. Eltis, *Britain's Economic Problems: Too Few Producers*, London, 1978.

25 CSE State Group, *Struggle over the State: Cuts and Restructuring in Contemporary Britain*, London, 1979, p. 112.

26 Raymond Williams, 'Towards a Socialist Society', in Perry Anderson and Robin Blackburn (eds), *Towards Socialism*, New York, 1966, p. 387.

27 *Nationalised Industries* (Cmnd 7131), 1978.

28 *State Intervention in Industry: a Workers' Inquiry*, Nottingham, 1980, p. 81.

29 Huw Beynon, *What Happened at Speke?*, Liverpool, 1978, p. 43.

30 Williams, op. cit., pp. 387–8.

31 Guglielmo Carchedi, *On the Economic Identification of Social Classes*, London, 1977, p. 130.
32 Ian Gough, *The Political Economy of the Welfare State*, London, 1979, p. 97.
33 See, in particular, Cockburn, op. cit.
34 K. Newton, cited in Howard Elcock, *Local Government: Politicians, Professionals and the Public in Local Authorities*, London, 1982, p. 8.
35 *The Pay and Conditions of Manual Workers in Local Authorities, The National Health Service, Gas and Water Supply*, National Board for Prices and Incomes, Report Number 29, HMSO, 1967.
36 Ibid., p. 24.
37 Committee on the Management of Local Government, *Management of Local Government* (Maud Report), HMSO, 1967; Committee on the Staffing of Local Government, *Staffing of Local Government* (Mallaby Report), HMSO, 1967; Royal Commission on Local Government in England, Report, (Redcliffe-Maud), Cmnd 4040, HMSO, 1969; Study Group on Local Authority Management Structures, *The New Local Authorities Management and Structure* (Bains Report), HMSO, 1972.
38 Cockburn, op. cit., p. 13.
39 Benington, op. cit., p. 12.
40 Elcock, op. cit., pp. 231–52.
41 Benington, op. cit., p. 41.
42 Elcock, op. cit., p. 236.
43 Yehezkel Dror, *Public Policy Making Re-Examined*, London, 1973, pp. 260–1.
44 Cockburn, op. cit., pp. 36–7.
45 Ibid., p. 38.
46 Benington, op. cit., p. 15.
47 Committee on Local Authority and Allied Personal Social Services, *Report* (Seebohm Report), HMSO, 1968, p. 11.
48 M. Kogan and J. Terry, cited in *Struggle over the State*, op. cit., pp. 105–6.
49 Both areas are represented in, for example, Bolger *et al.*, op. cit.
50 Bryan Glastonbury, 'Are Social Services Departments Bureaucracies?', in Bryan Glastonbury, David M. Cooper and Pearl Hawkins, *Social Work in Conflict: the Practitioner and the Bureaucrat*, London, 1980, p. 46.
51 Ibid.
52 Cited in Bolger *et al.*, op. cit., p. 66.
53 D. Gould, in ibid., p. 67.
54 Ibid., p. 66.
55 David M. Cooper, 'Managing Social Workers', in Glastonbury *et al.*, op. cit., pp. 73–85.
56 Bolger *et al.*, op. cit., p. 66.
57 David M. Cooper and Bryan Glastonbury, 'The Dilemma of the Professional Employee', in Glastonbury *et al.*, op. cit., p. 118.
58 Noel and José Parry, 'Professionalism and Unionism', *Sociological Review*, vol. 25, 1977, p. 830.

59 Paul Bellaby and Patrick Oribabor, 'The Growth of Trade Union Consciousness among General Hospital Nurses, Viewed as a Response to "Proletarianisation" ', *Sociological Review*, vol. 25, 1977, pp. 801–22.

60 *A Hospital Plan for England and Wales*, HMSO, Cmnd 1604, 1962.

61 Daniel Vulliamy and Roger Moore, *Whitleyism and Health: The NHS and its Industrial Relations*, Studies for Trade Unionists, vol. 5, no. 19, 1979, p. 17.

62 *Report of the Committee on Senior Nursing Staff Structure* (Salmon Report), HMSO, 1966.

63 Taken from Michael Carpenter, 'The New Managerialism and Professionalism in Nursing', in Margaret Stacey and Margaret Reid (eds), *Health and the Division of Labour*, London, 1977, p. 177. This organisation has subsequently been modified; see ibid., p. 183.

64 Salmon Report, op. cit., p. 24.

65 Carpenter, op. cit., p. 177.

66 Salmon Report, op. cit., p. 8.

67 Carpenter, op. cit., p. 183.

68 See pp. 114–22.

69 Bellaby and Oribabor, op. cit., p. 811.

70 Ibid., p. 812.

71 National Board for Prices and Incomes, Report No. 29, *The Pay and Conditions of Manual Workers in Local Authorities, the National Health Service, Gas and Water Supply*, Cmnd. 3199, January 1967; Report No. 166, *Pay and Conditions of Service of Ancillary Workers in National Health Service Hospitals*, Cmnd 4644, April 1971.

72 Vulliamy and Moore, op. cit., p. 18.

73 M. Carpenter, 'The Labour Movement in the National Health Service (NHS): UK', in A.S. Sehti and S. Dimmock (eds), *Industrial Relations and Health Services*, London, 1982, pp. 74–89.

74 Nicos Poulantzas, *State, Power, Socialism*, London, 1978, p. 154.

75 Ibid., pp. 156–7.

76 Cockburn, op. cit., pp. 44–5.

77 Peter Fairbrother, *Working for the State*, Studies for Trade Unionists, vol. 8, no. 29, 1982, p. 13.

78 Ibid.

79 Ian Gough, 'State Expenditure in Advanced Capitalism', *New Left Review*, 92, 1975, pp. 53–92.

80 Fine and Harris, op. cit., pp. 52–7.

81 For the distinction between condition and place in class analysis, see Theo Nichols, 'Social Class: Official, Sociological and Marxist', in John Irvine, Ian Miles and Jeff Evans (eds), *Demystifying Social Statistics*, London, 1979, pp. 152–71.

82 Kevin Harris, *Teachers and Classes: a Marxist Analysis*, London, 1982, p. 73.

5 The theory of middle-class trade unionism

1 Robert Price and George Sayers Bain, 'Union Growth Revisited: 1948–1974 in Perspective', *British Journal of Industrial Relations*, vol. XIV, no. 3, 1976, pp. 345–7.

2 The figures are taken from Robert Taylor, *The Fifth Estate*, London, 1978, pp. 10–11.

3 For an extensive bibliography, see George Sayers Bain, David Coates and Valerie Ellis, *Social Stratification and Trade Unionism*, London, 1973, pp. 161–74.

4 This distinction was made by Rosemary Crompton, 'Approaches to the Study of White Collar Unionism', *British Journal of Sociology*, vol. 10, no. 3, 1976, pp. 407–26.

5 For examples of this approach, see Duncan Hallas, 'White Collar Workers', *International Socialism*, no. 72, October 1974, pp. 14–18, David M. Patterson, *White Collar Militancy*, Studies for Trade Unionists, Workers Education Association, vol. 1, no. 2, July 1975, and Richard Maybin, 'NALGO: The New Unionism of Contemporary Britain', *Marxism Today*, January 1980, pp. 17–21.

6 V.L. Allen, *Militant Trade Unionism*, London, 1969, p. 13.

7 Ibid., p. 15.

8 V.L. Allen, *The Sociology of Industrial Relations*, London, 1971, p. 63.

9 Allen, op. cit., 1969, p. 17.

10 Ibid., pp. 16–17.

11 David Lockwood, *The Blackcoated Worker*, London, 1969, p. 15.

12 See Chapter 1, pp. 42–3.

13 Lockwood, op. cit., p. 13.

14 Ibid., pp. 194–8.

15 Ibid., pp. 137–8.

16 Ibid., p. 197.

17 See pp. 42–5, in this volume.

18 Blackburn, for instance, considered this of fundamental importance. See R.M. Blackburn, *Union Character and Social Class*, London, 1967, pp. 10–15.

19 Kenneth Prandy, *Professional Employees*, London, 1965, p.42.

20 Ibid., pp. 185–6.

21 Ibid., pp. 38–9.

22 Ibid., pp. 151–2.

23 Ibid., p. 151.

24 Ibid., p. 42.

25 Ibid., p. 42.

26 Blackburn, op. cit. Despite the differences between Prandy's and Blackburn's orientations, they combined to produce a joint work, 'White-Collar Unionization: A Conceptual Framework', *British Journal of Sociology*, vol. 16, 1965, pp. 111–22. This work essentially adopts Blackburn's framework. See also K. Prandy, A. Stewart and R.M. Blackburn, 'Concepts and Measures: the Example of Unionateness', *Sociology*, vol. 8, no. 3, September

1974, pp. 427–46. This latter article attempts to apply statistical techniques to the analysis and in so doing overwhelms the subject.

27 Blackburn, op. cit., p. 14.
28 Ibid., p. 18.
29 Ibid., pp. 18–19.
30 Ibid., p. 44.
31 Ibid., p. 265.
32 Ibid., p. 99.
33 Ibid., p. 258.
34 Ibid.
35 Ibid., p. 13.
36 Ibid., p. 265.
37 Ibid., p. 271.
38 Bain's major work, *The Growth of White Collar Unionism*, London, 1972, advanced his own explanation for the growth of white-collar unionism, which is examined below. A later work, undertaken with David Coates and Valerie Ellis, was essentially a critical attack on sociologists attempting to link social class to union growth and union character but the work is unfortunately marred by the crudity of their attack. The relationship between social class and unionism was characterised by the authors as a simple causal one, which allowed them to point to exceptions to this causal relationship and to conclude that such a mechanical model was inadequate. One example, but by no means an isolated one, should suffice to illustrate their method. Noting Lockwood's view that the character of blackcoated unionism, no less than its extent, is an outcome of the class situation of the clerk and that variations in character are to be understood in terms of variations in the class situations of clerks, Bain, Coates and Ellis gave a number of examples of groups with similar social positions that formed unions with different characters. One example cited was that 'English printers are affiliated to the Labour Party, but Scottish printers in the Scottish Typographical Association are not' (George Sayers Bain, David Coates and Valerie Ellis, *Social Stratification and Trade Unionism*, London, 1973, p. 69). Lockwood's position was thus transformed from one in which he claimed a relationship between social class position and union character, to one in which all identical social class positions must necessarily determine the character of unions in an identical fashion. The particular was used to refute the general with no allowance for intervening mediations. Furthermore, when some of these empirical refutations are further examined they themselves do not substantiate the criticisms which are based upon them. In the attempt to discredit Lockwood it was stated, for instance, that the National Union of Teachers (NUT) was affiliated to the TUC but that the National Association of Head Teachers (NAHT) was not, even though 80 per cent of its members belonged to the NUT (p. 69). This situation, however, is perfectly compatible with Lockwood's position. That the NUT was swayed to affiliate to the TUC by lower scale teachers, against the wishes of the majority of

joint NAHT/NUT members who are able to carry their own organisation against affiliation is not only quite understandable but also quite consistent with a relationship between social stratification and union character. Simiarly, Bain, Coates and Ellis claimed that because both the National Union of Bank Employees (NUBE) and various staff associations recruit bank clerks, but only NUBE was affiliated to the TUC, the relationship was again invalidated (pp. 69–70). This claim is doubly mistaken. Firstly it ignores the insistence of Blackburn, whose study provoked this particular refutation, that character and completeness had to be considered together. Blackburn's claim was that the affiliation of NUBE to the TUC was at the expense of completeness. Secondly, Blackburn noted that staff associations had a tendency to recruit the higher grades of bank workers, a fact which confirms a relationship between social position and union character.

This is not to suggest that all the criticisms made in the work were inaccurate or of no real import. But the statements declaring the necessity for a more sophisticated approach to the subject notwithstanding, the general approach of Bain, Coates and Ellis was essentially eclectic and negative. Where the authors point to a possible approach of their own, the conclusion was very much opposed to the position adopted throughout the rest of the book. They stated that the key to the explanation of union growth and character lay in both the union's abilities to control job regulation and in the methods they used to do so. The authors realised, however, that the power of unions to control job regulation and the methods they adopt, are not unconnected to the social position of their members, and they concluded: 'Yet, paradoxically, if power is seen to stratify society into groups, then the way is open for a reconsideration of the relationship between social stratification and trade unionism' (p. 160).

39 George Sayers Bain, *The Growth of White Collar Unionism*, London, 1972, p. 181.
40 Ibid., p. 188.
41 Ibid.
42 Ibid.
43 Ibid., p. 4.
44 Ibid., p. 187.
45 Both these developments are dealt with in Chapter 4.
46 *Royal Commission on Trade Unions and Employers' Associations*, George Sayers Bain, *Research Paper 6, Trade Union Growth and Recognition*, HMSO, 1967, p. 78.
47 George Bain, 'Management and white collar unions', in Sydney Kessler and Brian Weekes (eds), *Conflict at Work: Reshaping Industrial Relations*, London, 1971, pp. 22–3.
48 Ibid., p. 25.
49 Bain, op. cit., 1972, pp. 142–82.
50 Ibid., p. 181.
51 Roy J. Adams, 'The Recognition of White-Collar Worker Unions',

British Journal of Industrial Relations, vol. XIII, 1975, p. 103.

52 Ibid., p. 106.

53 Crompton, op. cit., p. 442.

54 Peter Fairbrother, 'The Bases of Collectivity: a Study of White-Collar Workplace Trade Unionism', unpublished paper, presented to Conference of Socialist Economist, Conference 1979, p. 8.

55 Figures from *British Labour Statistics, Historical Abstract 1886–1968*, Department of Employment, 1971, Table 197.

56 Ibid.

57 Ibid.

58 Figures from Steve Jeffreys, 'Striking into the 1980s – Modern British Trade Unionism: Its Limits and Potential', *International Socialism*, Series 2, no. 5, 1979, p. 23.

59 Colin Crouch, *The Politics of Industrial Relations*, London, 1979, p. 211.

60 Ibid., p. 212.

61 C.T.B. Smith, R. Clifton, P. Makeham, S.W. Creigh and R.B. Burn, *Strikes in Britain: a Research Study of Industrial Stoppages in the United Kingdom*, London, 1978, p. 38.

62 For an account of the Labour Party's relations with the trade unions, see Leo Panitch, *Social Democracy and Industrial Militancy*, Cambridge, 1976. The Conservative Party's attitudes since 1945 are dealt with in Nigel Harris, *Competition and the Corporate Society*, London, 1972.

63 *Royal Commission on Trade Unions and Employers' Associations, Written Evidence of the Ministry of Labour*, HMSO, 1965, p. 84.

64 *Royal Commission on Trade Unions and Employers' Associations, 1965–1968 Report*, HMSO, 1968, p. 57.

65 *Royal Commission on Trade Unions, Written Evidence of the Ministry of Labour*, HMSO, 1965, p. 99.

66 Sidney and Beatrice Webb, *The History of Trade Unionism*, London, 1911, p. 453.

67 Ibid., p. 186.

68 Ibid., pp. 456–7.

69 Robert Michels, *Political Parties*, New York, 1949.

70 See Royden Harrison, *Before the Socialists: Studies in Labour and Politics 1861 to 1881*, London, 1965.

71 Brian Pearce, 'Some Past Rank and File Movements', in Michael Woodhouse and Brian Pearce, *Essays on the History of Communism in Britain*, London, 1975, p. 105.

72 See James Hinton, *The First Shop Stewards' Movement*, London, 1973.

73 Christopher Farman, *The General Strike: May 1926*, London, 1972, p. 294.

74 Tony Cliff, 'The Bureaucracy Today', *International Socialism*, no. 48, June/July 1971, p. 32.

75 This analysis of the importance of trade union officials has been widely challenged. Both the Communist Party and the Labour Party Left have denied the significance of a division between rank and file

members and officials, preferring to see the decisive division between the left and the right within the unions. As an article in the Communist Party Journal, *Marxism Today*, states: 'the strategy of the Communist Party is one of strengthening and galvanizing the left trends throughout the movement in order that the Right, which has for so long held a dominant position, might be decisively challenged. To this end genuine left alliances are sought within each union and at a national level' (Geoff Roberts, 'The Strategy of Rank and Filism', *Marxism Today*, December 1976, p. 379). For a similar analysis from within the Labour Party, see *Trade Unions and Socialism*, Labour Co-ordinating Committee, n.d., pp. 16–17).

76 Richard Hyman, 'The Politics of Workplace Trade Unionism: Recent Tendencies and Some Problems for Theory', *Capital and Class*, no. 8, Summer 1979, p. 61. The need for democratic control and accountability at all levels of trade union organisation does not, however, detract from the fact that certain trade union officers are less open to rank and file influence than others. It may be possible to talk of the 'bureaucratisation of the rank and file' but it still remains the case that convenors are much more easily replaced than full-time officers located outside the factory environs and with a much wider constituency.

77 Ibid., p. 55.

78 Smith, Clifton, Makeham, Creigh and Burn, op. cit., p.31.

79 Ibid.

80 Adapted from Engineering Employers' Federation, Annual Reports, 1975 and 1976.

81 See Paul Blyton, Nigel Nicholson and Gill Ursell, 'Job Status and White Collar Members' Union Activity', *Journal of Occupational Psychology*, 55, 1981, pp. 33–45.

82 A survey carried out by the Department of Employment covering the period 1966–73 found that managerial, professional, scientific, technological and clerical strikes are much more likely to be made official. See Steven Creigh and Peter Makeham, 'Strikers' Occupations: an Analysis', *Employment Gazette*, vol. 88, no. 3, March 1980, pp. 237–9.

83 Clive Jenkins and Barrie Sherman, *White Collar Unionism: the Rebellious Salariat*, London, 1979, p. 6.

6 The practice of middle-class trade unionism

1 See I.G. McGivering, D.G.J. Matthews and W.H. Scott, *Management in Britain*, London, 1960, p. 79.

2 *Financial Times*, 19 June 1978.

3 Ibid., 10 March 1978.

4 Ibid.

5 Ibid., 10 November 1976.

6 Heinz Hartmann, 'Managerial Employees – New Participants in Industrial Relations', *British Journal of Industrial Relations*, vol. XII, 1973, pp. 268–81.

7 Ibid., p. 270.
8 Ibid.
9 Greg Bamber, 'Trade Unions for Managers', *Personnel Review*, vol. 5, no. 4, Autumn 1976, p. 38.
10 David Weir, 'Radical Managerialism: Middle Managers' Perceptions of Collective Bargaining', *British Journal of Industrial Relations*, vol. XIV, 1976, pp. 333–4.
11 Ibid., p. 336.
12 *Financial Times*, 19 June 1978.
13 Ibid., 28 January 1977.
14 AMPS recruiting leaflet, no date.
15 Ibid.
16 *AMPS Report*, February 1979.
17 Bill Price, 'Who Speaks for the Manager?', *Personnel Management*, November 1977, p. 29.
18 *Financial Times*, 24 October 1977.
19 SIMA recruiting leaflet, no date.
20 Bill Price, op. cit., p. 29.
21 *Financial Times*, 16 May 1980.
22 *Socialist Worker*, 24 May 1980.
23 '. . . introducing the EMA', EMA recruiting leaflet, no date.
24 H.A. Clegg, *The Changing System of Industrial Relations in Great Britain*, Oxford, 1979, p. 180.
25 R. Carter, 'Managerial and Supervisory Workers: Class, Unionism and Union Character', unpublished PhD thesis, Bristol University, 1980, pp. 292–4. The arguments in this section are given more extended treatment within this thesis.
26 Clive Jenkins and Barrie Sherman, *White Collar Unionism: the Rebellious Salariat*, London, 1979, p. 11. There is a close parallel between the imagery used here and that employed by AMPS noted above p. 188.
27 Clive Jenkins and Barrie Sherman, *Collective Bargaining*, London, 1977, p. 2.
28 Finance News, Spring 1977.
29 *Professional Scientists, Engineers and Technologists*, ASTMS recruiting brochure, no date.
30 ASTMS NEC Minutes, November 1975.
31 *ASTMS Journal*, March–April 1977.
32 Ibid.
33 See Carter, op. cit., p. 346.
34 ASTMS *Annual Report*, 1976.
35 ASTMS *Annual Report*, 1979.
36 Irving Richter, *Political Purpose in Trade Unions*, London, 1973, p. 182.
37 ASTMS NEC Minutes, July 1977.
38 Richter, op. cit., p. 183.
39 Ibid., p. 183.
40 Carter, op. cit., pp. 384–6.
41 See pp. 159–62 in this volume.
42 See pp. 157–9, 168–70 in this volume.

Conclusion

1 Important elements of state capitalism can be seen within the Alternative Economic Strategy favoured by not only the left wing of the Labour Party, but many socialists outside it. For an outline and criticism see Andrew Glyn and John Harrison, *The British Economic Disaster*, London, 1980, pp. 147–74.

2 Nicos Poulantzas, *Classes in Contemporary Capitalism*, London, 1978, p. 290.

3 John Goldthorpe, 'On the Service Class', in Anthony Giddens and Gavin Mackenzie (eds), *Social Class and the Division of Labour: Essays in Honour of Ilya Neustadt*, London, 1982, p. 164.

4 Raphael Samuel, 'The SDP and the New Political Class', *New Society*, 22 April 1982, p. 128.

5 Ibid., p. 124.

6 See, for example, F. Bechhofer and B. Elliot, 'The Voice of Small Business and the Politics of Survival', *Sociological Review*, vol. 26, no. 1, 1978, pp. 57–88.

7 Hugh Stephenson, *Claret and Chips*, London, 1982, p. 173.

8 Goldthorpe, op. cit., p. 168.

9 Ibid., p. 180.

10 Ibid., p. 171.

11 Serge Mallet, *The New Working Class*, Nottingham, 1975.

12 Harry Braverman, *Labor and Monopoly Capital*, New York, 1974, p. 408.

13 Ibid., p. 408.

14 Rosemary Crompton, 'Trade Unionism and the Insurance Clerk', *Sociology*, vol. 13, 1979, p. 406.

15 Ibid., pp. 403–6.

16 Ibid., p. 418.

17 Rosemary Crompton, 'Approaches to the Study of White Collar Unionism', *Sociology*, vol. 10, no. 3, 1976, pp. 407–26.

18 Duncan Gallie, *In Search of the New Working Class: Automation and Social Integration Within the Capitalist Enterprise*, Cambridge, 1978.

19 Ibid., p. 310.

20 See Perry Anderson, 'The Limits and Possibilities of Trade Union Action', in R. Blackburn and A. Cockburn (eds), *The Incompatibles: Trade Union Militancy and the Consensus*, London, 1967, pp. 263–80.

21 E. Anderson, cited in Colin Sparks, 'Fascism and the Working Class: Part 2 The National Front today', *International Socialism*, series 2, no. 3, 1978, p. 19.

22 Marco Revelli, 'Defeat at Fiat', *Capital and Class*, Spring 1982, pp. 95–108.

23 Ibid., p. 97.

24 Ibid., p. 108.

25 Michael Edwardes, *Back from the Brink*, London, 1983, pp. 73–91.

26 Ralf Dahrendorf, cited in Stephenson, op. cit., p. 173.

Bibliography

(A) Primary sources

(i) Commissions

Royal Commission on Trade Unions and Employers' Associations 1965—8 Chairman: Lord Donovan. Report. Cmnd 3623, HMSO, 1968.
Royal Commission on Local Government in England. Report (Redcliffe-Maud), Cmnd 4040, HMSO, 1969.

(ii) Reports

A Hospital Plan for England and Wales, HMSO, Cmnd 1604, 1962.
Report of the Committee on Senior Nursing Staff Structure (Salmon Report), HMSO, 1966.
The Pay and Conditions of Manual Workers in Local Authorities, The National Health Service, Gas and Water Supply, National Board for Prices and Incomes, Report Number 29, HMSO, 1967.
Committee on the Management of Local Government, *Management of Local Government* (Maud Report), HMSO, 1967.
Committee on the Staffing of Local Government, *Staffing of Local Government* (Mallaby Report), HMSO, 1967.
Committee on Local Authority and Allied Personal Social Services. *Report.* (Seebohm Report), HMSO, 1968.
Pay and Conditions of Service of Ancillary Workers in National Health Service Hospitals, Cmnd 4644, April 1971.
Study Group on Local Authority Management Structures, *The New Local Authorities' Management and Structure*, (Bains Report), HMSO, 1972.

(iii) Annual reports

Labour Party Conference 1963.
Engineering Employers' Federation, 1975, 1976.

(iv) Recruiting leaflets

Association of Managerial and Professional Staffs (ASTMS).
Association of Scientific, Technical and Managerial Staffs (ASTMS).
Engineers and Managers Association (EMA).
Steel Industry Management Association (SIMA).

(v) Newspapers and magazines

Financial Times
Socialist Worker

(vi) ASTMS documents

ASTMS Journal
Finance News
Annual Reports
NEC Minutes
ASTMS Pamphlets
Professional Scientists, Engineers and Technologists (n.d.)

(B) Books and articles

AARONOVITCH, SAM, *The Ruling Class*, London, 1961.
AARONOVITCH, SAM, 'The State and Production', in Sam Aaronovitch
    and Ron Smith (eds), *The Political Economy of British Capitalism*,
    London, 1981.
ADAMS, ROY J., 'The Recognition of White-Collar Worker Unions',
    British Journal of Industrial Relations, vol. XIII, 1975, pp. 102–6.
ALLEN, L.A., *Professional Management*, New York, 1973.
ALLEN, V.L., *Militant Trade Unionism*, London, 1969.
ALLEN, V.L., *The Sociology of Industrial Relations*, London, 1971.
ANDERSON, PERRY, 'Components of the National Culture', in Alexander
    Cockburn and Robin Blackburn (eds), *Student Power*, London, 1969,
    pp. 214–84.
ANDERSON, PERRY (ed), *Towards Socialism*, London, 1965.
ANDERSON, PERRY, 'The Limits and Possibilities of Trade Union
    Action', in R. Blackburn and A. Cockburn, *The Incompatibles: Trade
    Union Militancy and the Consensus*, London, 1967, pp. 263–80.
ANTHONY, P.D., *The Ideology of Work*, London, 1977.
ARGYRIS, C., *Understanding Organizational Behaviour*, London, 1960.
BACON, R. and ELTIS, W., *Britain's Economic Problems: Too Few
    Producers*, London, 1978.
BAILEY, D.T., 'The Business of Accountancy: East and West', *Journal of
    Management Studies*, vol. 12, 1975, pp. 28–44.
BAIN, GEORGE SAYERS, *Trade Union Growth and Recognition. Research
    Papers 6, Royal Commission on Trade Unions and Employers
    Associations*, London, HMSO, 1967.

BAIN, GEORGE SAYERS, 'Management and White Collar Unions', in Sidney Kessler and Brian Weekes (eds), *Conflict at Work: Reshaping Industrial Relations*, London, 1971, pp. 15−30.

BAIN, GEORGE SAYERS, *The Growth of White Collar Unionism*, London, 1972.

BAIN, GEORGE SAYERS, COATES, DAVID, and ELLIS, VALERIE, *Social Stratification and Trade Unionism*, London, 1973.

BAIN, GEORGE SAYERS, and PRICE, ROBERT, 'Who is a White Collar Employee?', *British Journal of Industrial Relations*, vol. X, 1972, pp. 325−39; see also Price, Robert.

BAMBER, GREG, 'Trade Unions for Managers', *Personnel Review*, vol. 5, no. 4, Autumn 1976, pp. 36−41.

BANKS, OLIVE, see Mumford, Enid.

BARAN, PAUL, and SWEEZY, PAUL, *Monopoly Capitalism*, London, 1966.

BECHOFER, F., and ELLIOT, B., 'The Voice of Small Business and the Politics of Survival', *Sociological Review*, vol. 26, no. 1, 1978, pp. 57−88.

BELL, DANIEL, *The Coming of the Post-Industrial Society: a Venture in Social Forecasting*, London, 1976.

BELLABY, PAUL, and ORIBABOR, PATRICK, 'The Growth of Trade Union Consciousness among General Hospital Nurses, Viewed as a Response to "Proletarianisation" ', *Sociological Review*, vol. 25, 1977, pp. 801−22.

BENINGTON, JOHN, *Local Government Becomes Big Business*, London, 1976.

BERNSTEIN, EDUARD, *Evolutionary Socialism*, New York, 1909.

BERTHOUD, RICHARD, *Unemployed Professionals and Executives, Policy Studies Institute*, vol. XLV, no. 528, May 1979.

BETTELHEIM, CHARLES, *Economic Calculation and Forms of Property*, London, 1976.

BEYNON, HUW, *Working for Ford*, London, 1973.

BEYNON, HUW, *What Happened at Speke?*, Liverpool, 1978.

BEYNON, HUW, and WAINWRIGHT, HILARY, *The Workers' Report on Vickers*, London, 1979; see also Nichols, Theo.

BLACKBURN, R.M., *Union Character and Social Class*, London, 1967.

BLACKBURN, R.M., and PRANDY, KENNETH, 'White-Collar Unionization: a Conceptual Framework', *British Journal of Sociology*, vol. 16, 1965, pp. 111−22; see also Prandy, K.

BLACKBURN, ROBIN, 'The New Capitalism', in Perry Anderson (ed.), *Towards Socialism*, London, 1965, pp. 114−45; see also Cockburn, Alexander.

BLYTON, PAUL, NICHOLSON, NIGEL, and URSELL, GILL, 'Job Status and White Collar Members' Union Activity', *Journal of Occupational Psychology*, 55, 1981, pp. 33−45.

BOLGER, STEVE, CORRIGAN, PAUL, BOOKING, JAN, and FROST, NICK, *Towards Socialist Welfare Work*, London, 1981.

BOSQUET, MICHEL, 'The Prison Factory', *New Left Review*, no. 73, May 1972, pp. 23−34.

BOTTOMORE, T.B., *Classes in Modern Society*, London, 1965.

BOTTOMORE, T.B., and GOODE, P., *Austro-Marxism*, Oxford, 1978.

BRAVERMAN, HARRY, *Labor and Monopoly Capital*, New York, 1974.

British Labour Statistics, Historical Abstract 1856–1968, London, Department of Employment, 1971.

BROOK, EVE, and FINN, DAN, 'Working Class Images of Society and Community Studies', in *On Ideology: Working Papers in Cultural Studies*, 10, 1977, pp. 77–105.

BROWN, MICHAEL BARRATT, 'The Controllers', *Universities and Left Review*, no. 5, 1959, pp. 53–61.

BURNHAM, JAMES, *The Managerial Revolution*, London, 1962.

BUTLER, ROSEMARY, 'Employment of the Highly Qualified 1971–1986', *Unit of Manpower Studies Research Paper, no. 2*, London, Department of Employment, 1978.

CARCHEDI, GUGLIELMO, *On the Economic Identification of Social Classes*, London, 1977.

CARPENTER, MICHAEL, 'The New Managerialism and Professionalism in Nursing', in Margaret Stacey and Margaret Reid (eds), *Health and the Division of Labour*, London, 1977, pp. 165–95.

CARPENTER, M., 'The Labour Movement in the National Health Service (NHS): UK', in A.S. Sethi and S. Dimmock (eds), *Industrial Relations and Health Services*, London, 1982, pp. 74–89.

CARTER, R., 'Managerial and Supervisory Workers: Class, Unionisation and Union Character', unpublished PhD thesis, University of Bristol, 1980.

CHANDLER, ALFRED D., JNR, *Strategy and Structure: Chapters in the History of the Industrial Enterprise*, Cambridge, Mass., 1972.

CHANDLER, ALFRED D., JNR, *The Visible Hand: the Managerial Revolution in American Business*, Cambridge, Mass., 1977.

CHANDLER, ALFRED D., JNR, and DAEMS, HERMAN (eds), *Managerial Hierarchies: Comparative Perspectives on the Rise of the Modern Industrial Enterprises*, Cambridge, Mass., 1980.

CHANNON, DEREK, *The Structure of British Enterprise*, London, 1973.

CHILD, JOHN, *British Management Thought*, London, 1969.

CHILD, JOHN. 'Organisation Structure and Strategies of Control', *Administrative Science Quarterly*, vol. 17, no. 2, 1972, pp. 163–76.

CHILD, JOHN (ed.), *Man and Organisation*, London, 1973.

CHILD, JOHN, 'The Industrial Supervisor', in Geoff Esland, Graeme Salaman and Mary-Anne Speakman (eds), *People and Work*, Edinburgh, 1975, pp. 70–87.

CLAPHAM, J.H., *The Economic Development of France and Germany 1815–1914*, Cambridge, 1923.

CLARKE, SIMON, 'The Value of Value: Rereading *Capital*', *Capital and Class*, 10, Spring 1980, pp. 1–17.

CLAWSON, DAN, *Bureaucracy and the Labor Process: the Transformation of US Industry, 1860–1920*, New York, 1980.

CLEGG, H.A., *The Changing System of Industrial Relations in Great Britain*, Oxford, 1979.

CLIFF, TONY, *The Employers' Offensive: Productivity Deals and How to Fight Them*, London, 1970.

CLIFF, TONY, 'The Bureaucracy Today', *International Socialism*, no. 48, June/July 1971.

COATES, DAVID, *Labour Party and the Struggle for Socialism*, London, 1975.

COATES, DAVID, see Bain, George Sayers.

COCKBURN, ALEXANDER, and BLACKBURN, ROBIN, *Student Power*, London, 1969.

COCKBURN, CYNTHIA, *The Local State: Management of Cities and People*, London, 1977.

COLE, G.D.H., *Studies in Class Structure*, London, 1968.

COOLEY, M.J.E., 'Taylor in the Office', in R.N. Ottaway (ed.), *Humanising Work*, London, 1977, pp. 50—85.

COOPER, DAVID M., 'Managing Social Workers', in Bryan Glastonbury, David M. Cooper and Pearl Hawkins, *Social Work in Conflict: the Practitioner and the Bureaucrat*, London, 1980, pp. 73—85.

COOPER, DAVID M., and GLASTONBURY, BRYAN, 'The Dilemma of the Professional Employee', in Bryan Glastonbury, David M. Cooper and Pearl Hawkins, *Social Work in Conflict: the Practitioner and the Bureaucrat*, London, 1980, pp. 116—28.

CORRIGAN, PAUL, see Bolger, Steve.

Coventry, Liverpool, Newcastle and North Tyneside Trades Councils, *State Intervention in Industry: a Workers' Inquiry*, Nottingham, 1980.

CREIGH, STEVEN, and MAKEHAM, PETER, 'Strikers' Occupations: an Analysis', *Employment Gazette*, vol. 88, no. 3, March 1980, pp. 237—9.

CROMPTON, ROSEMARY, 'Approaches to the Study of White Collar Unionism', *Sociology*, vol. 10, no. 3, 1976, pp. 407—26.

CROMPTON, ROSEMARY, 'Trade Unionism and the Insurance Clerk', *Sociology*, vol. 13, 1979, pp. 403—26.

CROMPTON, ROSEMARY, and GUBBAY, JON, *Economy and Class Structure*, London, 1977.

CRONER, FRITZ, *Die Angestellten in der modernen Gesellschaft*, Frankfurt, 1954.

CRONER, FRITZ, 'Salaried Employees in Modern Society', *International Labour Review*, LXIX, February 1954, pp. 97—110.

CROSLAND, C.A.R., *The Future of Socialism*, London, 1956.

CROSLAND, C.A.R., *The Conservative Enemy*, London, 1962.

CROSSICK, GEOFFREY, 'The Emergence of the Lower Middle Class in Britain', in Geoffrey Crossick (ed.), *The Lower Middle Class in Britain 1870—1914*, London, 1978, pp. 11—60.

CROUCH, COLIN, *The Politics of Industrial Relations*, London, 1979.

CROUCH, COLIN, and PIZZORNO, ALESSANDRO (eds), *The Resurgence of Class Conflict in Western Europe Since 1968*, vol. 2, London, 1978.

CSE STATE GROUP, *Struggle Over the State: Cuts and Restructuring in Contemporary Britain*, London, 1979.

DAEMS, HERMAN, see Chandler, Alfred D.

DAHRENDORF, RALF, *Conflict after Class: New Perspectives on the Theory of Social and Political Conflict*, London, 1967.

DAHRENDORF, RALF, *Class and Class Conflict in an Industrial Society*,

London, 1972.

DALTON, MELVILLE, *Men Who Manage*, New York, 1959.

DOBB, MAURICE, *Studies in the Development of Capitalism*, London, 1978.

DOCKING, JAN, see Bolger, Steve.

DRAPER, HAL, *Karl Marx's Theory of Revolution*, vol. 1, New York, 1977.

DROR, YEHEZKEL, *Public Policy Making Re-Examined*, London, 1973.

DRUCKER, PETER F., *Management*, London, 1979.

ECKSTEIN, HARRY, *The English Health Service*, Cambridge, Mass., 1958.

EDWARDES, MICHAEL, *Back from the Brink*, London, 1983.

EDWARDS, RICHARD, *Contested Terrain: the Transformation of the Workplace in the Twentieth Century*, New York, 1979.

EHRENREICH, BARBARA and JOHN, 'The Professional-Managerial Class', in Pat Walker (ed.), *Between Labour and Capital*, Hassocks, Sussex, 1979, pp. 5–45.

ELCOCK, HOWARD, *Local Government: Politicians, Professionals and the Public in Local Authorities*, London, 1982.

ELLIOTT, B., see Bechofer, F.

ELLIS, VALERIE A., see Bain, George Sayers.

ELTIS, W., see Bacon, R.

FAIRBROTHER, PETER, 'Consciousness and Collective Action: a Study of the Social Organisation of Unionised White Collar Factory Workers', unpublished PhD thesis, Oxford, 1978.

FAIRBROTHER, PETER, 'The Bases of Collectivity: a Study of White-Collar Workplace Trade Unionism', unpublished paper presented to Conference of Socialist Economists, Conference 1979.

FAIRBROTHER, PETER, *Working for the State*, Studies for Trade Unionists, vol. 8, no. 29, 1982.

FARMAN, CHRISTOPHER, *The General Strike, May 1926*, London, 1972.

FINE, BEN, and HARRIS, LAURENCE, *Rereading Capital*, London, 1979.

FINN, DAN, see Brook, Eve.

FLETCHER, COLIN, 'The End of Management', in John Child (ed.), *Man and Organisation*, London, 1973, pp. 135–57.

FLETCHER, COLIN, 'Men in the Middle: a Reformulation of the Thesis', *Sociological Review*, vol. 17, no. 3, 1969, pp. 341–54.

FOOT, PAUL, 'Parliamentary Socialism', in Nigel Harris and John Palmer (eds), *World Crisis*, London, 1971, pp. 76–114.

FRANKEL, H., *Capitalist Society and Modern Sociology*, London, 1970.

The Front-Line Manager, British Institute of Management, London, 1976.

FROST, NICK, see Bolger, Steve.

GALBRAITH, JOHN KENNETH, *The New Industrial State*, London, 1969.

GALLIE, DUNCAN, *In Search of the New Working Class: Automation and Social Integration Within the Capitalist Enterprise*, Cambridge, 1978.

GAY, PETER, *The Dilemma of Democratic Socialism*, New York, 1970.

GERTH, H.H., and MILLS, C. WRIGHT (eds), *From Max Weber*, London, 1967.

GIDDENS, ANTHONY, *The Class Structure of Advanced Societies*, London,

1973.

GIDDENS, ANTHONY, see Stanworth, Philip.

GLASTONBURY, BRYAN, 'Are Social Services Departments Bureaucracies?', in Bryan Glastonbury, David M. Cooper and Pearl Hawkins, *Social Work in Conflict: the Practitioner and the Bureaucrat*, London, 1980, pp. 42–52.

GLASTONBURY, BRYAN, see also Cooper, David M.

GLYN, ANDREW, and HARRISON, JOHN, *The British Economic Disaster*, London, 1980.

GOLDTHORPE, JOHN, 'On the Service Class', in Anthony Giddens and Gavin Mackenzie (eds), *Social Class and the Division of Labour: Essays in Honour of Ilya Neustadt*, London, 1982, pp. 162–85.

GOLDTHORPE, JOHN H., and LOCKWOOD, DAVID, 'Affluence and the British Class Structure', *Sociological Review*, vol. 11, no. 2, July 1963, pp. 133–63.

GOLDTHORPE, JOHN H., LOCKWOOD, DAVID, BECHOFER, FRANK, and PLATT, JENNIFER, *The Affluent Worker in the Class Structure*, Cambridge, 1969.

GOODE, P., see Bottomore, T.B.

GORZ, ANDRÉ, *Farewell to the Working Class*, London, 1982.

GOUGH, IAN, 'State Expenditure and Capital', *New Left Review*, 92, August 1975, pp. 53–92.

GOUGH, IAN, *The Political Economy of the Welfare State*, London, 1979.

GRAHAM, K., 'Union Attitudes to Job Satisfaction', in Mary Weir (ed.), *Job Satisfaction*, London, 1976, pp. 265–72.

GUÉRIN, DANIEL, *Fascism and Big Business*, New York, 1973.

HALL, STUART, 'The "Political" and the "Economic" in Marx's Theory of Classes', in Alan Hunt (ed.), *Class and Class Structure*, London, 1977, pp. 15–60.

HALLAS, DUNCAN, 'White Collar Workers', *International Socialism*, no. 72, October 1974, pp. 14–18.

HANNAH, LESLIE, 'Visible and Invisible Hands in Great Britain: the Advent of the Modern Cooperation in Britain', in Alfred D. Chandler and Herman Daems (eds), *Managerial Hierarchies: Comparative Perspectives on the Rise of the Modern Industrial Enterprise*, Cambridge, Mass., 1980, pp. 41–76.

HARRIS, ABRAM L., 'Pure Capitalism and the Disappearance of the Middle Class', *Journal of Political Economy*, 1939, pp. 238–56.

HARRIS, KEVIN, *Teachers and Classes: a Marxist Analysis*, London, 1982.

HARRIS, LAURENCE, see Fine, Ben.

HARRIS, NIGEL, and PALMER, JOHN (eds), *World Crisis*, London, 1971.

HARRIS, NIGEL, *Competition and the Corporate Society*, London, 1972.

HARRISON, JOHN, see Glyn, Andrew.

HARRISON, ROYDEN, *Before the Socialists: Studies in Labour and Politics 1861 to 1881*, London, 1965.

HARTMANN, HEINZ, 'Managerial Employees – New Participants in Industrial Relations', *British Journal of Industrial Relations*, vol. XII, 1973, pp. 268–81.

HAYWARD, HELENA, and KIRKHAM, PAT, *William and John Linnell*.

Eighteenth Century London Furniture Makers, London, 1980.

HERZBERG, FREDERICK, *Work and the Nature of Man*, London, 1968.

HILL, STEPHEN, 'Supervisory Roles and the Man in the Middle: Dock Foremen', *British Journal of Sociology*, vol. XXIV, no. 2, June 1973, pp. 205–21.

HINTON, JAMES, *The First Shop Stewards' Movement*, London, 1973.

HMSO, *Supervisory Training: a New Approach for Management*, London, 1966.

HMSO, *Nationalised Industries*, London, 1978.

HMSO, *Strikes in Britain: a Research Study of Industrial Stoppages in the United Kingdom*, London, 1978.

HOBSBAWM, E.J., *Labouring Men: Studies in the History of Labour*, London, 1968.

HODGSKIN, THOMAS, *Labour Defended Against the Claims of Capital: or the Unproductiveness of Capital proved. By a Labourer*, London, 1825.

HOLLAND, STUART, *The Socialist Challenge*, London, 1975.

HUGHES, JOHN, *The Nationalized Industries*, London, 1955.

HUNT, ALAN, 'Class Structure in Britain Today', *Marxism Today*, June 1970, pp. 167–73.

HUNT, ALAN (ed.), *Class and Class Structure*, London, 1977.

HYMAN, RICHARD, 'Occupational Structure, Collective Organisation and Industrial Militancy', in Colin Crouch and Alessandro Pizzorno (eds), *The Resurgence of Class Conflict in Western Europe Since 1968*, vol. 2, London, 1978, pp. 35–70.

HYMAN, RICHARD, 'The Politics of Workplace Trade Unionism: Recent Tendencies and Some Problems for Theory', *Capital and Class*, no. 8, Summer 1979, pp. 54–67.

JACKSON, BRIAN, *Working Class Community*, London, 1968.

JEFFREYS, STEVE, 'Striking into the 1980s – Modern British Trade Unionism: Its Limits and Potential', *International Socialism*, series 2, no. 5, 1979, pp. 1–52.

JENKINS, CLIVE, and SHERMAN, BARRIE, *Collective Bargaining*, London, 1977.

JENKINS, CLIVE, and SHERMAN, BARRIE, *White Collar Unionism: the Rebellious Salariat*, London, 1979.

JESSOP, BOB, 'The Transformation of the State in Post-War Britain', in Richard Scase (ed.), *The State in Western Europe*, London, 1980, pp. 23–93.

JESSOP, BOB, *The Capitalist State*, London, 1982.

JOHNSON, TERRY, 'The Professions in the Class Structure', in Richard Scase (ed.), *Industrial Society: Class, Cleavage and Control*, London, 1977, pp. 93–110.

JOHNSON, TERRY, 'What is to be Known?', *Economy and Society*, vol. 6, 1977, pp. 194–223.

JOHNSON, TERRY, 'The Professions', in Geoffrey Hurd (ed.), *Human Societies*, London, 1978, pp. 120–35.

KAUTSKY, KARL, *Bernstein und das sozialdemokratische Programm*, Stuttgart, 1899.

KENDALL, WALTER, *The Labour Movement in Europe*, London, 1975.

KESSLER, SIDNEY, and WEEKES, BRIAN (eds), *Conflict at Work: Reshaping Industrial Relations*, London, 1971.

KIRKHAM, PAT, see Hayward, Helena.

KLINGENDER, F.D., *The Condition of Clerical Labour in Great Britain*, London, 1935.

KOLKO, GABRIEL, *Wealth and Power in America*, London, 1962.

KORNHAUSER, WILLIAM, *Scientists in Industry: Conflict and Accommodation*, Berkeley, 1962.

LABOUR CO-ORDINATING COMMITTEE, *Trade Unions and Socialism*, London, n.d.

LEAVITT, H., and WHISLER, L., 'Management in the 1980s', *Harvard Business Review*, vol. 36, no. 6, Nov./Dec. 1958, pp. 41–8.

LEBOVICS, H., *Social Conservatism and the Middle Classes in Germany*, Princeton, 1969.

LEDERER, EMIL, *The Problem of the Modern Salaried Employee: Its Theoretical and Statistical Basis*, W.P.A. Project no. 165–6999–6027, New York, 1937.

LEDERER, EMIL, *State of the Masses*, New York, 1940.

LEDERER, EMIL, and MARSCHAK, JACOB, *The New Middle Class*, WPA Project no. 165–97–6999–6027, New York, 1937.

LENIN, V.I., 'The Proletarian Revolution and the Renegade Kautsky', in *Collected Works*, vol. 28, Moscow, 1964, pp. 231–50.

LICHTHEIM, GEORGE, *Marxism*, London, 1964.

LITTLER, CRAIG R., 'Understanding Taylorism', *British Journal of Sociology*, vol. 29, no. 2, June 1978, pp. 185–202.

LITTLER, CRAIG R., 'Deskilling and the Changing Structures of Control', in Stephen Wood, *The Degradation of Work? Skill, Deskilling and the Labour Process*, London, 1982.

LOCKWOOD, DAVID, 'Sources of Variations in Working Class Images of Society', *Sociological Review*, vol. 14, no. 4, November 1966, pp. 249–67.

LOCKWOOD, DAVID, *The Blackcoated Worker*, London, 1969; see also Goldthorpe, John H.

LONGSTRETH, FRANK, 'The City, Industry and the State', in Colin Crouch (ed.), *State and Economy in Contemporary Capitalism*, London, 1979, pp. 157–90.

LOREN, C., *Classes in the United States: Workers against Capitalism*, California, 1977.

LUKÁCS, GEORG, *History and Class Consciousness*, London, 1971.

MCGIVERING, I.C., MATTHEWS, D.G.J., and SCOTT, W.H., *Management in Britain*, London, 1960.

MCGREGOR, DOUGLAS, *The Human Side of Enterprise*, New York, 1960.

MALLET, SERGE, *The New Working Class*, Nottingham, 1975.

MANDEL, ERNEST, Introduction to Leon Trotsky, *The Struggle Against Fascism in Germany*, London, 1975.

MANDEL, ERNEST, *Late Capitalism*, London, 1975.

MARX, KARL, *Theories of Surplus Value*, London, Lawrence & Wishart, 1969.

MARX, KARL, *The Eighteen Brumaire of Louis Bonaparte*, in Karl Marx, *Surveys from Exile*, Harmondsworth, Pelican, 1973.

MARX, KARL, *The Poverty of Philosophy*, in Karl Marx and Friedrich Engels, *Collected Works*, vol. 6, London, 1976.

MARX, KARL, *Capital*, vol. 3, London, Lawrence & Wishart, 1974.

MARX, KARL, 'Results of the Immediate Process of Production', in *Capital*, vol. 1, Harmondsworth, Pelican, 1976.

MARX, KARL, *Capital*, vol. 1, Harmondsworth, Pelican, 1976.

MARX, KARL, *Capital*, vol. 2, Harmondsworth, Pelican, 1978.

MARX, KARL, and ENGELS, FRIEDRICH, *Manifesto of the Communist Party*, in *The Communist Manifesto*, Harmondsworth, Pelican, 1967.

MASLOW, A.H., *Motivation and Personality*, London, 1970.

MAYBIN, RICHARD, 'NALGO: The New Unionism of Contemporary Britain', *Marxism Today*, January 1980, pp. 17–21.

MELMAN, SEYMOUR, *Decision-Making and Productivity*, Oxford, 1958.

MICHELS, ROBERT, *Political Parties*, New York, 1949.

MILIBAND, RALPH, *Marxism and Politics*, Oxford, 1977.

MILLS, C. WRIGHT, *The Power Elite*, London, 1959.

MILLS, C. WRIGHT, *White Collar. The American Middle Classes*, New York, 1972; see also Gerth, H.H.

MOORE, ROGER, see Vulliamy, Daniel.

MOORE, WILBERT E., see Davis, Kingsley.

MUMFORD, ENID, and BANKS, OLIVE, *The Computer and the Clerk*, London, 1967.

NELSON, DANIEL, *Managers and Workers: Origins of the New Factory System in the United States 1880–1920*, Madison, 1975.

NELSON, RALPH, *Merger Movements in American Industry 1895–1956*, Princeton, 1959.

NEWBOULD, GERALD, *Management and Merger*, London, 1970.

NEWBOULD, GERALD, and JACKSON, ANDREW, *The Receding Ideal*, Liverpool, 1972.

NICHOLS, THEO, *Ownership, Control and Ideology*, London, 1969.

NICHOLS, THEO, 'The "Socialism" of Management: some comments on the New "Human Relations" ', *Sociological Review*, vol. 23, no. 2, May 1975, pp. 245–65.

NICHOLS, THEO, 'Social Class: Official, Sociological and Marxist', in J. Irvine, I. Miles and J. Evans (eds), *Demystifying Social Statistics*, London, 1979, pp. 152–71.

NICHOLS, THEO (ed.), *Capital and Labour: a Marxist Primer*, London, 1980.

NICHOLS, THEO, and BEYNON, HUW, *Living with Capitalism. Class Relations and the Modern Factory*, London, 1977.

NICHOLSON, NIGEL, see Blyton, Paul.

NICOLAUS, MARTIN, 'Proletariat and Middle Class in Marx: Hegelian Choreography and the Capitalist Dialectic', *Studies on the Left*, 7, 1967, pp. 22–49.

NIGHTINGALE, MARTYN, 'UK Productivity Dealing in the 1960s', in Theo Nichols (ed.), *Capital and Labour: A Marxist Primer*, London, 1980, pp. 316–33.

OLLMAN, BERTELL, *Social and Sexual Revolution*, London, 1979.

ORIBABOR, PATRICK, see Bellaby, Paul.

OTTAWAY, R.N. (ed.), *Humanising Work*, London, 1977.

PAHL, R.E., and WINKLER, J.T., 'The Economic Elite: Theory and Practice', in Philip Stanworth and Anthony Giddens, *Elites and Power in British Society*, London, 1974, pp. 102–22.

PALMER, JOHN, see Harris, Nigel.

PANITCH, LEO, *Social Democracy and Industrial Militancy*, Cambridge, 1976.

PARKIN, FRANK, *Class, Inequality and Political Order*, London, 1972.

PARKIN, FRANK (ed.), *The Social Analysis of Class Structure*, London, 1974.

PARKIN, FRANK, 'Strategies of Social Closure in Class Formation', in Frank Parkin (ed.), *The Social Analysis of Class Structure*, London, 1974, pp. 1–18.

PARKIN, FRANK, *Marxism and Class Theory*, London, 1979.

PARRY, NOEL and JOSÉ, 'Professionalism and Unionism', *Sociological Review*, vol. 25, 1977, pp. 823–41.

PATTERSON, DAVID M., *White Collar Militancy*, Studies for Trade Unionists, Workers Educational Association, vol. 1, no. 2, July 1975.

PINCHBECK, IVY, *Women Workers and the Industrial Revolution 1750–1850*, London, 1969.

PIZZORNO, ALLESSANDRO, see Crouch, Colin.

POLLARD, SIDNEY, *The Genesis of Modern Management: a Study of the Industrial Revolution in Great Britain*, London, 1965.

POULANTZAS, NICOS, *Classes in Contemporary Capitalism*, London, 1975.

POULANTZAS, NICOS, *State, Power, Socialism, London, 1978.*

PRANDY, KENNETH, *Professional Employees*, London, 1965.

PRANDY, KENNETH, and BLACKBURN, R.M., 'White-Collar Unionization: a Conceptual Framework', *British Journal of Sociology*, vol. 16, 1965, pp. 111–22.

PRANDY, K., STEWART, A., and BLACKBURN, R.M., 'Concepts and Measures: the Example of Unionateness', *Sociology*, vol. 8, no. 3, September 1974, pp. 427–46; see also Blackburn, R.M.

PRICE, BILL, 'Who Speaks for the Manager?', *Personnel Management*, November 1977, pp. 27–31.

PRICE, ROBERT, and BAIN, GEORGE SAYERS, 'Union Growth Revisited: 1948–1974 in Perspective', *British Journal of Industrial Relations*, vol. XIV, no. 3, 1976, pp. 339–55.

RENNER, KARL, 'The Service Class', in T.B. Bottomore and P. Goode, *Austro-Marxism*, Oxford, 1978, pp. 249–52.

REVELLI, MARCO, 'Defeat at Fiat', *Capital and Class*, Spring 1982, pp. 95–108.

RICHTER, IRVING, *Political Purpose in Trade Unions*, London, 1973.

ROBERTS, B.C., LOVERIDGE, RAY, and GENNARD, JOHN, *Reluctant Militants*, London, 1972.

ROBERTS, GEOFF, 'The Strategy of Rank and Filism', *Marxism Today*, December 1976, pp. 375–83.

ROBERTSON, KEITH, 'Managing People and Jobs', in Mary Weir (ed.), *Job Satisfaction*, London, 1976, pp. 32—43.

ROSE, MICHAEL, *Industrial Behaviour: Theoretical Developments Since Taylor*, London, 1975.

ROSS, G., 'Marxism and the New Middle Classes', *Theory and Society*, vol. 5, 1978, pp. 163—90.

SAMUEL, RAPHAEL, 'The SDP and the New Political Class', *New Society*, 22 April 1982.

SCHAEFFER, ROBERT, and WEINSTEIN, JAMES, 'Between the Lines', in Pat Walker (ed.), *Between Labour and Capital*, Hassocks, Sussex, 1979, pp. 143—72.

SCHONFIELD, ANDREW, *Modern Capitalism: the Changing Balance of Public and Private Power*, London, 1978.

SEABROOK, JEREMY, *Unemployment*, London, 1982.

SLOAN, A.P., JNR, *My Years with General Motors*, New York, 1965.

SMITH, C.T.B., CLIFTON, R., MAKEHAM, P., CREIGH, S.W., and BURN, R.B., *Strikes in Britain: a Research Study of Industrial Stoppages in the United Kingdom*, HMSO, 1978.

SOFER, C., *Men in Mid-Career: a Study of British Managers and Technical Specialists*, Cambridge, 1970.

SPARKS, COLIN, 'Fascism and the Working Class; Part 2 The National Front Today', *International Socialism*, series 2, no. 3, 1978, pp. 17—38.

SPEIER, HANS, 'The Salaried Employee in Modern Society', *Social Research*, vol. 1, no. 1, 1934, pp. 111—33.

SPEIER, HANS, *The Salaried Employee in German Society*, WPA Project no. 465—97—0391, New York, 1939.

STANWORTH, PHILIP, and GIDDENS, ANTHONY, 'An Economic Elite: a Demographic Profile of Company Chairmen', in Philip Stanworth and Anthony Giddens (eds), *Elites and Power in British Society*, London, 1974, pp. 81—101.

STEPHENSON, HUGH, *Claret and Chips*, London, 1982.

STEWART, A., see Prandy, K.

STEWART, ROSEMARY, *Managers and their Jobs*, London, 1967.

STEWART, ROSEMARY, *The Reality of Management*, London, 1967.

STRUVE, WALTER, *Elites against Democracy*, Princeton, 1973.

SWEEZY, PAUL, see Baran, Paul.

TAYLOR, A.J.P., Introduction to *The Communist Manifesto*, Harmondsworth, Pelican, 1967.

TAYLOR, F.W., *The Principles of Scientific Management*, New York, 1911.

TAYLOR, F.W., *Scientific Management*, New York, 1947.

TAYLOR, ROBERT, *The Fifth Estate*, London, 1978.

THOMPSON, E.P., *The Making of the English Working Class*, Harmondsworth, 1968.

TROTSKY, LEON, 'The Turn in the Communist International and the Situation in Germany', in Leon Trotsky, *The Struggle Against Fascism in Germany*, London, 1975.

URE, ANDREW, *The Philosophy of Manufacturers*, London, 1835.

URRY, JOHN, 'New Theories of the New Middle Class', unpublished paper, University of Lancaster, May 1975.

URSELL, GILL, see Blyton, Paul.

VROEY, MICHEL DE, 'A Marxist View of Ownership and Control', in Theo Nichols (ed.), *Capital and Labour*, London, 1980, pp. 218–36.

VULLIAMY, DANIEL, and MOORE, ROGER, *Whiteleyism and Health: The NHS and its Industrial Relations*, Studies for Trade Unionists, vol. 5, no. 19, September 1979.

WAINWRIGHT, HILARY, see Beynon, Huw.

WALKER, PAT (ed.), *Between Labour and Capital*, Hassocks, Sussex, 1979.

WEBB, SIDNEY and BEATRICE, *The History of Trade Unionism*, London, 1911.

WEDDERBURN, DOROTHY, *White Collar Redundancy: a Case Study*, Cambridge, 1964.

WEEKES, BRIAN, see Kessler, Sidney.

WEINSTEIN, JAMES, see Schaeffer, Robert.

WEIR, DAVID, 'Radical Managerialism: Middle Managers' Perceptions of Collective Bargaining', *British Journal of Industrial Relations*, vol. XIV, 1976, pp. 324–38.

WEIR, MARY, 'Are Computer Systems and Humanised Work Compatible?', in R.N. Ottaway (ed.), *Humanising Work*, London, 1977.

WEIR, MARY (ed.), *Job Satisfaction*, London, 1976.

WESTERGAARD, JOHN, and RESLER, HENRIETTA, *Class in a Capitalist Society*, London, 1975.

WHISLER, L., see Leavitt, H.

WILLIAMS, RAYMOND, 'Towards a Socialist Society', in Perry Anderson and Robin Blackburn (eds), *Towards Socialism*, New York, 1966.

WILMOTT, P., and YOUNG, M., *Family and Kinship in East London*, London, 1957.

WILMOTT, P., and YOUNG, M., *Family and Class in a London Suburb*, London, 1960.

WINKLER, J.T., see Pahl, R.E.

WRAY, DONALD E., 'Marginal Men of Industry: the Foremen', *American Journal of Sociology*, vol. 54, 1949, pp. 298–301.

WRIGHT, ERIK OLIN, *Class, Crisis and the State*, London, 1978.

YOUNG, M., see Wilmott, P.

ZEITLIN, I.M., *Ideology and the Development of Sociological Theory*, New Jersey, 1968.

ZWEIG, F., *The Worker in an Affluent Society*, London, 1961.

Index

accountancy, 98–9
Adams, Roy, 167–8
AEI, 97
Allen, L.A., 108–9
Allen, V.L., 154–5
American Tobacco, 91
Anderson, E., 211–12
Argyris, C., 105
Arkwright, Richard, 86
Association of Managerial Electrical
  Executives, 191
Association of Managerial and Professional
  Staffs, 187–9
Association of Scientific, Technical and
  Managerial Staffs, 153, 182, 201, 205;
  appeal of, 193–5; policies of, 196–7; and
  politics, 197–200; structure of, 195–6
Association of Scientific Workers, 159
Association of Supervisory and Executive
  Engineers, 192
Association of Supervisory Staffs,
  Executives and Technicians, 168, 193, 198

Bacon, R. and Eltis, W., 133
Bain, George Sayers, 163–8, 170, 234–5
Bains Report, 137
Bamber, Greg, 185
Bellaby, Paul and Oribabor, Patrick, 144
Benington, John, 137, 139–40
Bernstein, Eduard, 17–19, 32
Bettelheim, Charles, 66, 97, 104, 122
Beynon, Huw, 99–100, 103, 118
Blackburn, R.M., 159–63, 201, 235
Braverman, Harry, 6, 82, 106, 208–9
British Institute of Managers, 114–15,
  118–19, 182–4
British Leyland, 134–5, 213–14
British Steel Corporation, 191
Brittan, Samuel, 131–2
Bullock Report, 187, 190
Burnham, James, 95–6

Callard, Sir Jack, 184
Capital, method of, 54–64
capital, function of, 61–8, 70, 75, 88, 95, 99,
  119–20, 168–9, 209
capitalism: and the growth of factory
  production, 84–7; periodisation of, 125–8
capitalists, role of, 61–5
Carchedi, Guglielmo, 5, 66–70, 83, 121,
  135–6, 152, 168
Carpenter, Michael, 146
Channon, Derek, 93
Child, John, 104, 109–10, 117
class: in British sociology, 36–51;
  consciousness, 1, 14, 22, 38–9, 148, 151,
  159, 162–3, 169, 212; debate in Germany,
  16–31; debate outside Germany, 31–6;
  Marx on, 52–64; orthodox Marxist
  accounts of, 8–14; in public sector,
  136–51; Weberian accounts of, 37–48
Clawson, Dan, 87
clerks, *see* commercial workers
Coates, David, 234–5
Cockburn, Cynthia, 148
Cole, G.D.H., 9
collective worker, 60–1, 66–7, 70, 120, 168–9
commercial workers, 21, 23, 36, 50, 57–8,
  68, 74, 76, 155–7, 160, 164, 209
Communist Party of Great Britain, 7, 12
Confederation of British Industry, 183–4
Confederation of Health Service Employees,
  147
conflict theory, 34–5
Conservative Party, 131, 133–4, 173, 202,
  205
contradictory class locations, 79–81
Cooper, David, 143
corporate planning, 137–47
corporate structures, 91–3
Crompton, Rosemary, 168–70, 201, 209
Croner, Fritz, 32–3
Crosland, Anthony, 44, 94, 124

Routledge Social Science Series

Routledge & Kegan Paul
London, Boston, Melbourne and Henley

39 Store Street, London WC1E 7DD
9 Park Street, Boston, Mass 02108
296 Beaconsfield Parade, Middle Park,
Melbourne, 3206 Australia
Broadway House, Newtown Road,
Henley-on-Thames, Oxon RG9 1EN

Contents

*Authors wishing to submit manuscripts for any series
in this catalogue should send them to the Social Science Editor,
Routledge & Kegan Paul plc, 39 Store Street,
London WC1E 7DD.*
● *Books so marked are available in paperback also.*
○ *Books so marked are available in paperback only.*
*All books are in metric Demy 8vo format (216 × 138mm approx.)
unless otherwise stated.*

International Library of Sociology
General Editor John Rex

Strong, P. Ceremonial Order of the Clinic. *267 pp.*
Urry, J. Reference Groups and the Theory of Revolution. *244 pp.*
Weinberg, E. Development of Sociology in the Soviet Union. *173 pp.*

FOREIGN CLASSICS OF SOCIOLOGY

● **Gerth, H. H.** and **Mills, C. Wright.** From Max Weber: *Essays in Sociology.*
502 pp.
● **Tönnies, Ferdinand.** Community and Association (*Gemeinschaft und Gesell-schaft*). *Translated and Supplemented by Charles P. Loomis. Foreword by Pitirim A. Sorokin. 334 pp.*

SOCIAL STRUCTURE

Andreski, Stanislav. Military Organization and Society. *Foreword by Professor A. R. Radcliffe-Brown. 226 pp. 1 folder.*
Bozzoli, B. The Political Nature of a Ruling Class. *Capital and Ideology in South Africa 1890–1939. 396 pp.*
Bauman, Z. Memories of Class. *The Prehistory and After life of Class. 240 pp.*
Broom, L., Lancaster Jones, F., McDonnell, P. and **Williams, T.** The Inheritance of Inequality. *208 pp.*
Carlton, Eric. Ideology and Social Order. *Foreword by Professor Philip Abrahams. 326 pp.*
Clegg, S. and **Dunkerley, D.** Organization, Class and Control. *614 pp.*
Coontz, Sydney H. Population Theories and the Economic Interpretation. *202 pp.*
Coser, Lewis. The Functions of Social Conflict. *204 pp.*
Crook, I. and **D.** The First Years of the Yangyi Commune. *304 pp., illustrated.*
Dickie-Clark, H. F. Marginal Situation: *A Sociological Study of a Coloured Group. 240 pp. 11 tables.*
Fidler, J. The British Business Elite. *Its Attitudes to Class, Status and Power. 332 pp.*
Giner, S. and **Archer, M. S.** (Eds) Contemporary Europe: *Social Structures and Cultural Patterns. 336 pp.*
● **Glaser, Barney** and **Strauss, Anselm L.** Status Passage: *A Formal Theory. 212 pp.*
Glass, D. V. (Ed.) Social Mobility in Britain. *Contributions by J. Berent, T. Bottomore, R. C. Chambers, J. Floud, D. V. Glass, J. R. Hall, H. T. Himmelweit, R. K. Kelsall, F. M. Martin, C. A. Moser, R. Mukherjee and W. Ziegel. 420 pp.*
Kelsall, R. K. Higher Civil Servants in Britain: *From 1870 to the Present Day. 268 pp. 31 tables.*
● **Lawton, Denis.** Social Class, Language and Education. *192 pp.*
McLeish, John. The Theory of Social Change. *Four Views Considered. 128 pp.*
● **Marsh, David C.** The Changing Social Structure of England and Wales, 1871–1961. *Revised edition. 288 pp.*
Menzies, Ken. Talcott Parsons and the Social Image of Man. *206 pp.*
● **Mouzelis, Nicos.** Organization and Bureaucracy. *An Analysis of Modern Theories. 240 pp.*
● **Ossowski, Stanislaw.** Class Structure in the Social Consciousness. *210 pp.*
● **Podgórecki, Adam.** Law and Society. *302 pp.*
Ratcliffe, P. Racism and Reaction. *A Profile of Handsworth. 388 pp.*
Renner, Karl. Institutions of Private Law and Their Social Functions. *Edited, with an Introduction and Notes, by O. Kahn-Freud. Translated by Agnes Schwarzschild. 316 pp.*
Rex, J. and **Tomlinson, S.** Colonial Immigrants in a British City. *A Class Analysis. 368 pp.*
Smooha, S. Israel. *Pluralism and Conflict. 472 pp.*
Strasser, H. and **Randall, S. C.** An Introduction to Theories of Social Change. *300 pp.*

Wesolowski, W. Class, Strata and Power. *Trans. and with Introduction by G. Kolankiewicz. 160 pp.*
Zureik, E. Palestinians in Israel. *A Study in Internal Colonialism. 264 pp.*

SOCIOLOGY AND POLITICS

Acton, T. A. Gypsy Politics and Social Change. *316 pp.*
Burton, F. Politics of Legitimacy. *Struggles in a Belfast Community. 250 pp.*
Crook, I. and **D.** Revolution in a Chinese Village. *Ten Mile Inn. 216 pp., illustrated.*
de Silva, S. B. D. The Political Economy of Underdevelopment. *640 pp.*
Etzioni-Halevy, E. Political Manipulation and Administrative Power. *A Comparative Study. 228 pp.*
Fielding, N. The National Front. *260 pp.*
● **Hechter, Michael.** Internal Colonialism. *The Celtic Fringe in British National Development, 1536–1966. 380 pp.*
Levy, N. The Foundations of the South African Cheap Labour System. *367 pp.*
Kornhauser, William. The Politics of Mass Society. *272 pp. 20 tables.*
● **Korpi, W.** The Working Class in Welfare Capitalism. *Work, Unions and Politics in Sweden. 472 pp.*
Kroes, R. Soldiers and Students. *A Study of Right- and Left-wing Students. 174 pp.*
Martin, Roderick. Sociology of Power. *214 pp.*
Merquior, J. G. Rousseau and Weber. *A Study in the Theory of Legitimacy. 286 pp.*
Myrdal, Gunnar. The Political Element in the Development of Economic Theory. *Translated from the German by Paul Streeten. 282 pp.*
Preston, P. W. Theories of Development. *296 pp.*
Varma, B. N. The Sociology and Politics of Development. *A Theoretical Study. 236 pp.*
Wong, S.-L. Sociology and Socialism in Contemporary China. *160 pp.*
Wootton, Graham. Workers, Unions and the State. *188 pp.*

CRIMINOLOGY

Ancel, Marc. Social Defence: *A Modern Approach to Criminal Problems. Foreword by Leon Radzinowicz. 240 pp.*
Athens, L. Violent Criminal Acts and Actors. *104 pp.*
Cain, Maureen E. Society and the Policeman's Role. *326 pp.*
Cloward, Richard A. and **Ohlin, Lloyd E.** Delinquency and Opportunity: *A Theory of Delinquent Gangs. 248 pp.*
Downes, David M. The Delinquent Solution. *A Study in Subcultural Theory. 296 pp.*
Friedlander, Kate. The Psycho-Analytical Approach to Juvenile Delinquency: *Theory, Case Studies, Treatment. 320 pp.*
Gleuck, Sheldon and **Eleanor.** Family Environment and Delinquency. *With the statistical assistance of Rose W. Kneznek. 340 pp.*
Lopez-Rey, Manuel. Crime. *An Analytical Appraisal. 288 pp.*
Mannheim, Hermann. Comparative Criminology: *A Text Book. Two volumes. 442 pp. and 380 pp.*
Morris, Terence. The Criminal Area: *A Study in Social Ecology. Foreword by Hermann Mannheim. 232 pp. 25 tables. 4 maps.*
Rock, Paul. Making People Pay. *338 pp.*
● **Taylor, Ian, Walton, Paul** and **Young, Jock.** The New Criminology. *For a Social Theory of Deviance. 325 pp.*
● **Taylor, Ian, Walton, Paul** and **Young, Jock.** (Eds) Critical Criminology. *268 pp.*

SOCIAL PSYCHOLOGY

Bagley, Christopher. The Social Psychology of the Epileptic Child. *320 pp.*
Brittan, Arthur. Meanings and Situations. *224 pp.*
Carroll, J. Break-Out from the Crystal Palace. *200 pp.*
● **Fleming, C. M.** Adolescence: Its Social Psychology. *With an Introduction to recent findings from the fields of Anthropology, Physiology, Medicine, Psychometrics and Sociometry. 288 pp.*
● The Social Psychology of Education: *An Introduction and Guide to Its Study. 136 pp.*
Linton, Ralph. The Cultural Background of Personality. *132 pp.*
● **Mayo, Elton.** The Social Problems of an Industrial Civilization. *With an Appendix on the Political Problem. 180 pp.*
Ottaway, A. K. C. Learning Through Group Experience. *176 pp.*
Plummer, Ken. Sexual Stigma. *An Interactionist Account. 254 pp.*
● **Rose, Arnold M.** (Ed.) Human Behaviour and Social Processes: *an Interactionist Approach. Contributions by Arnold M. Rose, Ralph H. Turner, Anselm Strauss, Everett C. Hughes, E. Franklin Frazier, Howard S. Becker et al. 696 pp.*
Smelser, Neil J. Theory of Collective Behaviour. *448 pp.*
Stephenson, Geoffrey M. The Development of Conscience. *128 pp.*
Young, Kimball. Handbook of Social Psychology. *658 pp. 16 figures. 10 tables.*

SOCIOLOGY OF THE FAMILY

Bell, Colin R. Middle Class Families: *Social and Geographical Mobility. 224 pp.*
Burton, Lindy. Vulnerable Children. *272 pp.*
Gavron, Hannah. The Captive Wife: *Conflicts of Household Mothers. 190 pp.*
George, Victor and **Wilding, Paul.** Motherless Families. *248 pp.*
Klein, Josephine. Samples from English Cultures.
    1. Three Preliminary Studies and Aspects of Adult Life in England. *447 pp.*
    2. Child-Rearing Practices and Index. *247 pp.*
Klein, Viola. The Feminine Character. *History of an Ideology. 244 pp.*
McWhinnie, Alexina M. Adopted Children. *How They Grow Up. 304 pp.*
● **Morgan, D. H. J.** Social Theory and the Family. *188 pp.*
● **Myrdal, Alva** and **Klein, Viola.** Women's Two Roles: *Home and Work. 238 pp. 27 tables.*
Parsons, Talcott and **Bales, Robert F.** Family: Socialization and Interaction Process. *In collaboration with James Olds, Morris Zelditch and Philip E. Slater. 456 pp. 50 figures and tables.*

SOCIAL SERVICES

Bastide, Roger. The Sociology of Mental Disorder. *Translated from the French by Jean McNeil. 260 pp.*
Carlebach, Julius. Caring for Children in Trouble. *266 pp.*
George, Victor. Foster Care. *Theory and Practice. 234 pp.*
    Social Security: *Beveridge and After. 258 pp.*
George, V. and **Wilding, P.** Motherless Families. *248 pp.*
● **Goetschius, George W.** Working with Community Groups. *256 pp.*
Goetschius, George W. and **Tash, Joan.** Working with Unattached Youth. *416 pp.*
Heywood, Jean S. Children in Care. *The Development of the Service for the Deprived Child. Third revised edition. 284 pp.*
King, Roy D., Ranes, Norma V. and **Tizard, Jack.** Patterns of Residential Care. *356 pp.*
Leigh, John. Young People and Leisure. *256 pp.*
● **Mays, John.** (Ed.) Penelope Hall's Social Services of England and Wales. *368 pp.*

Morris Mary. Voluntary Work and the Welfare State. *300 pp.*
Nokes. P. L. The Professional Task in Welfare Practice. *152 pp.*
Timms, Noel. Psychiatric Social Work in Great Britain (1939–1962). *280 pp.*
● Social Casework: *Principles and Practice. 256 pp.*

SOCIOLOGY OF EDUCATION

Banks, Olive. Parity and Prestige in English Secondary Education: a Study in
Educational Sociology. *272 pp.*
● **Blyth, W. A. L.** English Primary Education. *A Sociological Description.*
2. Background. *168 pp.*
Collier, K. G. The Social Purposes of Education: *Personal and Social Values in
Education. 268 pp.*
Evans, K. M. Sociometry and Education. *158 pp.*
● **Ford, Julienne.** Social Class and the Comprehensive School. *192 pp.*
Foster, P. J. Education and Social Change in Ghana. *336 pp. 3 maps.*
Fraser, W. R. Education and Society in Modern France. *150 pp.*
Grace, Gerald R. Role Conflict and the Teacher. *150 pp.*
Hans, Nicholas. New Trends in Education in the Eighteenth Century. *278 pp.*
19 tables.
● Comparative Education: *A Study of Educational Factors and Traditions. 360 pp.*
● **Hargreaves, David.** Interpersonal Relations and Education. *432 pp.*
● Social Relations in a Secondary School. *240 pp.*
School Organization and Pupil Involvement. *A Study of Secondary Schools.*
● **Mannheim, Karl** and **Stewart, W. A. C.** An Introduction to the Sociology of
Education. *206 pp.*
● **Musgrove, F.** Youth and the Social Order. *176 pp.*
● **Ottaway, A. K. C.** Education and Society: An Introduction to the Sociology of
Education. *With an Introduction by W. O. Lester Smith. 212 pp.*
Peers, Robert. Adult Education: *A Comparative Study. Revised edition. 398 pp.*
Stratta, Erica. The Education of Borstal Boys. *A Study of their Educational
Experiences prior to, and during, Borstal Training. 256 pp.*
● **Taylor, P. H., Reid, W. A.** and **Holley, B. J.** The English Sixth Form. *A Case
Study in Curriculum Research. 198 pp.*

SOCIOLOGY OF CULTURE

● **Eppel, E. M.** and **M.** Adolescents and Morality: *A Study of some Moral Values
and Dilemmas of Working Adolescents in the Context of a changing Climate
of Opinion. Foreword by W. J. H. Sprott. 268 pp. 39 tables.*
● **Fromm, Erich.** The Fear of Freedom. *286 pp.*
● The Sane Society. *400 pp.*
Johnson, L. The Cultural Critics. *From Matthew Arnold to Raymond Williams.
233 pp.*
Mannheim, Karl. Essays on the Sociology of Culture. *Edited by Ernst
Mannheim in co-operation with Paul Kecskemeti. Editorial Note by Adolph
Lowe. 280 pp.*
Structures of Thinking. *Edited by David Kettler, Volker Meja and Nico Stehr.
304 pp.*
Merquior, J. G. The Veil and the Mask. *Essays on Culture and Ideology.
Foreword by Ernest Gellner. 140 pp.*
Zijderfeld, A. C. On Clichés. *The Supersedure of Meaning by Function in
Modernity. 150 pp.*
Reality in a Looking Glass. *Rationality through an Analysis of Traditional
Folly. 208 pp.*

SOCIOLOGY OF RELIGION

Argyle, Michael and **Beit-Hallahmi, Benjamin.** The Social Psychology of Religion. *256 pp.*

Glasner, Peter E. The Sociology of Secularisation. *A Critique of a Concept. 146 pp.*

Hall, J. R. The Ways Out. *Utopian Communal Groups in an Age of Babylon. 280 pp.*

Ranson, S., Hinings, B. and **Bryman, A.** Clergy, Ministers and Priests. *216 pp.*

Stark, Werner. The Sociology of Religion. *A Study of Christendom.*
  Volume II. *Sectarian Religion. 368 pp.*
  Volume III. *The Universal Church. 464 pp.*
  Volume IV. *Types of Religious Man. 352 pp.*
  Volume V. *Types of Religious Culture. 464 pp.*

Turner, B. S. Weber and Islam. *216 pp.*

Watt, W. Montgomery. Islam and the Integration of Society. 230 pp.

Pomian-Srzednicki, M. Religious Change in Contemporary Poland. *Sociology and Secularization. 280 pp.*

SOCIOLOGY OF ART AND LITERATURE

Jarvie, Ian C. Towards a Sociology of the Cinema. *A Comparative Essay on the Structure and Functioning of a Major Entertainment Industry. 405 pp.*

Rust, Frances S. Dance in Society. *An Analysis of the Relationships between the Social Dance and Society in England from the Middle Ages to the Present Day. 256 pp. 8 pp. of plates.*

Schücking, L. L. The Sociology of Literary Taste. *112 pp.*

Wolff, Janet. Hermeneutic Philosophy and the Sociology of Art. *150 pp.*

SOCIOLOGY OF KNOWLEDGE

Diesing, P. Patterns of Discovery in the Social Sciences. *262 pp.*

● **Douglas, J. D.** (Ed.) Understanding Everyday Life. *270 pp.*

● **Hamilton, P.** Knowledge and Social Structure. *174 pp.*

Jarvie, I. C. Concepts and Society. *232 pp.*

Mannheim, Karl. Essays on the Sociology of Knowledge. *Edited by Paul Kecskemeti. Editorial Note by Adolph Lowe. 353 pp.*

Remmling, Gunter W. The Sociology of Karl Mannheim. *With a Bibliographical Guide to the Sociology of Knowledge, Ideological Analysis, and Social Planning. 255 pp.*

Remmling, Gunter W. (Ed.) Towards the Sociology of Knowledge. *Origin and Development of a Sociological Thought Style. 463 pp.*

Scheler, M. Problems of a Sociology of Knowledge. *Trans. by M. S. Frings. Edited and with an Introduction by K. Stikkers. 232 pp.*

URBAN SOCIOLOGY

Aldridge, M. The British New Towns. *A Programme Without a Policy. 232 pp.*

Ashworth, William. The Genesis of Modern British Town Planning: *A Study in Economic and Social History of the Nineteenth and Twentieth Centuries. 288 pp.*

Brittan, A. The Privatised World. *196 pp.*

Cullingworth, J. B. Housing Needs and Planning Policy: *a Restatement of the Problems of Housing Need and 'Overspill' in England and Wales. 232 pp. 44 tables. 8 maps.*

Dickinson, Robert E. City and Region: *A Geographical Interpretation. 608 pp. 125 figures.*
  The West European City: *A Geographical Interpretation. 600 pp. 129 maps. 29 plates.*

Humphreys, Alexander J. New Dubliners: *Urbanization and the Irish Family. Foreword by George C. Homans. 304 pp.*

Jackson, Brian. Working Class Community: *Some General Notions raised by a Series of Studies in Northern England. 192 pp.*

● **Mann, P. H.** An Approach to Urban Sociology. *240 pp.*

Mellor, J. R. Urban Sociology in an Urbanized Society. *326 pp.*

Morris, R. N. and **Mogey, J.** The Sociology of Housing. *Studies at Berinsfield. 232 pp. 4 pp. plates.*

Mullan, R. Stevenage Ltd. *438 pp.*

Rex, J. and **Tomlinson, S.** Colonial Immigrants in a British City. *A Class Analysis. 368 pp.*

Rosser, C. and **Harris, C.** The Family and Social Change. *A Study of Family and Kinship in a South Wales Town. 352 pp. 8 maps.*

● **Stacey, Margaret, Batsone, Eric, Bell, Colin** and **Thurcott, Anne.** Power, Persistence and Change. *A Second Study of Banbury. 196 pp.*

RURAL SOCIOLOGY

● **Mayer, Adrian C.** Peasants in the Pacific. *A Study of Fiji Indian Rural Society. 248 pp. 20 plates.*

Williams, W. M. The Sociology of an English Village: *Gosforth. 272 pp. 12 figures. 13 tables.*

SOCIOLOGY OF INDUSTRY AND DISTRIBUTION

Dunkerley, David. The Foreman. *Aspects of Task and Structure. 192 pp.*

Eldridge, J. E. T. *Industrial Disputes. Essays in the Sociology of Industrial Relations. 288 pp.*

Hollowell, Peter G. The Lorry Driver. *272 pp.*

● **Oxaal, I., Barnett, T.** and **Booth, D.** (Eds) Beyond the Sociology of Development. *Economy and Society in Latin America and Africa. 295 pp.*

Smelser, Neil J. Social Change in the Industrial Revolution: *An Application of Theory to the Lancashire Cotton Industry, 1770–1840. 468 pp. 12 figures. 14 tables.*

Watson, T. J. The Personnel Managers. *A Study in the Sociology of Work and Employment, 262 pp.*

ANTHROPOLOGY

Brandel-Syrier, Mia. Reeftown Elite. *A Study of Social Mobility in a Modern African Community on the Reef. 376 pp.*

Dickie-Clark, H. F. The Marginal Situation. *A Sociological Study of a Coloured Group. 236 pp.*

Dube, S. C. Indian Village. *Foreword by Morris Edward Opler. 276 pp. 4 plates.*

India's Changing Villages: *Human Factors in Community Development. 260 pp. 8 plates. 1 map.*

Fei, H.-T. Peasant Life in China. *A Field Study of Country Life in the Yangtze Valley. With a foreword by Bronislaw Malinowski. 328 pp. 16 pp. plates.*

Firth, Raymond. Malay Fishermen. *Their Peasant Economy. 420 pp. 17 pp. plates.*

Gulliver, P. H. Social Control in an African Society: a Study of the Arusha, Agricultural Masai of Northern Tanganykia. *320 pp. 8 plates. 10 figures. Family Herds. 288 pp.*

Jarvie, Ian C. The Revolution in Anthropology. *268 pp.*

Little, Kenneth L. Mende of Sierra Leone. *308 pp. and folder.*

Negroes in Britain. *With a New Introduction and Contemporary Study by Leonard Bloom. 320 pp.*

Tambs-Lyche, H. London Patidars. *168 pp.*
Madan, G. R. Western Sociologists on Indian Society. *Marx, Spencer, Weber, Durkheim, Pareto. 384 pp.*
Mayer, A. C. Peasants in the Pacific. *A Study of Fiji Indian Rural Society. 248 pp.*
Meer, Fatima. Race and Suicide in South Africa. *325 pp.*
Smith, Raymond T. The Negro Family in British Guiana: *Family Structure and Social Status in the Villages. With a Foreword by Meyer Fortes. 314 pp. 8 plates. 1 figure. 4 maps.*

SOCIOLOGY AND PHILOSOPHY

● **Adriaansens, H.** Talcott Parsons and the Conceptual Dilemma. *200 pp.*
Barnsley, John H. The Social Reality of Ethics. *A Comparative Analysis of Moral Codes. 448 pp.*
Diesing, Paul. Patterns of Discovery in the Social Sciences. *362 pp.*
● **Douglas, Jack D.** (Ed.) Understanding Everyday Life. *Toward the Reconstruction of Sociological Knowledge. Contributions by Alan F. Blum, Aaron W. Cicourel, Norman K. Denzin, Jack D. Douglas, John Heeren, Peter McHugh, Peter K. Manning, Melvin Power, Matthew Speier, Roy Turner, D. Lawrence Wieder, Thomas P. Wilson and Don H. Zimmerman. 370 pp.*
Gorman, Robert A. The Dual Vision. *Alfred Schutz and the Myth of Phenomenological Social Science. 240 pp.*
Jarvie, Ian C. Concepts and Society. *216 pp.*
Kilminster, R. Praxis and Method. *A Sociological Dialogue with Lukács, Gramsci and the Early Frankfurt School. 334 pp.*
Outhwaite, W. Concept Formation in Social Science. *255 pp.*
● **Pelz, Werner.** The Scope of Understanding in Sociology. *Towards a More Radical Reorientation in the Social Humanistic Sciences. 283 pp.*
Roche, Maurice, Phenomenology, Language and the Social Sciences. *371 pp.*
Sahay, Arun. Sociological Analysis. *212 pp.*
● **Slater, P.** Origin and Significance of the Frankfurt School. *A Marxist Perspective. 185 pp.*
Spurling, L. Phenomenology and the Social World. *The Philosophy of Merleau-Ponty and its Relation to the Social Sciences. 222 pp.*
Wilson, H. T. The American Ideology. *Science, Technology and Organization as Modes of Rationality. 368 pp.*

International Library of Anthropology
General Editor Adam Kuper

● **Ahmed, A. S.** Millennium and Charisma Among Pathans. *A Critical Essay in Social Anthropology. 192 pp.*
Pukhtun Economy and Society. *Traditional Structure and Economic Development. 422 pp.*
Barth, F. Selected Essays. *Volume 1. 256 pp.* Selected Essays. *Volume II. 200 pp.*
Brown, Paula. The Chimbu. *A Study of Change in the New Guinea Highlands. 151 pp.*
Duller, H. J. Development Technology. *192 pp.*
Foner, N. Jamaica Farewell. *200 pp.*
Gudeman, Stephen. Relationships, Residence and the Individual. *A Rural Panamanian Community. 288 pp. 11 plates, 5 figures, 2 maps, 10 tables.*
The Demise of a Rural Economy. *From Subsistence to Capitalism in a Latin American Village. 160 pp.*

Hamnett, Ian. Chieftainship and Legitimacy. *An Anthropological Study of Executive Law in Lesotho. 163 pp.*
Hanson, F. Allan. Meaning in Culture. *127 pp.*
Hazan, H. The Limbo People. *A Study of the Constitution of the Time Universe Among the Aged. 208 pp.*
Humphreys, S. C. Anthropology and the Greeks. *288 pp.*
Karp, I. Fields of Change Among the Iteso of Kenya. *140 pp.*
Kuper, A. Wives for Cattle. *Bridewealth in Southern Africa. 224 pp.*
Lloyd, P. C. Power and Independence. *Urban Africans' Perception of Social Inequality. 264 pp.*
Malinowski, B. and **de la Fuente, J.** Malinowski in Mexico. *The Economics of a Mexican Market System. Edited and Introduced by Susan Drucker-Brown. About 240 pp.*
Parry, J. P. Caste and Kinship in Kangra. *352 pp. Illustrated.*
Pettigrew, Joyce. Robber Noblemen. *A Study of the Political System of the Sikh Jats. 284 pp.*
Street, Brian V. The Savage in Literature. *Representations of 'Primitive' Society in English Fiction, 1858–1920. 207 pp.*
Van Den Berghe, Pierre L. Power and Privilege at an African University. *278 pp.*

International Library of Phenomenology and Moral Sciences
General Editor John O'Neill

Adorno, T. W. Aesthetic Theory. Translated by C. Lenhardt.
Apel, K.-O. Towards a Transformation of Philosophy. *308 pp.*
Bologh, R. W. Dialectical Phenomenology. *Marx's Method. 287 pp.*
Fekete, J. The Critical Twilight. *Explorations in the Ideology of Anglo-American Literary Theory from Eliot to McLuhan. 300 pp.*
Green, B. S. Knowing the Poor. *A Case Study in Textual Reality Construction. 200 pp.*
McHoul, A. W. How Texts Talk. *Essays on Reading and Ethnomethodology. 163 pp.*
Medina, A. Reflection, Time and the Novel. *Towards a Communicative Theory of Literature. 143 pp.*
O'Neill, J. Essaying Montaigne. *A Study of the Renaissance Institution of Writing and Reading. 244 pp.*
Schutz. A. Life Forms and Meaning Structure. *Translated, Introduced and Annotated by Helmut Wagner. 207 pp.*

International Library of Social Policy
General Editor Kathleen Jones

Bayley, M. Mental Handicap and Community Care. *426 pp.*
Bottoms, A. E. and **McClean, J. D.** Defendants in the Criminal Process. *284 pp.*
Bradshaw, J. The Family Fund. *An Initiative in Social Policy. 248 pp.*
Butler, J. R. Family Doctors and Public Policy. *208 pp.*
Davies, Martin. Prisoners of Society. *Attitudes and Aftercare. 204 pp.*
Gittus, Elizabeth. Flats, Families and the Under-Fives. *285 pp.*
Holman, Robert. Trading in Children. *A Study of Private Fostering. 355 pp.*
Jeffs, A. Young People and the Youth Service. *160 pp.*
Jones, Howard and **Cornes, Paul.** Open Prisons. *288 pp.*
Jones, Kathleen. History of the Mental Health Service. *428 pp.*

Jones, Kathleen with **Brown, John, Cunningham, W. J., Roberts, Julian** and **Williams, Peter.** Opening the Door. *A Study of New Policies for the Mentally Handicapped. 278 pp.*

Karn, Valerie. Retiring to the Seaside. *400 pp. 2 maps. Numerous tables.*

King, R. D. and **Elliot, K. W.** Albany: Birth of a Prison—End of an Era. *294 pp.*

Thomas, J. E. The English Prison Officer since 1850. *258 pp.*

Walton, R. G. Women in Social Work. *303 pp.*

● **Woodward, J.** To Do the Sick No Harm. *A Study of the British Voluntary Hospital System to 1875. 234 pp.*

International Library of Welfare and Philosophy
General Editors Noel Timms and David Watson

○ **Campbell, J.** The Left and Rights. *A Conceptual Analysis of the Idea of Socialist Rights. About 296 pp.*

● **McDermott, F. E.** (Ed.) Self-Determination in Social Work. *A Collection of Essays on Self-determination and Related Concepts by Philosophers and Social Work Theorists. Contributors: F. P. Biestek, S. Bernstein, A. Keith-Lucas, D. Sayer, H. H. Perelman, C. Whittington, R. F. Stalley, F. E. McDermott, I. Berlin, H. J. McCloskey, H. L. A. Hart, J. Wilson, A. I. Melden, S. I. Benn. 254 pp.*

● **Plant, Raymond.** Community and Ideology. *104 pp.*

● **Plant, Raymond, Lesser, Harry** and **Taylor-Gooby, Peter.** Political Philosophy and Social Welfare. *Essays on the Normative Basis of Welfare Provision. 276 pp.*

Ragg, N. M. People Not Cases. *A Philosophical Approach to Social Work. 168 pp.*

Timms, Noel (Ed.) Social Welfare. *Why and How? 316 pp. 7 figures.*

● **Timms, Noel** and **Watson, David** (Eds) Talking About Welfare. *Readings in Philosophy and Social Policy. Contributors: T. H. Marshall, R. B. Brandt, G. H. von Wright, K. Nielsen, M. Cranston, R. M. Titmuss, R. S. Downie, E. Telfer, D. Donnison, J. Benson, P. Leonard. A. Keith-Lucas, D. Walsh, I. T. Ramsey. 230 pp.*

● Philosophy in Social Work. *250 pp.*

● **Weale, A.** Equality and Social Policy. *164 pp.*

Library of Social Work
General Editor Noel Timms

● **Baldock, Peter.** Community Work and Social Work. *140 pp.*

○ **Beedell, Christopher.** Residential Life with Children. *210 pp. Crown 8vo.*

● **Berry, Juliet.** Daily Experience in Residential Life. *A Study of Children and their Care-givers. 202 pp.*

○ Social Work with Children. *190 pp. Crown 8vo.*

● **Brearley, C. Paul.** Residential Work with the Elderly. *116 pp.*

● Social Work, Ageing and Society. *126 pp.*

● **Cheetham, Juliet.** Social Work with Immigrants. *240 pp. Crown 8vo.*

● **Cross, Crispin P.** (Ed.) Interviewing and Communication in Social Work. *Contributions by C. P. Cross, D. Laurenson, B. Strutt, S. Raven. 192 pp. Crown 8vo.*

● **Curnock, Kathleen** and **Hardiker, Pauline.** Towards Practice Theory. *Skills and Methods in Social Assessments. 208 pp.*

● **Davies, Bernard.** The Use of Groups in Social Work Practice. *158 pp.*

Davies, Bleddyn and **Knapp, M.** Old People's Homes and the Production of Welfare. *264 pp.*

● **Davies, Martin.** Support Systems in Social Work. *144 pp.*
    Ellis, June. (Ed.) West African Families in Britain. *A Meeting of Two Cultures. Contributions by Pat Stapleton, Vivien Biggs. 150 pp. 1 map.*
○ **Ford, J.** Human Behaviour. *Towards a Practical Understanding. About 160 pp.*
● **Hart, John.** Social Work and Sexual Conduct. *230 pp.*
    Heraud, Brian. Training for Uncertainty. *A Sociological Approach to Social Work Education. 138 pp.*
    Holder, D. and **Wardle, M.** Teamwork and the Development of a Unitary Approach. *212 pp.*
● **Hutten, Joan M.** Short-Term Contracts in Social Work. *Contributions by Stella M. Hall, Elsie Osborne, Mannie Sher, Eva Sternberg, Elizabeth Tuters. 134 pp.*
    Jackson, Michael P. and **Valencia, B. Michael.** Financial Aid Through Social Work. *140 pp.*
● **Jones, Howard.** The Residential Community. *A Setting for Social Work. 150 pp.*
● (Ed.) Towards a New Social Work. *Contributions by Howard Jones, D. A. Fowler, J. R. Cypher, R. G. Walton, Geoffrey Mungham, Philip Priestley, Ian Shaw, M. Bartley, R. Deacon, Irwin Epstein, Geoffrey Pearson. 184 pp.*
    Jones, Ray and **Pritchard, Colin.** (Eds) Social Work With Adolescents. *Contributions by Ray Jones, Colin Pritchard, Jack Dunham, Florence Rossetti, Andrew Kerslake, John Burns, William Gregory, Graham Templeman, Kenneth E. Reid, Audrey Taylor.*
○ **Jordon, William.** The Social Worker in Family Situations. *160 pp. Crown 8vo.*
◐ **Laycock, A. L.** Adolescents and Social Work. *128 pp. Crown 8vo.*
● **Lees, Ray.** Politics and Social Work. *128 pp. Crown 8vo.*
◐ Research Strategies for Social Welfare. *112 pp. Tables.*
○ **McCullough, M. K.** and **Ely, Peter J.** Social Work with Groups. *127 pp. Crown 8vo.*
● **Moffett, Jonathan.** Concepts in Casework Treatment. *128 pp. Crown 8vo.*
    Parsloe, Phyllida. Juvenile Justice in Britain and the United States. *The Balance of Needs and Rights. 336 pp.*
● **Plant, Raymond.** Social and Moral Theory in Casework. *112 pp. Crown 8vo.*
    Priestley, Philip, Fears, Denise and **Fuller, Roger.** Justice for Juveniles. *The 1969 Children and Young Persons Act: A Case for Reform? 128 pp.*
● **Pritchard, Colin** and **Taylor, Richard.** Social Work: Reform or Revolution? *170 pp.*
○ **Pugh, Elisabeth.** Social Work in Child Care. *128 pp. Crown 8vo.*
● **Robinson, Margaret.** Schools and Social Work. *282 pp.*
○ **Ruddock, Ralph.** Roles and Relationships. *128 pp. Crown 8vo.*
● **Sainsbury, Eric.** Social Diagnosis in Casework. *118 pp. Crown 8vo.*
● **Sainsbury, Eric, Phillips, David** and **Nixon, Stephen.** Social Work in Focus. *Clients' and Social Workers' Perceptions in Long-Term Social Work. 220 pp.*
● Social Work with Families. *Perceptions of Social Casework among Clients of a Family Service. 188pp.*
    Seed, Philip. The Expansion of Social Work in Britain. *128 pp. Crown 8vo.*
● **Shaw, John.** The Self in Social Work. *124 pp.*
    Smale, Gerald G. Prophecy, Behaviour and Change. *An Examination of Self-fulfilling Prophecies in Helping Relationships. 116 pp. Crown 8vo.*
    Smith, Gilbert. Social Need. *Policy, Practice and Research. 155 pp.*
● Social Work and the Sociology of Organisations. *124 pp. Revised edition.*
● **Sutton, Carole.** Psychology for Social Workers and Counsellors. *An Introduction. 248 pp.*
● **Timms, Noel.** Language of Social Casework. *122 pp. Crown 8vo.*

● Recording in Social Work. *124 pp. Crown 8vo.*
● **Todd, F. Joan.** Social Work with the Mentally Subnormal. *96 pp. Crown 8vo.*
● **Walrond-Skinner, Sue.** Family Therapy. *The Treatment of Natural Systems.*
   172 pp.
● **Warham, Joyce.** An Introduction to Administration for Social Workers.
   Revised edition. 112 pp.
● An Open Case. *The Organisational Context of Social Work. 172 pp.*
○ **Wittenberg, Isca Salzberger.** Psycho-Analytic Insight and Relationships.
   A Kleinian Approach. 196 pp. Crown 8vo.

Primary Socialization, Language and Education
General Editor   Basil Bernstein

Adlam, Diana S., *with the assistance of Geoffrey Turner and Lesley Lineker.*
   Code in Context. *272 pp.*
Bernstein, Basil. Class, Codes and Control. *3 volumes.*
●   1. *Theoretical Studies Towards a Sociology of Language. 254 pp.*
     2. *Applied Studies Towards a Sociology of Language. 377 pp.*
●   3. *Towards a Theory of Educational Transmission. 167 pp.*
Brandis, Walter and **Henderson, Dorothy.** Social Class, Language and
   Communication. *288 pp.*
Cook-Gumperz, Jenny. Social Control and Socialization. *A Study of Class
   Differences in the Language of Maternal Control. 290 pp.*
● **Gahagan, D. M.** and **G. A.** Talk Reform. *Exploration in Language for Infant
   School Children. 160 pp.*
Hawkins, P. R. Social Class, the Nominal Group and Verbal Strategies. *About
   220 pp.*
Robinson, W. P. and **Rakstraw, Susan D. A.** A Question of Answers.
   2 volumes. 192 pp. and 180 pp.
Turner, Geoffrey J. and **Mohan, Bernard A.** A Linguistic Description and
   Computer Programme for Children's Speech. *208 pp.*

Reports of the Institute of Community Studies

Baker, J. The Neighbourhood Advice Centre. A Community Project in
   Camden. *320 pp.*
● **Cartwright, Ann.** Patients and their Doctors. *A Study of General Practice.
   304 pp.*
Dench, Geoff. Maltese in London. *A Case-study in the Erosion of Ethnic
   Consciousness. 302 pp.*
Jackson, Brian and **Marsden, Dennis.** Education and the Working Class: *Some
   General Themes Raised by a Study of 88 Working-class Children in a
   Northern Industrial City. 268 pp. 2 folders.*
Madge, C. and **Willmott, P.** Inner City Poverty in Paris and London. *144 pp.*
Marris, Peter. The Experience of Higher Education. *232 pp. 27 tables.*
● Loss and Change. *192 pp.*
Marris, Peter and **Rein, Martin.** Dilemmas of Social Reform. *Poverty and
   Community Action in the United States. 256 pp.*
Marris, Peter and **Somerset, Anthony.** African Businessmen. *A Study of
   Entrepreneurship and Development in Kenya. 256 pp.*
Mills, Richard. Young Outsiders: *a Study in Alternative Communities. 216 pp.*
Runciman, W. G. Relative Deprivation and Social Justice. *A Study of Attitudes
   to Social Inequality in Twentieth-Century England. 352 pp.*

14

Willmott, Peter. Adolescent Boys in East London. *230 pp.*
Willmott, Peter and Young, Michael. Family and Class in a London Suburb. *202 pp. 47 tables.*
Young, Michael and McGeeney, Patrick. Learning Begins at Home. *A Study of a Junior School and its Parents. 128 pp.*
Young, Michael and Willmott, Peter. Family and Kinship in East London. *Foreword by Richard M. Titmuss. 252 pp. 39 tables.*
The Symmetrical Family. *410 pp.*

Reports of the Institute for Social Studies in Medical Care

Cartwright, Ann, Hockey, Lisbeth and Anderson, John J. Life Before Death. *310 pp.*
Dunnell, Karen and Cartwright, Ann. Medicine Takers, Prescribers and Hoarders. *190 pp.*
Farrell, C. My Mother Said. . . *A Study of the Way Young People Learned About Sex and Birth Control. 288 pp.*

Medicine, Illness and Society
General Editor W. M. Williams

Hall, David J. Social Relations & Innovation. *Changing the State of Play in Hospitals. 232 pp.*
Hall, David J. and Stacey M. (Eds) Beyond Separation. *234 pp.*
Robinson, David. The Process of Becoming Ill. *142 pp.*
Stacey, Margaret *et al.* Hospitals, Children and Their Families. *The Report of a Pilot Study. 202 pp.*
Stimson, G. V. and Webb, B. Going to See the Doctor. *The Consultation Process in General Practice. 155 pp.*

Monographs in Social Theory
General Editor Arthur Brittan

● Barnes, B. Scientific Knowledge and Sociological Theory. *192 pp.*
Bauman, Zygmunt. Culture as Praxis. *204 pp.*
● Dixon, Keith. Sociological Theory. *Pretence and Possibility. 142 pp.*
The Sociology of Belief. *Fallacy and Foundation. 144 pp.*
Goff, T. W. Marx and Mead. *Contributions to a Sociology of Knowledge. 176 pp.*
Meltzer, B. N., Petras, J. W. and Reynolds, L. T. Symbolic Interactionism. *Genesis, Varieties and Criticisms. 144 pp.*
● Smith, Anthony D. The Concept of Social Change. *A Critique of the Functionalist Theory of Social Change. 208 pp.*
● Tudor, Andrew. Beyond Empiricism. *Philosophy of Science in Sociology. 224 pp.*

Routledge Social Science Journals

The British Journal of Sociology. *Editor – Angus Stewart; Associate Editor – Leslie Sklair. Vol. 1, No. 1 – March 1950 and Quarterly. Roy. 8vo. All back issues available. An international journal publishing original papers in the field of sociology and related areas.*

Community Work. *Edited by David Jones and Majorie Mayo. 1973. Published annually.*
Economy and Society. *Vol. 1, No. 1. February 1972 and Quarterly. Metric Roy. 8vo. A journal for all social scientists covering sociology, philosophy, anthropology, economics and history. All back numbers available.*
Ethnic and Racial Studies. *Editor – John Stone. Vol. 1 – 1978. Published quarterly.*
Religion. Journal of Religion and Religions. *Chairman of Editorial Board, Ninian Smart. Vol. 1, No. 1, Spring 1971. A journal with an interdisciplinary approach to the study of the phenomena of religion. All back numbers available.*
Sociological Review. *Chairman of Editorial Board, S. J. Eggleston. New Series. August 1982, Vol. 30, No. 1. Published quarterly.*
Sociology of Health and Illness. *A Journal of Medical Sociology. Editor – Alan Davies; Associate Editor – Ray Jobling. Vol. 1, Spring 1979. Published 3 times per annum.*
Year Book of Social Policy in Britain. *Edited by Kathleen Jones. 1971. Published annually.*

Social and Psychological Aspects of Medical Practice
Editor Trevor Silverstone

Lader, Malcolm. Psychophysiology of Mental Illness. *280 pp.*
● **Silverstone, Trevor** and **Turner, Paul.** Drug Treatment in Psychiatry. *Third edition. 256 pp.*
Whiteley, J. S. and **Gordon, J.** Group Approaches in Psychiatry. *240 pp.*